NURYOGHDI TOSHOV (ED.)

ĪSH MURĀD B. ĀDĪNA MUḤAMMAD AL-ʿALAVĪ: JAMSHĪDĪ ṬAVĀYIFĪ FATḤĪ

(THE SUBJUGATION OF THE JAMSHĪDĪS)

ÖSTERREICHISCHE AKADEMIE DER WISSENSCHAFTEN
PHILOSOPHISCH-HISTORISCHE KLASSE
SITZUNGSBERICHTE, 888. BAND

VERÖFFENTLICHUNGEN ZUR IRANISTIK
HERAUSGEGEBEN VON BERT G. FRAGNER UND FLORIAN SCHWARZ

NR. 82

STUDIES AND TEXTS ON CENTRAL ASIA
HERAUSGEGEBEN VON PAOLO SARTORI

BAND 1

NURYOGHDI TOSHOV (ED.)

ĪSH MURĀD B. ĀDĪNA MUḤAMMAD AL-ʿALAVĪ

JAMSHĪDĪ ṬAVĀYIFĪ FATḤĪ

(The Subjugation of the Jamshīdīs)

VERLAG DER
ÖSTERREICHISCHEN
AKADEMIE DER
WISSENSCHAFTEN

Angenommen durch die Publikationskommission
der philosophisch-historischen Klasse der ÖAW:
Michael Alram, Bert Fragner, Hermann Hunger, Sigrid Jalkotzy-Deger, Brigitte Mazohl,
Franz Rainer, Oliver Jens Schmitt, Peter Wiesinger und Waldemar Zacharasiewicz

Umschlaggestaltung: Bettina Hofleitner

Lektorat: Thomas Welsford

Diese Publikation wurde einem anonymen, internationalen
Peer-Review-Verfahren unterzogen.

This publication has undergone the process of anonymous, international peer review.

Die verwendete Papiersorte ist aus chlorfrei gebleichtem Zellstoff hergestellt,
frei von säurebildenden Bestandteilen und alterungsbeständig.

ISBN 978-3-7001-7977-1

Druck und Bindung: Sowa Sp., Zo.o.
https://epub.oeaw.ac.at/7977-1
https://verlag.oeaw.ac.at
Printed and bound in the EU

CONTENTS

Acknowledgments 7

Preface 9

Introduction 11

Plates 49

Text ٣

Indexes ١٣٥

Persons ١٣٧
Places ١٤١
Groups and communities ١٤٥
Technical terms ١٤٧

ACKNOWLEDGMENTS

The present book was produced within the framework of the research project "Seeing like an Archive: Documents and Forms of Governance in Islamic Central Asia (18th – 19th Centuries)" (START-Project Y 704), funded by the Austrian Science Fund (FWF) and based at the Institute of Iranian Studies of the Austrian Academy of Sciences, Vienna. I want to thank these two institutions for providing material support for my research in Uzbekistan, Russia, and Austria. I am grateful to Dr. Paolo Sartori and Dr. Ulfat Abdurasulov for commenting on previous versions of the Introduction to this book at various stages of drafting; thanks are also due to Dr. Hamidulla Aminov for his insightful comments on the preparation of the edition of Īsh Murād's text. Their suggestions proved helpful in clarifying some of the issues that I faced while working on the book. I also took on board the recommendations of three anonymous reviewers who read the book for the Austrian Academy of Sciences Press, to whom I am naturally grateful. I further wish to express my gratitude to the directors of the Center of Oriental Studies in Tashkent and the Institute of Iranian Studies of the Austrian Academy of Sciences for providing the facilities to carry out my research. Bettina Hofleitner deserves particular mention here for taking on the burden of transforming my text into a real book. I am deeply grateful to her. Finally, I want to thank my wife Sharifa Toshova, without whose support this book would never have seen the light of day.

Nuryoghdi Toshov

PREFACE

The present volume introduces a new subseries of the *Veröffentlichungen zur Iranistik* (Iranian Studies Monographs), a series published under this name by the Austrian Academy of Sciences Press since 2003. *Studies and texts on Central Asia* directs the spotlight on the necessity for state-of-the-art editions and presentations of various types of sources and for studies on the history of Central Asia that are as richly documented as they are theoretically informed. Two recent monographs in the *Veröffentlichungen zur Iranistik* series, Jeff Eden's annotated translation of "The Life of Muḥammad Sharīf: A Central Asian Sufi Hagiography in Chaghatay" (2015) and Andreas Wilde's three-volume monograph "What is Beyond the River? Power, Authority, and Social Order in Transoxania, 18th-20th Centuries" (2016) prepared the path for a focused publication program, underwritten by Paolo Sartori as subseries editor and the main series editors Bert G. Fragner and Florian Schwarz. Covering a wide range of source genres and historical approaches, and publishing books in English as well as occasionally in Russian, the series intends to build bridges between diverse approaches to academic publishing in the field of Central Asian studies.

The editors wish to thank Nuryoghdi Toshov for introducing Īsh Murād ibn Ādīna Muḥammad al-ʿAlavī's *Jamshīdī ṭavāyifī fatḥī* to historians of Central Asia (and beyond) and for preparing a diligent and well-presented edition of this Chaghatay-language account of a military campaign of the Khorezmian ruler Allah-Quli Khan into Khorasan in 1841 as the opening volume of *Studies and texts on Central Asia*. Historically of high relevance, *Jamshīdī ṭavāyifī fatḥī* also sheds light on the processes of crafting historiographical texts. The editors could not have wished for an opening publication that better represents the goals of the series.

Bert G. Fragner　　Paolo Sartori　　Florian Schwarz

INTRODUCTION

The material published here comprises a detailed description of the Khivan campaign against Khurasan, carried out in 1257–1258/1841–1842 under the command of Prince Raḥīm-Qulī and resulting directly in the resettlement of the Jamshīdīs of Bādghīs, on the territory of present-day Afghanistan, in Khorezm. The text has come to us as a single manuscript, which was discovered a few years ago among the holdings of the Institute of Oriental Studies at the Academy of Sciences of the Republic of Uzbekistan.[1]

Allāh-Qulī Khān (1240–1258/1825–1842), at the end of whose reign this expedition took place, was the third ruler from the Qungrat dynasty, which officially reigned in Khorezm from 1804 until 1920. He inherited a centralized state with a more or less established system of governance and an efficient army from his father, Muḥammad Raḥīm Khān I (1221–1240/1806–1825). Relying on this army, whose main striking force consisted of bellicose Turkmen, Allāh-Qulī Khān continued the aggressive and successful foreign policy of his predecessor. His rule saw especially frequent expeditions against Khurasan, which, as particularly underlined in local sources, took on an almost annual character. These expeditions continued under Allāh-Qulī Khān's immediate successors and were invariably presented by court historians as "holy war" against "infidels". In addition to other benefits, they were sometimes crowned by the resettlement into Khorezm of various Turkmen tribes and the inhabitants of entire Khurasani villages and fortresses. The Khivan *khān*s settled these migrants along newly reconstructed canals so that they would engage in agriculture. The male Turkmen population, meanwhile, was drawn into military service in exchange for the cancelling of tax and labor obligations.[2]

After the establishment of direct control over the Merv oasis in 1832, a development of great strategic and economic value, Allāh-Qulī Khān had the

---

[1] In 2014 this institute has been reorganized as the Al-Biruni Center for Oriental Manuscripts at the Tashkent State Institute of Oriental Studies, Ministry of Higher and Specialized Secondary Education of Uzbekistan.

[2] On Khorezm under the first Qungrats, see Yu. Bregel, "The New Uzbek States: Bukhara, Khiva and Khoqand: c. 1750–1886," in *The Cambridge History of Inner Asia: The Chinggisid Age*, ed. N. Di Cosmo, A. J. Frank and P. B. Golden (Cambridge, 2009), 398–400; *Khorezm v istorii gosudarstvennosti Uzbekistana*, ed. É. V. Rtveladze and D. A. Alimova (Tashkent, 2013), 166–179.

opportunity to wield more effective influence over events in Khurasan and northwestern Afghanistan.[3] This was particularly evident during the Herat crisis of 1837–1841, when this small dominion became an arena of conflict between several world and regional powers – Britain, Russia, Iran, and others.[4]

The Khivan *khān*s had already maintained friendly relations with Herat's Sadūzai dynasty earlier,[5] something that was largely motivated by the presence of a common enemy in the form of Qājār Iran. When Muḥammad Shāh Qājār (1834–1848) besieged Herat in 1837, the city's ruler Shāh Kāmrān b. Shāh Maḥmūd (1828–1842) turned to Allāh-Qulī Khān for help, receiving not only military assistance but also significant food aid. Although the Persians were forced to lift the siege of Herat primarily because of stubborn resistance on the part of its defenders and pressure from the British, who threatened the *shāh* with war in the Persian Gulf, Khivan authors attribute Herat's victory entirely to Khivan weaponry.[6]

Be that as it may, this was followed by an unprecedentedly frequent exchange of embassies between the Persian *shāh* and the Khivan *khān*. According to Āgahī, the *shāh* was the first to send his messenger with expressions of friendship and even agreed to the *khān*'s request that he persecute those who engaged in public cursing (*sabb*) of the Companions of the Prophet in his domains. But this nascent improvement in relations between the two countries was nullified, in the words of this historian, through the

---

[3] W. A. Wood, *The Sariq Turkmens of Merv and the Khanate of Khiva in the Early Nineteenth Century* (PhD diss., Indiana University, 1999), 136.

[4] V. M. Masson and V. A. Romodin, *Istoriia Afganistana*, vol. II (Moscow, 1965); Ch. Noelle-Karimi, *The Pearl in its Midst: Herat and the Mapping of Khurasan (15th – 19th Centuries)* (Vienna, 2014).

[5] Shīr Muḥammad Mīrāb Mūnis and Muḥammad Riżā Mīrāb Āgahī, *Firdaws al-iqbāl: History of Khorezm*, trans. Yu. Bregel (Leiden/Boston/Köln, 1999), 457, 505, 536; Muḥammad Riżā Mīrāb Āgahī b. Īr Niyāz Bīk, *Riyāż al-dawla*, MS IOM, inv. no. D 123, ff. 35b, 161b, 168b.

[6] Āgahī, *Riyāż al-dawla*, ff. 208a–224a; Muḥammad Taqī Lisān al-Mulk Sipihr, *Nāsikh al-tavārīkh: Tārīkh-i qājārīya*, ed. J. Kiyanfar, vol. 2 (Tehran, 1377/1998), 682–683, 691 (his information is repeated in: *The History of Afghanistan*: Fayż Muḥammad Kātib Hazāra's *Sirāj al-tavārīkh*, vol. 1, trans. R. D. McChesney (Leiden/Boston, 2013), 216, 226–227); Wood, *The Sariq Turkmens of Merv*, 161–165. Recently the author of this introduction discovered a text devoted to the campaign in question at the National Library of Russia (see below, "Determining the genre of the work").

fault of the *shāh*, who ordered the *khān*s of Kurdistan to arrange a raid against the Akhal Taka, the Khivan *khān*'s vassals. In response, the *khān* granted the Turkmen permission to resume periodic raids into Iranian territory, and in the fall of 1841 he set out on another expedition into Khurasan.[7]

The work published here is dedicated to the details of that campaign. Written by an eyewitness to the events it describes, the account contains many facts and details that are absent from other sources, both Eastern and European. This includes the text of numerous letters, the originals of which appear to be no longer extant. The author's evaluation of various events is also of interest from the point of view of understanding the peculiarities of the Khivan historiographical school. Finally, this text is of great interest as a significant literary work composed in Khorezm and written in Central Asian Turki.

I. THE AUTHOR

1. Establishing Īsh Murād's authorship

The text of the manuscript is missing the usual author's preface, from which it follows that either the work was not completed by the author, or it has come down to us in incomplete form. Whatever the case, the existing text includes neither the author's name nor the original title of the work. The card catalogue assigns it the provisional title *Raḥīm-Qulī Khānnīng ṭavāyif-i a'ādī üstīgā yibārīlīshī* ("Raḥīm-Qulī Khān's expedition against hostile tribes"), and the potential author is listed as Muḥammad Riżā Mīrāb b. Īr Niyāz Bīk Āgahī (1809–1874), with the following annotation: "The *Zubdat al-tavārīkh* and the *Jāmi' al-vāqi'āt* include similar content, but the wording is not identical."[8]

Given the ineffective provisional title, I propose a different name for this text: the *Jamshīdī ṭavāyifī fatḥī* (see below, the section "The Jamshīdī ṭavāyifī fatḥī"). As for the author, the card catalogue attributes the text to Āgahī without sufficient grounds for doing so. There is indeed indirect evi-

[7] Āgahī, *Riyāż al-dawla*, ff. 224b–226a, 230a, 233a, 238b.

[8] This refers to Āgahī's historical texts, the *Zubdat al-tavārīkh* and the *Jāmi' al vāqi'āt i sulṭānī*. Nevertheless, *Jāmi' al-vāqi'āt-i sulṭānī* does not contain any references to the campaign in question.

dence against Āgahī's authorship. First of all, it should be noted that Āgahī does not include this work in the list of his writings and translations contained in the preface to his *dīvān*, entitled *Ta'vīdh al-'āshiqīn.*[9] Moreover, Āgahī composed two separate works on the rule of Allāh-Qulī Khān and Raḥīm-Qulī Khān (1258–1262/1842–1846), the *Riyāż al-dawla* and the *Zubdat al-tavārīkh*, respectively, the second of which contains a section dedicated to the military campaign in question.[10] The language and the writing style also contradict the card catalogue's compilers. For example, the text I offer here in edition contains words, phrases, and blessing formulas that are not found in any of Āgahī's historical works (see below, the subsection "Some remarks on the language and style of the work").

Leaving aside this type of circumstantial evidence against Āgahī's authorship, as one piece of information provided by the anonymous author makes a convincing attribution possible. According to this information, during the campaign in question, in the locality Band-i Nādir, Prince Raḥīm-Qulī sent the author and Qārlī Maḥram to collect the *zakāt* from the Chārshangī and Īrsārī tribes living in the vicinity of the fortress of Panjdih; having fulfilled this assignment, they joined the army in the locality of Ūrūshtūshgān.[11] The author does not provide his name, limiting himself to the traditional formula of self-abasement, "the poor and insignificant" (*faqīr al-ḥaqīr*). In order to identify the author, therefore, there remains only one small thing – to identify Qārlī Maḥram's companion through other sources, provided, of course, that such sources exist. Fortunately, such a source is available to us in the form of the *Zubdat al-tavārīkh*, Āgahī's text on the history of Raḥīm-Qulī Khān's reign.

Āgahī also mentions the 1257–1258/1841–1842 campaign in another of his works, dedicated to the history of Allāh-Qulī Khān, but only very briefly, in one long sentence, promising the reader that he will relate the details of this event in his history of Raḥīm-Qulī Khān.[12] Indeed, in the *Zubdat al-*

[9] See: Muḥammad Riżā Mīrāb Āgahī, *Jāmi' al-vāqi'āt-i sulṭānī*, ed. N. Tashev (Samarkand/Tashkent, 2012), XIII-XVI.

[10] On the connections between the *Zubdat al-tavārīkh* and the text under consideration, see below, "The Jamshīdī ṭavāyifī fatḥī."

[11] [Īsh Murād b. Ādīna Muḥammad al-'Alavī], [*Jamshīdī ṭavāyifī fatḥī*], MS COM permanent collection, inv. no. 9981, ff. 79a–80b.

[12] Āgahī, *Riyāż al-dawla*, f. 238b.

tavārīkh considerable space is devoted to this campaign,[13] and a certain interesting fact is related. Āgahī writes: "On Tuesday [Raḥīm-Qulī Tūra] appointed the refuge of wisdom, the abode of eloquence, the friend of grace, Dāmullā Īsh Murād Ra'īs, who occupies, like fortune, a position in the royal retinue of His Majesty, together with the expresser of sincerity, the mirror of devotion, the attendant of faith, Qārlī Maḥram, for the collection, in accordance with *sharī'a* law, of *zakāt* on large and small livestock (*amvāl va mavāshī*) that had achieved the taxable minimum and was [therefore] subject to taxation, from the Chārshangī clan living in the vicinity of Panjdiha."[14] As is evident from Āgahī's words, Qārlī Maḥram's companion – and therefore the author of the text in question – was Dāmullā Īsh Murād b. Mullā Ādīna Muḥammad al-'Alavī, already known as the author of two other historical works.

A further irrefutable proof of Dāmullā Īsh Murād's authorship lies in the fact that one of the poems written by the author contains Īsh Murād's literary name (see below).

2. The author's biography

Information on the life of Dāmullā Īsh Murād is extremely scarce. As evidenced by the various components of his name (al-'Alavī, *makhdhūm*, *mullā*, *dāmullā*, *ākhūnd*) and the posts he occupied, he was a member of the clergy. Although it is difficult to say with certainty, it seems that he was a native of Khiva.[15] Judging by the lack of a component indicating any government office in his father's name, the latter was never involved in royal service.[16]

---

13 Muḥammad Riżā Mīrāb Āgahī, *Zubdat al-tavārīkh*, ed. Kh. Nazirova (Tashkent/Samarkand, 2016), 32–73. For an abbreviated Russian translation, see *Materialy po istorii turkmen i Turkmenii, II: Iranskie, bukharskie i khivinskie istochniki* (Moscow/Leningrad, 1938), 477–486.

14 Āgahī, *Zubdat al-tavārīkh*, 61–62.

15 For example, one Mullā Ādīna Muḥammad figures as a witness on a Khivan deed of purchase from 1205/1791, see *Katalog khivinskikh kaziĭskikh dokumentov XIX – nachala XX vv.*, ed. A. Urunbaev et al. (Tashkent/Kyoto, 2001), no. 615. We cannot be completely certain, however, that this is the same person as our author's father.

16 In the Khanate of Khiva a title became part of its bearer's name, see Āgahī, *Jāmi' al-vāqi'āt-i sulṭānī*, VII. However, it should be mentioned that there were exceptions to this rule. For example, if a person served as the *imām* of a mosque, this might not be reflected in his name.

As discussed above, in 1257/1841, Īsh Murād held the post of *ra'īs*, but it is unclear in which province he performed his duties. The two most likely options are Khiva and Hazārasp. The latter is worthy of consideration based on the fact that Raḥīm-Qulī, as heir to the throne, was the governor of Hazārasp, and Īsh Murād might have accompanied his patron as *ra'īs* of this *vilāyat*.[17]

Īsh Murād relates a very interesting fact from his biography, pertaining to the same period, in the text published here. He writes that he composed a chronogram (*tārīkh*) dedicated to this campaign, and presented it to Raḥīm-Qulī. The verse met with the latter's approval, and he immediately appointed the author to the post of *muftī* for the duration of the campaign (literally, "until the time of return").[18] According to another source, on Sunday, 4 Rabī' I 1262/1 March 1846, Muḥammad Amīn Khān (1262–1271/1846–1855) sent Dāmullā Īsh Murād Ra'īs and Allāh-Bīrdī Ṣūfī as ambassadors to Bukhara in order to announce the death of his brother and his own accession to the throne.[19] If the Dāmullā Īsh Murād Ra'īs mentioned here is our author, which there seems to be no serious reason to doubt, then in 1262/1846, he still held the same post. It is not known how long he served as *ra'īs* and whether he was appointed to other positions,[20] but on 27 Rabī' I 1278/2 October 1861 Sayyid Muḥammad Khān (1272–1281/1856–1864) appointed him as a teacher (*mudarris*) at the Qūtlūq Murād Īnāq Madrasa in Khiva.[21]

---

[17] The *khān* was certainly accompanied on his various trips by members of the so-called "Khān's Council", see Āgahī, *Jāmi' al-vāqi'āt-i sulṭānī*, X. The same could easily have been true at the residence of the heir to the throne.

[18] Īsh Murād 'Alavī, *Jamshīdī ṭavāyifī fatḥī*, f. 42a. If I am not mistaken, other Khivan sources do not provide information on such a practice, which, of course, does not rule out its existence.

[19] Āgahī, *Jāmi' al-vāqi'āt-i sulṭānī*, 36.

[20] According to Āgahī, at the beginning of 1282 (May 1865), Muḥammad Raḥīm Khān II (1281–1328/1864–1910) organized a type of civil service exam at which the supreme *qāżī* 'Abd al-Raḥīm Īshān and Īsh Murād Ra'īs served as experts (*mumayyiz*) (Muḥammad Riżā Mīrāb Āgahī b. Īr Niyāz Bīk, *Shāhid al-iqbāl*, MS IOM, inv. no. C 572, f. 26b). It is difficult to say whether this is our author. If so, this can mean only one thing: After Muḥammad Raḥīm Khān II came to power, Īsh Murād was again appointed as *ra'īs*, and two years later, as *qāżī-yi 'askar* (see below).

[21] Īsh Murād Ākhūnd b. Ādīna Muḥammad al-'Alavī, *Tārīkh-i Sayyid Muḥammad-Khānī*, MS IOM, inv. no. C 573, f. 3b. In the catalogue the *madrasa* in question is incorrectly called the Qūtlūq Murād Khān Madrasa, L. V. Dmitrieva, A. M. Muginov and S. N. Muratov, *Opisanie tiurkskikh rukopiseĭ Instituta narodov Azii*, vol. 1 (Moscow, 1965), no.

From that point on, the title of *ākhūnd* was appended to his name.[22] By that time, Īsh Murād's father was no longer alive, as in the preface to the *Tārīkh-i Sayyid Muḥammad-Khānī* his name is followed by the word "deceased" (*marḥūmī*).

The seal on one legal opinion (a *fatwā* or *rivāyat*) reads "Dāmullā Īsh Murād Ākhūnd Muftī ibn-i Mullā ... (?) Muḥammad marḥūmī."[23] Unfortunately, none of the three stamps is dated, so the time of the document's origin cannot be established, as the date was usually not specified in legal opinions. There are four other documents, dated 1283–1284/1866–1868, stamped by Qāżī-yi 'askar Īsh Murād Ākhūnd b. Mullā Ādīna Muḥammad marḥūmī.[24] All of them are private deeds (a *vaqf* deed, a relinquishment of claim, a sale deed, and a debenture); one is from Khiva, one from Pīshkānīk, which is in the vicinity of Khiva, while the place of origin of the other two is unknown. The seal on the debenture includes a date, 1283/1866–1867, from which we can conclude that it was in that year that its bearer was appointed to this position. So is this person our author? The answer should be in the affirmative. In addition to the name and the title, the chronology also supports a clear-cut answer to the above question. There is only one potential point of confusion – the seal lacks the *nisba* 'Alavī, while the legends of a number of other stamps contain such an element.[25] However, this counterargument is too weak to cast doubt on the conclusion that in 1283/1866–67, our author was appointed as a military judge in the capital city of Khiva.

This is the extent of our information on the career of Īsh Murād. The dates of his death and birth remain unknown, and nothing is known about his descendants. It cannot be excluded, however, that 'Abdallāh Ākhūnd b. Qāżī Īsh Murād, appointed as *ra'īs* in 1296/1878–79, was the author's son.

---

103. On Qūtlūq Murād Īnāq Madrasa, see P. Sartori, "On Madrasas, Legitimation, and Islamic Revival in 19th-Century Khorezm: Some Preliminary Observations," *Eurasian Studies* 14 (2016): 98–134.

22 In one register (*daftar*) from the archive of the Khivan *khāns*, relating to the year 1272/1856, there is a record according to which Īsh Murād Ākhūnd was paid 10 *ṭilā*, see Central State Archive of the Republic of Uzbekistan, f. I-125, op. 2, d. 526, t. 86. Unfortunately, his position is not given, and there is no firm basis for a positive identification of this person as our author.

23 For a description of the document, see *Katalog khivinskikh kaziĭskikh dokumentov*, no. 1117. Because of a blemish it is impossible to read the first part of the *nasab*.

24 *Katalog khivinskikh kaziĭskikh dokumentov*, nos. 211, 217, 534, 798a.

25 See, e.g.: *Katalog khivinskikh kaziĭskikh dokumentov*, nos. 49, 56, 556b, 948.

As evident from the last line of his long poem glorifying Raḥīm-Qulī, Īsh Murād used the poetic pseudonym (*takhalluṣ)* Murādī.[26] Although Īsh Murād himself does not employ this nom de plume anywhere else, neither in this text nor in any other, it is used to refer to him in the *Tūy-nāma* composed by Shīr Muḥammad Mūnis (1778–1829). This *Tūy-nāma* contains verses by many Khivan poets, including Mūnis himself, written in honor of the celebration organized by Allāh-Qulī Khān in Sha'bān 1244/February 1829 on the occasion of the marriage and circumcision (*khatna*) of a number of princes, the *khān*'s sons and brothers. The poem of our author, named by the compiler as Mullā Īsh Murād Makhdhūm Murādī, comes towards the end of the collection.[27]

3. The author's works

As noted above, Dāmullā Īsh Murād has long been known as the author of two historical texts. In recent years, several other of his works have been discovered, which allows us to rank him as a relatively prolific author. In addition to the text published here, he composed the following original works, as well as one translation.

A) *Tārīkh-i Sayyid Muḥammad-Khānī.*
Written in 1278/1861–62 on the orders of Sayyid Muḥammad Khān, who charged the author, indebted to the ruler for his appointment to the post of *mudarris* (see above), with writing a history of his ancestors, bringing the story up to the time of his own reign.[28] Īsh Murād began his history with the fourth chapter of Shīr Muḥammad Mūnis and Muḥammad Riżā Āgahī's *Firdaws al-iqbāl,* entitled "The enumeration of His Majesty's noble ancestors and venerable forefathers,"[29] significantly abridging its initial sections. So, having mentioned Naghadāy Bī in a few words, the author immediately

[26] Īsh Murād 'Alavī, *Jamshīdī ṭavāyifī fatḥī*, f. 4a.

[27] Mūnis Shīr Muḥammad, *Tūy-nāma*, MS NLR, inv. no. T.n.s. 88, ff. 75b–78a. This is the earliest reference to Īsh Murād in the sources.

[28] Īsh Murād 'Alavī, *Tārīkh-i Sayyid Muḥammad-Khānī*, ff. 2b–3a.

[29] Shīr Muḥammad Mīrāb Mūnis and Muḥammad Riżā Mīrāb Āgahī, *Firdaws al-iqbāl: History of Khorezm*, ed. Yu. Bregel (Leiden/New York, 1988), 193.

proceeds to Īsh Muḥammad Bī.[30] Through the reign of Muḥammad Raḥīm Khān I (f. 510b), Īsh Murād recapitulates the *Firdaws al-iqbāl*. This is followed by a brief history of the reigns of Allāh-Qulī Khān (ff. 510b–515b), Raḥīm-Qulī Khān (ff. 515b–518b), Muḥammad Amīn Khān, 'Abdallāh Khān (1271/1855), and Qūtlūq Murād Khān (1271–1272/1855–1856) (ff. 518b–524a), as well as the circumstances of the accession of Sayyid Muḥammad Khān (ff. 524b–526b). It is possible that in these latter sections the author made use of Āgahī's works on the history of these *khān*s, with the exception, perhaps, of *Gulshan-i dawlat*, although for some reason the manuscript cataloguers name that work (along with *Firdaws al-iqbāl*) as Īsh Murād's source.[31]

The only known extant manuscript of this text is held by the St. Petersburg Institute of Oriental Manuscripts at the Russian Academy of Sciences.[32] It was copied out in 1279/1862–63, meaning that the text was composed in about one year.

B) *Tārīkhcha-yi Muḥammad Ya'qūb Khwāja.*

This work was begun in 1280/1864 at the request of Sayyid Muḥammad Khān and dedicated to the history of his rule. The author's name and the name of this work are absent from the text. Īsh Murād's authorship can be established thanks to the author's preface to this work, in which he states that he had recently completed, on the orders of Sayyid Muḥammad Khān, a work entitled *Tārīkh-i Sayyid Muḥammad-Khānī*, which contains that ruler's genealogy and relates the events of the reigns of his ancestors, ending with his ascension to the throne.[33] The provisional and, it must be said, ineffective title given above was assigned by one of the manuscript's readers, and

30 Īsh Murād 'Alavī, *Tārīkh-i Sayyid Muḥammad-Khānī*, ff. 3b–4a. Cf.: Mūnis/Āgahī, *Firdaws al-iqbāl*, text, 204–206, 219.

31 Dmitrieva et al., *Opisanie tiurkskikh rukopiseĭ*, no. 103.

32 For a description, see Dmitrieva et al., *Opisanie tiurkskikh rukopiseĭ*, no. 103; L. V. Dmitrieva, *Katalog tiurkskikh rukopiseĭ Instituta vostokovedeniia Rossiĭskoĭ akademii nauk* (Moscow, 2002), no. 71.

33 Īsh Murād Ākhūnd b. Ādīna Muḥammad al-'Alavī, *Tārīkhcha-yi Muḥammad Ya'qūb Khwāja*, MS IOM, inv. no. C 574, ff. 1b–2b. As the result of an error, the description of the manuscript gives the information in reverse, as if the author had written about his *Tārīkhcha-yi Muḥammad Ya'qūb Khwāja* in the *Tārīkh-i Sayyid Muḥammad-Khānī*, see Dmitrieva et al., *Opisanie tiurkskikh rukopiseĭ*, no. 104.

adopted by K. G. Zalemann.[34] The only basis for this strange title is the fact that the *khān*'s orders to compose the text were transmitted to the author by Muḥammad Ya'qūb Khwāja (ff. 2b–3a).[35]

The St. Petersburg manuscript, C 574, whose ending is defective, was long considered unique. In fact, the manuscript held by the Al-Biruni Center for Oriental Manuscripts under inventory number 845 contains the same text and, judging by the numerous amendments and additions it includes, is the author's draft.[36] According to the compilers of the catalogue, the end of manuscript C 574 is missing "about one or two folios; the narration cuts off on the events preceding Sayyid Muḥammad Raḥīm Khān's ascension to the throne."[37] But a comparison of this manuscript with the Tashkent manuscript and with Āgahī's *Gulshan-i dawlat* shows that this assertion is mistaken. The end of manuscript C 574 corresponds to the beginning of folio 31b of manuscript 845, which comprises 42 folios, and to folio 150b of the Tashkent manuscript of the *Gulshan-i dawlat* (MS 7572), which describes the events of Rajab 1274/February-March 1858. The text of manuscript 845 covers events through the end of 1275/mid-1859, which corresponds to folio 201a of the *Gulshan-i dawlat* manuscript. Thus, even in the more complete text of manuscript 845, events concerning a further six years of Sayyid Muḥammad Khān's reign remain unaddressed. It appears that the work remained unfinished, but it is difficult to say why. According to Īsh Murād, when the narration of events had reached Jumādā I 1274/December 1857, Sayyid Muḥammad Khān died and work on the text was suspended; the work was later continued on the orders of the newly enthroned Sayyid

34 Iu. É. Bregel', "Sochinenie Baiani 'Shadzhara-yi khorezmshakhi' kak istochnik po istorii turkmen," *Kratkie soobshcheniia Instituta narodov Azii* XLIV (1961): 129; Dmitrieva et al., *Opisanie tiurkskikh rukopiseĭ*, no. 104.

35 On Muḥammad Ya'qūb Khwāja Dīvān b. Ibrāḥīm Khwāja (died 1287/1870), see N. Toshov, "Povtoriaemost' imen i psevdonimov kak faktor nedorazumeniĭ: primer khorezmskogo poéta Khalisa" (forthcoming).

36 In the first volume of the Tashkent catalogue, this manuscript is described as one of the copies of Āgahī's work, *Riyāż al-dawla*, see *Sobranie vostochnykh rukopiseĭ Akademii nauk Uzbekskoĭ SSR*, vol. I (Tashkent, 1952), no. 213. The thematic catalog corrects this error and gives the title of the text as the *Tārīkh-i Sayyid Muḥammad-Khān* [*Sobranie vostochnykh rukopiseĭ Akademii nauk Respubliki Uzbekistan: Istoriia*, ed. D. Iu. Iusupova and R. P. Dzhalilova (Tashkent, 1998), no. 649], but the work was not identified.

37 Dmitrieva et al., *Opisanie tiurkskikh rukopiseĭ*, no. 104. See also: Bregel', "Sochinenie Baiani," 130.

Muḥammad Raḥīm Khān II (1281–1328/1864–1910).[38] We can conclude, therefore, that the work was completed after 1281/1864.

Yuri Bregel posited that both works by Īsh Murād, as well as the writings of Bābājān Thanā'ī and Muḥammad Yūsuf Bayānī, were abbreviated and simplified retellings of texts by Mūnis and Āgahī, completed in order to popularize the latter, as these two historians wrote in highly stylized language accessible only to a narrow circle of educated people.[39] As a forthcoming book on the historiography of the Khanate of Khiva will seek to demonstrate,[40] this thesis requires serious refinement. In the meantime, without delving into this multi-faceted issue, I note only that in relation to the works of Īsh Murād, it is more appropriate to talk about modifications to the style and language of Mūnis and Āgahī's chronicles, rather than their simplification, although a degree of abbreviation is indeed present. Īsh Murād carefully replaces words and phrases used by the sources with his own expressions, even when this means that his style becomes more flowery and verbose than that of the original. In an effort to make the text distinct from its sources, Īsh Murād goes so far – and this is somewhat troubling – as to edit the texts of documents (see below).

C) *Sulṭān al-lughāt.*

This work is an Arabic-Turkic-Persian dictionary, compiled in 1280/1863 on the basis of other dictionaries and organized alphabetically. It is noteworthy that the manuscript does not include the author's name. Attribution is possible thanks to the compiler's mentioning of the fact that about a month after completing a translation of the *Mu'nis al-insān*, in the middle of Jumādā II 1280/late November 1863, he was commissioned by Allāh-Bīrgān Maḥram, on behalf of Sayyid Muḥammad Khān, to compile a dictionary.[41] There can

38 Īsh Murād 'Alavī, *Tārīkhcha-yi Muḥammad Ya'qūb Khwāja*, MS COM, inv. no. 845, f. 25a–b; MS IOM, inv. no. C 574, ff. 93b–95a.

39 Bregel', "Sochinenie Baiani," 129–130; Yu. Bregel, "The Tawārīkh-i Khōrazmshāhīya by Thanā'ī: The Historiography of Khiva and the Uzbek Literary Language," in *Aspects of Altaic Civilization II: Proceedings of the XVIII PIAC, Bloomington, June 29–July 5, 1975*, ed. L. V. Clark and P. A. Draghi (Bloomington, 1978), 21–22. See also: Dmitrieva et al., *Opisanie tiurkskikh rukopiseĭ*, no. 103; H. F. Hofman, *Turkish Literature: A Bio-bibliographical Survey* III (Utrecht, 1969), 333–334.

40 N. Toshov, *Khorezmian Historiography (19th – 20th Centuries)* (provisional title).

41 Īsh Murād Ākhūnd b. Adīna Muḥammad al-'Alavī, *Sulṭān al-lughāt*, MS from the private collection of Anbara Atamuradova and Allanazar Abdurahimov, ff. 2a–3b.

be no doubt that the *Mu'nis al-insān* refers to the *Mayāmin al-tarjumān va mu'nis al-insān*, a translation of which was completed by Īsh Murād Ākhūnd more than a month before work was begun on the *Sulṭān al-lughāt* (see below).

The structure of the dictionary cannot be characterized as systematic. Entries can be under Arabic, Persian, Turkic, or even Mongol words (as determined by the author, of course), and it is completely unclear what criteria guided the compiler's selection of terms. Sometimes a word is translated only into one language, not into both "proposed" languages. It should also be noted that the origins of some words are incorrectly related by the compiler, for which, of course, he should not be harshly judged. For example, the word *barānghar* ("the right flank of the army"), which is of Mongolian origin, is given as Persian (f. 18a). Despite its obvious flaws, the dictionary is not without a certain value, mainly as guide to Khorezmian dialects. For example, in the *Jamshīdī ṭavāyifī fatḥī* we encounter the word *sūyghūn* (ff. 15b, 21a), which does not appear in well-known dictionaries, including in a dictionary of Khorezmian dialects.[42] From the *Sulṭān al-lughāt* we learn that this word means "deer" (f. 19a).

There are three known manuscripts of the *Sulṭān al-lughāt*. Two are held by the Institute of Oriental Manuscripts in St. Petersburg;[43] one manuscript found its way there from the collection of Alexander L. Kun[44], while the other comes from the collection of Konstantin P. von Kaufman, meaning that both manuscripts came from the library of the Khivan *khān*s and were taken from Khiva after its occupation by the Russian troops in 1873. The third manuscript is stored in the personal library of Anbara Atamuradova and Allanazar Abdurahimov.[45]

---

[42] F. A. Abdullaev, *Ŭzbek tilining Xorazm shevalari* (Tashkent, 1961).

[43] Dmitrieva, *Katalog tiurkskikh rukopiseĭ*, nos. 881–882. The description incorrectly gives the hijri date as 1285.

[44] On him and his collection, see O. Yastrebova and A. Azad, "Reflections on an Orientalist: Alexander Kuhn (1840–88), the Man and his Legacy," *Iranian Studies* 48:5 (2015): 675–694.

[45] I would like to take this opportunity to express my sincere gratitude to them for allowing me access to the manuscript.

D) *Mayāmin al-tarjumān va mu'nis al-insān tarjumasī.*
The Arabic original of this text was written by Abū Muṭī' Makḥūl b. Fażl-Allāh al-Nasafī (died 318/930) and bears the title *Lu'lu'iyāt* or the *Lu'lu'iyāt fī'l-mavā'iẓ*.[46] The work was translated from Arabic into Persian by Maḥmūd b. Ḥasan b. Qāżī A'rāj, who entitled his translation the *Mayāmin al-tarjumān va mu'nis al-insān*.[47] The translation from Persian into Turki was begun by Īsh Murād Ākhūnd b. Mullā Ādīna Muḥammad marḥūmī al-'Alavī in 1277/1861 and completed at the beginning of Jumādā I 1280/mid-October 1863 at the Qūtlūq Murād Īnāq Madrasa.[48] The translation was commissioned by Sayyid Muḥammad Khān, whose order was transmitted to the translator through Pahlavān Niyāz Dīvān (ff. 2b–3a).[49]

II. The Jamshīdī Ṭavāyifī Fatḥī

1. Title

As mentioned above, the card catalogue assigns the work the provisional title of the *Raḥīm-Qulī Khānnīng ṭavāyif-i a'ādī ūstīgā yibārīlīshī* ("Raḥīm-Qulī Khān's expedition against hostile tribes"). The above title should be considered ineffective for several reasons. First of all, the campaign in ques-

[46] For more on the Arabic original, see C. Brockelmann, *Geschichte der arabischen Litteratur*, Supplementband I (Leiden, 1996), 293.

[47] For more on the Persian translation, see *Sobranie vostochnykh rukopiseĭ Akademii nauk Uzbekskoĭ SSR*, vol. III (Tashkent, 1955), no. 2010; *Persidskie i tadzhikskie rukopisi Instituta narodov Azii AN SSSR (Kratkiĭ alfavitnyĭ katalog)*, ed. N. D. Miklukho-Maklaĭ, part 1 (Moscow, 1964), no. 4361. In the Tashkent catalogue, this work is described in the "Ethics" section, while in the St. Petersburg catalogue it is classified as theological.

[48] Īsh Murād Ākhūnd b. Ādīna Muḥammad al-'Alavī, *Mayāmin al-tarjumān va mu'nis al-insān tarjumasī*, MS NLR, inv. no. T.n.s. 16, ff. 2a–5a, 447a–b. For some reasons Dmitrieva [L. V. Dmitrieva, "Tiurkskie rukopisi kollektsii 'novaia seriia' sobraniia Gosudarstvennoĭ Publichnoĭ biblioteki im. M. E. Saltykova-Shchedrina," *Vostochnyĭ sbornik* 3 (1973): 81] states that the translator into Turki is unknown. She also gives incorrect dates for the translation (1267–1285/1860–1868) and the manuscript (1285/1868).

[49] The Pahlavān Niyāz Dīvān mentioned here is, of course, no other than Pahlavān Niyāz Mīrzābāshī b. Dāmullā 'Abdallāh Ākhund, of the poetic nom de plume Kāmil (1825–1899), who for several years served as a scribe at the court of Sayyid Muḥammad Khān and his son and successor Sayyid Muḥammad Raḥīm Khān II, see Toshov, "Povtoriaemost' imen i psevdonimov"; Hofman, *Turkish literature* IV, 10–11.

tion was carried out during the reign of Allāh-Qulī Khān, the father of Raḥīm-Qulī, and the latter, while still heir to the throne, only led this campaign. This yields a semantic absurdity, with the *khān* being dispatched somewhere by someone else. Moreover, the proposed title does not accord with the tradition of naming works, and in some ways fails to accurately and fully reflect the content of the work. Based on these considerations, a different title has been proposed – the *Khurāsān fatḥī tārīkhī*,[50] which still leaves unaddressed the important fact that the author begins his text with the words "The conquest of the Jamshīdī tribes," which adequately reflect its content. With this in mind, I have decided to entitle the work the *Jamshīdī ṭavāyifī fatḥī.*

2. Date of compilation

Although no date is given in the text indicating when it was written, a chronological range can be established with reasonable accuracy. Given that the author was a participant in the events he describes, it is natural to assume that he began outlining or even writing the text during the campaign. Therefore, the *terminus post quem* can be assumed to be the date of the beginning of the campaign, 6 Shavvāl 1257/21 November 1841. The *terminus ante quem* should be recognized as 3 Dhū'l-qa'da 1258/6 December 1842, the date of Allāh-Qulī Khān's death, as he figures throughout the text as alive and well. The fact that the *Jamshīdī ṭavāyifī fatḥī* bestows lush titles and epithets upon Raḥīm-Qulī, including the title of *sulṭān*, does not prove that he had already begun to rule when the text was written. According to Muḥammad 'Īsā Tūra (1841–1894), the only son of Raḥīm-Qulī Khān, while the latter served as Īnāq and governor of Hazārasp, his seal bore the following inscription:

در اکلیل خسرو دوران
شهزاده رحیم قلی سلطان

(The pearl in the crown of the king of the era –
Prince Raḥīm-Qulī Sulṭān).[51]

---

[50] N. Toshov, "Khiva khonligi tarikhiga oid yangi manbalar: Éshmurod Alaviyning "Khuroson fathi tarikhi" asari," *Sharqshunoslik* 16 (2013): 69–70.

[51] Muḥammad 'Īsā Tūra b. Raḥīm-Qulī Khān, *Sayāḥat-nāma* (or *Ḥajj-nāma*), MS COM permanent collection, inv. no. 7695, ff. 166b–167a. In the manuscript the legend is given

This is further confirmed by Āgahī.[52]

3. The *Jamshīdī ṭavāyifī fatḥī* and Āgahī's *Zubdat al-tavārīkh*

Since the *Jamshīdī ṭavāyifī fatḥī* was written before the *Zubdat al-tavārīkh*, the question automatically arises: Did Āgahı use the text of his predecessor? If so, we would be witness to a rather rare and interesting case, in which two authors make use of each other's work; as noted above, Īsh Murād wrote his *Tārīkh-i Sayyid Muḥammad-Khānī* and the *Tārīkhcha-yi Muḥammad Ya'qūb Khwāja* based on the chronicles of Mūnis and Āgahī. A comparison of the *Jamshīdī ṭavāyifī fatḥī* against the corresponding part of the *Zubdat al-tavārīkh*[53] gives us complete certainty that this was indeed the case. Maintaining the order of his source's account and following it almost exactly as far as facts are concerned, Āgahī enumerates people and places in the same order as does Īsh Murād, with the sole difference that he sometimes rearranges the components of a given name (for instance, Khalīfa Isḥāq – Isḥāq Khalīfa). As his description of the campaign draws to a close, Āgahī's dependence on Īsh Murād becomes increasingly obvious. At the same time, the connection between the two texts is not immediately apparent, which can be explained as follows. Firstly, as a contemporary, and at one point even a participant in the campaign, as part of Allāh-Qulī Khān's retinue,[54] Āgahī relates facts that are absent from Īsh Murād's text. Secondly, in some places Āgahī significantly abbreviates the text of his source, omitting not only copies of numerous letters, but also other details, such as, for instance, the description of the Jamshīdīs' "subjugation".[55] Thirdly, Āgahī never reproduces Īsh Murād's text word for word, but rather rephrases it, as a result of which

with orthographical errors, which is generally characteristic of the manuscript, see N. Toshev, "Khorezmiĭskiĭ prints 'Isa Tora i ego novonaĭdennoe Saĭakhat-nama," in *Istoriografiia i istochnikovedenie srednevekovogo Vostoka* (Baku, 2012), 206.

52 Āgahī, *Zubdat al-tavārīkh*, 48.

53 Āgahī, *Zubdat al-tavārīkh*, 32–73.

54 Āgahī, *Zubdat al-tavārīkh*, 42–49 (see p. 46, which relates how Āgahī presented the *khān* with a chronogram devoted to this campaign). The part of the road that the *khān* and the prince covered together is described in the *Jamshīdī ṭavāyifī fatḥī* on folios 11b–19b. Īsh Murād does not mention Āgahī.

55 Īsh Murād 'Alavī, *Jamshīdī ṭavāyifī fatḥī*, ff. 57a–58b.

there is no complete textual coincidence. This is illustrated by the following phrases:

Īsh Murād	Āgahī	Folios
و همولکوندا اخلاص‌نشان میرزا خان خلیفه‌نی هرات خانی شاه کامرانغه‌کیم بو دولت‌خانه‌نینک قدیمی دوستی‌دور ایلچی یوسونیدا محبت‌نامه‌لارین تاپشوروب ییباردی‌لار	و همول کون اخلاص‌نشان خذمتکارلاردین میرزا خان خلیفه‌نی هرات ولایتی‌نینک والئ والاشانی شاه کامران‌غه‌کیم بو خاندان عزت‌مکان نینک قدیمی اخلاص‌کیش‌لاریدین ایردی ایلچی‌لیک یوسونیدا عنایت‌نامه تاپشوروب ارسال ایتی	The *Jamshīdī ṭavāyifī fatḥī*, ff. 37b–38a; The *Zubdat al-tavārīkh*, 55.
یول اثناسیدا بیرام علی خان‌نینک خراب بولغان قلعه‌سین تماشا قیلیب سلطان قلعه‌سی محاذی‌سیدین عبور ایتیب قوی قلعه‌سی آتلیغ جایغه‌کیم قلعهٔ مذکوره‌نینک جنوبی طرفیدا واقع‌دور نزول قیلدی‌لار	یول اثناسیدا بیرام علی خان‌نینک قلعه سین تماشا قیلیب سلطان قلعه‌سی مقابله‌سیدین اوتوب قویون قلعه‌سی آتلیغ موضع‌داکیم مذکور قلعه‌نینک جنوبی طرفیدا واقع‌دور بارکاه اقبال نی برپای قیلدوروب نزول اجلال کورکوزدی	The *Jamshīdī ṭavāyifī fatḥī*, f. 108b; The *Zubdat al-tavārīkh*, 65.

A more complete analysis of this question, which is of key importance in terms of evaluating Āgahī as a historian, will be undertaken in a separate study.[56]

4. Content

In the form in which it has come down to us, the *Jamshīdī ṭavāyifī fatḥī* is dedicated to one sole event, i.e. the Khivan army's campaign under the command of the heir to the throne, Raḥīm-Qulī Īnāq, which took place from 6 Shavvāl 1257/21 November 1841 to 28 Ṣafar 1258/10 April 1842.

Īsh Murād's account and interpretation of these events can be broadly summarized as follows. Initially the aim of this campaign was a routine raid on Khurasan and Iran. Two pieces of information received from Merv inspired Raḥīm-Qulī Īnāq to adjust his plans, however. The first of these con-

---

[56] See above, footnote 40. See also the recently published work, Āgahī, *Zubdat al-tavārīkh*, xxvi–xxviii.

cerned the enmity between the ruler of Herat, Shāh Kāmrān, and his vizier Yār Muḥammad Khān (d. 1267/1851). Rumors reached Raḥīm-Qulī Khān that Yār Muḥammad Khān, having besieged Shāh Kāmrān in the citadel of Herat, was undertaking efforts to capture the fortress. The second piece of information also concerned Herat, and more specifically the Jamshīdīs, who lived in the vicinity of the city. For unknown reasons, the Jamshīdīs had begun to entreat the *qīzīlbāsh* to resettle them from Bādghīs to Mashhad, promising that in return they would become loyal subjects of the Iranian ruler and accept his religion. In his replies, Āṣaf al-Dawla, the governor of Mashhad and a maternal uncle of Muḥammad Shāh Qājār, expressed his willingness to fulfill their request, offering them the fortress of Zīra-Ābād in the vicinity of Mashhad together with all of its land and water resources. Having learned of these events, Raḥīm-Qulī decided, on the one hand, to reconcile Shāh Kāmrān and his vizier, and on the other, to set the Jamshīdīs on the path of righteousness. Upon arriving in the locality of Ūrūshtūshgān, Raḥīm-Qulī dispatched part of his army against the Jamshīdīs in order to resettle them. After several days the news arrived that Raḥīm-Qulī's forces had been victorious, and that the Jamshīdīs had been subjugated without any effort. The Jamshīdīs, numbering about 16 thousand households,[57] were resettled to Khorezm.

In order to realize his second goal, Raḥīm-Qulī engaged in a correspondence with both Shāh Kāmrān and Yār Muḥammad Khān, calling on them to reconcile. Nevertheless, later events would show the futility of these efforts: Shāh Kāmrān did not evade the fate of being killed by his vizier. This undoubtedly occurred before the end of the campaign,[58] although Īsh Murād is silent on this rather inconvenient fact. In his last letter, addressed to Maḥmūd Khān, the ruler of Sar-i Pul, Raḥīm-Qulī promised to return during the harvest in order to punish "certain recalcitrants."[59] The letter does not specify the name of the recalcitrant in question, but he could quite well be Yār Muḥammad Khān.

---

[57] From Īsh Murād's text it is not entirely clear how many Jamshīdīs were ultimately resettled, see Īsh Murād 'Alavī, *Jamshīdī ṭavāyifi fatḥī*, ff. 62a, 68b, 73a, 76b.

[58] By some accounts Shāh Kāmrān was killed at the beginning of 1842, according to others in 1256/1840–1841 (see: M. E. Yapp, "Kāmrān Shāh Durrānī," *EI*[2] IV: 523–524; Noelle-Karimi, *The Pearl in its Midst*, 131, note 225). As can be seen from the *Jamshīdī ṭavāyifi fatḥī,* the second date is certainly wrong.

[59] Īsh Murād 'Alavī, *Jamshīdī ṭavāyifi fatḥī*, f. 109b.

This information as related by Īsh Murād does not entirely correspond to evidence found in other sources, including, among others, a text originating from among the Jamshīdīs themselves. This was written at the beginning of the 20th century at the order of Alexander A. Semenov by Khān Āghā b. Yalangtūsh Khān II, the grandson of Mahdī-Qulī Khān (for more on whom see below), and is entitled the *Tārīkh-i Jamshīdīhā* (or the *Tārīkh-nāma-yi Jamshīdīhā*).[60]

The first inconsistency concerns the reasons behind the Jamshīdīs' resettlement in Khorezm and affects even Āgahī, whose writings on this issue are based on the *Jamshīdī ṭavāyifī fatḥī.* Unlike Īsh Murād, who accuses the Jamshīdīs of willingness to convert, Āgahī takes their side and writes that Shāh Kāmrān continually subjected this people to violence and pillaging, selling their women and children into slavery in neighboring lands, presenting them as *qīzīlbāsh*;[61] unable to endure such oppression, the Jamshīdīs turned to the Khivan government, entreating that they be resettled.[62] According to the above-mentioned Muḥammad 'Īsā Tūra, Raḥīm-Qulī resorted to this measure because of the Jamshīdīs' disobedience (*mukhālifat*). A forced resettlement is also mentioned by some European sources, which incorrectly date this event to 1839–1840 or 1844–46.[63] The author of the *Tārīkh-i Jamshīdīhā*, Khān Āghā, whose words, I must assume, reflect the ideas and attitudes of his fellow-tribesmen, relates that Yār Muḥammad Khān, having killed Shāh Kāmrān and assumed power in Herat in 1260/1844 [*sic*], moved against the *ūymāq*s of Bādghīs (on them see below) and won a victory over them, after which 12,000 Jamshīdī households, headed by their leaders, were

---

[60] Khān Āghā b. Yalangtūsh Khān, *Tārīkh-i Jamshīdīhā*, Institute of History, Archeology, and Ethnography at the Tajikistani Academy of Sciences, MS A. A. Semenov Library, inv. no. 68. On its contents, see A. A. Semenov, "Dzhemshidy i ikh strana (Po dzhemshidskoĭ rukopisi nachala XX veka)," *Izvestiia Turkestanskogo otdeleniia Russkogo geograficheskogo obshchestva* XVI (1923): 165–173.

[61] For more on Shāh Kāmrān's participation in the slave trade, see Noelle-Karimi, *The Pearl in its Midst*, 159.

[62] Āgahī, *Zubdat al-tavārīkh*, 57–58.

[63] N. Veselovskiĭ, *Ocherk istoriko-geograficheskikh svedeniĭ o Khivinskom khanstve ot drevneĭshikh vremen do nastoiashchego* (St. Petersburg, 1877), 307–308; *Materialy po istorii turkmen i Turkmenii*, 481, note 3; Wood, *The Sariq Turkmens of Merv*, 168, note 100; Noelle-Karimi, *The Pearl in its Midst*, 176–177.

forced to flee to Khorezm, where they lived for 16 years, enjoying the protection and hospitality of the Khivan *khān*.[64]

As we can see, opinions differ to the point of contradiction. It is perhaps possible to smooth over this contradiction through the testimony of the Khivan prince Sayyid Ḥāmid Tūra, according to whom the Jamshīdīs, having committed an offence against the ruler of Herat, turned to the *khān* of Khiva, requesting that they be given lands in Merv; the *khān* promised to fulfill their request, but when the Jamshīdīs reached Merv, he ordered that they be resettled in Khorezm.[65] In light of this evidence, it seems by no means coincidental that, during their "subjugation" by the Khivan army, the Jamshīdīs did not offer any resistance,[66] but before advancing from Merv to Khorezm, Raḥīm-Qulī sent ahead 1000 Jamshīdī hostages.[67]

The second major inconsistency is connected to the number of Jamshīdīs resettled in Khorezm. European sources give their number as 5000, 7000, and 10,000.[68] Although this may appear somewhat strange, Khivan sources not only fail to clarify this point, they introduce even more confusion. Āgahī writes of 15,000 households,[69] although in his previous work he gave a larger figure – 20,000.[70] According to Muḥammad 'Īsā Tūra, the number of settlers reached 10,000 families.[71] We find a more likely figure in the work of Sayyid Ḥāmid Tūra, who gives the number of migrants as 5,000–6,000 households.[72]

It should be noted here that European sources give the total number of Jamshīdīs residing in the Herat Valley in the relevant period as not exceeding 12,000 families.[73] Meanwhile it was not all the Jamshīdīs who resettled

---

64 Khān Āghā, *Tārīkh-i Jamshīdīhā*, ff. 3b–4a; Semenov, "Dzhemshidy i ikh strana," 166.

65 Sayyid Ḥāmid Tūra Kāmyāb b. Sayyid Muḥammad Khān, *Tavārīkh al-khavānīn*, MS COM permanent collection, inv. no. 7717, f. 115a. Cf.: Wood, *The Sariq Turkmens of Merv*, 168–169, note 101.

66 Īsh Murād 'Alavī, *Jamshīdī ṭavāyifī fatḥī*, f. 58a.

67 Īsh Murād 'Alavī, *Jamshīdī ṭavāyifī fatḥī*, ff. 84b, 88b, 89a.

68 Veselovskiĭ, *Ocherk istoriko-geograficheskikh svedeniĭ*, 307. Wood, *The Sariq Turkmens of Merv*, 169, note 103; Noelle-Karimi, *The Pearl in its Midst*, 176

69 Āgahī, *Zubdat al-tavārīkh*, 61.

70 Āgahī, *Riyāż al-dawla*, f. 238b.

71 Muḥammad 'Īsā Tūra, *Sayāḥat-nāma*, ff. 167a–168a.

72 Sayyid Ḥāmid Tūra, *Tavārīkh al-khavānīn*, f. 115a.

73 Veselovskiĭ, *Ocherk istoriko-geograficheskikh svedeniĭ*, 307; Semenov, "Dzhemshidy i ikh strana," 162–163.

to Khorezm, but only those who inhabited Qarā Tīfa (i.e. Qarā Tīpa) and Kūshk, although they did comprise the majority of the tribes. Understandably, Īsh Murād and most other Khivan historians strive to present the resettlement of the Jamshīdīs as a great victory by the Khivan army, exaggerating the number of migrants. Indeed, in the figure of 12,000 families, related in the *Tārīkh-i Jamshīdīhā*, we must recognize the Jamshīdīs' tendency to present themselves as a populous nation. Overall, the number of those resettled to Khorezm likely did not exceed 5,000–6,000 families, as testified by Sayyid Ḥāmid Tūra.

A few words about the Jamshīdīs and their life in Khorezm are in order. The Jamshīdīs were an Iranian-speaking tribe who led a semi-nomadic life and professed Sunni Islam. They constituted one of the main subgroups of the so-called "four tribes" (*chahār ūymāq* or *chahār aymāq*), together with the Fīrūzkūhī, the Taymanī, and the Taymūrī (or Tīmūrī).[74] Residing to the east of Herat, the Jamshīdīs periodically took active part in the political life of the region.[75]

The Jamshīdīs we encounter in Khorezm settled on the banks of one of the branches of the Qīlīch Niyāz Bāy canal, roughly ten kilometers southwest of Manghīt. Of their number, 2000 soldiers began to perform military service for the Khivan *khāns*.[76] The Jamshīdīs' role in the state's military and political affairs gradually increased, a development which ultimately had far-reaching consequences for Khiva. Under Muḥammad Amīn Khān, the Jamshīdī leader Mīr Aḥmad Khān,[77] having ingratiated himself with the Khivan ruler, began to influence the latter's decisions and to lead the united army, and a division of Jamshīdīs began to fight in the vanguard of the army[78] – a privilege usually reserved for the Yūmūds and one that they valued

[74] Th. Barfield, *Afghanistan: A Cultural and Political History* (Princeton, 2010), 28. There are also other definitions of the *chahār aymāq*s, see Noelle-Karimi, *The Pearl in its Midst*, 118–119.

[75] See, e.g.: Noelle-Karimi, *The Pearl in its Midst*, 176–177.

[76] Āgahī, *Zubdat al-tavārīkh*, 73.

[77] Āgahī consistently refers to him as Mīr Muḥammad Khān, see Āgahī, *Zubdat al-tavārīkh*, 56, 173; Āgahī, *Jāmi' al-vāqi'āt-i sulṭānī* (see index); Āgahī Muḥammad Riżā Mīrāb b. Īr Niyāz Bīk, *Gulshan-i dawlat*, MS COM permanent collection, inv. no. 7572, f. 30a.

[78] Āgahī, *Jāmi' al-vāqi'āt-i sulṭānī*, 64–65, 69, 114, 116, inter alia.

highly. Moreover, the Jamshīdī Dāmullā Khāl Naẓar was appointed to the vacant post of *ra'īs*.[79]

We can find an explanation for this policy in the works of Sayyid Ḥāmid Tūra and Bayānī. According to these authors, Muḥammad Amīn Khān, having quarreled with the Yūmūds, a development to which the above-mentioned Mīr Aḥmad Khān contributed, began to favor the Jamshīdīs in order to counteract the Yūmūds. Thus, in a contravention of the tradition that had been established under the first Qungrats, he placed the Jamshīdīs, rather than the Yūmūds, at the head of the army. The Yūmūds were indignant, saying that the *khān* "wants to place our own prisoners (*yasīrlārīmīz*) above us."[80] According to the above-mentioned historians, such actions on the part of Muḥammad Amīn Khān served as one of the main reasons for his defeat and death in the battle of Sarakhs in the spring of 1855.[81]

Evidently Mīr Aḥmad Khān enjoyed so much influence that Muḥammad Ya'qūb Mihtar, the all-powerful Khivan vizier, consulted with him on the question of Muḥammad Amīn Khān's successor; after this meeting, they announced the new *khān*, 'Abdallāh Bīk b. Qūtlūq Murād Īnāq, right on the battlefield.[82] The latter, a member of a collateral branch of the Qungrat dynasty, did not figure on the list of contenders for the throne in any capacity, and when in 1856 the reins of power were returned to the "lawful" occupants of the Khivan throne, Muḥammad Ya'qūb Mihtar paid for his misdeed with his life.[83] Mīr Aḥmad Khān died at the hands of rebellious Turkmens even earlier, at the beginning of September 1855.[84] Under the next *khān*, Qūtlūq Murād, when the Turkmen and the Qaraqalpaqs rebelled and the country was

---

[79] Āgahī, *Jāmi' al-vāqi'āt-i sulṭānī*, 178.

[80] Sayyid Ḥāmid Tūra, *Tavārīkh al-khavānīn*, f. 126a. The Yūmūds took part in the resettlement of the Jamshīdīs, see Īsh Murād 'Alavī, *Jamshīdī ṭavāyifi fatḥī*, f. 58b.

[81] For more on this, see Sayyid Ḥāmid Tūra, *Tavārīkh al-khavānīn*, ff. 125b–129a; Bayānī Muḥammad Yūsuf, *Shajara-yi khwārazmshāhī*, MS COM permanent collection, inv. no. 9596, ff. 330a–b, 346b–351b; Bregel', "Sochinenie Baiani," 141–144.

[82] Bayānī, *Shajara-yi khwarazmshāhī*, f. 352b. Sayyid Ḥāmid Tūra does not say anything about Mīr Aḥmad Khān's involvement in this conspiracy and writes that 'Abdallāh Bīk became *khān* through the efforts of Muḥammad Ya'qūb Mihtar, see Sayyid Ḥāmid Tūra, *Tavārīkh al-khavānīn*, f. 129a.

[83] Āgahī, *Gulshan-i dawlat*, ff. 91b–95b.

[84] Āgahī, *Jāmi' al-vāqi'āt-i sulṭānī*, 216–217. Iranian sources mistakenly relate that Mīr Aḥmad Khān died in the battle of Sarakhs, see Noelle-Karimi, *The Pearl in its Midst*, 177. In fact he was only wounded.

engulfed by chaos, Mīr Aḥmad Khān's brother, Mahdī-Qulī Bīk (executed in 1880), having taken the former's place as leader of the Jamshīdīs, also rose up in rebellion and captured several fortresses.[85] A week after Sayyid Muḥammad Khān's accession to the throne, on 12 Jumādā II 1272/18 February 1856, the Jamshīdīs left Khorezm,[86] evidently fearing retaliation for the actions they had undertaken during Khiva's time of troubles.[87]

5. Determining the genre of the work

The content of the *Jamshīdī ṭavāyifī fatḥī* presents us with the complex challenge of determining the genre of the text. The practice of composing a historical work devoted to a single event, even a significant one, is very rare, not only in Central Asian historiography, but in the Muslim historiographical tradition more generally. This raises the question: is the *Jamshīdī ṭavāyifī fatḥī* part of a larger work conceived by the author, or was it originally planned as an independent work? Given the absence of a preface, which would generally make the author's intentions known to readers, we must seek the answer to the above question using indirect evidence, and that evidence seems to suggest that we are dealing with a unique type of composition.

In my opinion, one of the decisive arguments in favor of this hypothesis is the fact that, although the manuscript lacks an opening (at least the *dībācha* is missing), the end of the text is in completely finished form: having related the return of troops led by Raḥīm-Qulī to Khiva, the author adds a *mathnavī* under the heading "A Petition in the Form of a Blessing," in which, after presenting his best wishes to the *khān* – and this was, apparently, Allāh-Qulī Khān (see below) – he asks the latter to show him mercy.[88] The text clearly ends here because it is not followed by another history of

85 Āgahī, *Jāmi' al-vāqi'āt-i sulṭānī*, 223, 232–234.

86 Āgahī, *Gulshan-i dawlat*, ff. 28b–33b. A few days later the above-mentioned Dāmullā Khāl Naẓar, who lived in the capital and who was therefore unable to leave with his tribesmen, was removed from the post of Khivan *ra'is*, see Āgahī, *Gulshan-i dawlat*, f. 45b.

87 On the Jamshīdīs' further fate, see in particular: Noelle-Karimi, *The Pearl in its Midst*; Semenov, "Dzhemshidy i ikh strana".

88 Īsh Murād 'Alavī, *Jamshīdī ṭavāyifī fatḥī*, f. 124a–b.

Allāh-Qulī Khān and Raḥīm-Qulī Khān: the former's rule continued past these events, and the latter's rule had not yet begun.

Another strong argument lies in the high degree of detail with which the history of the campaign is related. This thoroughness is reflected primarily in the fact the text contains copies of nearly 37 letters (see below).[89] The texts of letters and other documents, and, more often, paraphrasings of them, can be found in almost in all historical works originating in the Khanate of Khiva,[90] but not with such regularity and not in such large numbers. Letters themselves are mentioned quite often, especially in relation to the exchange of embassies with various countries, references to which abound in Khivan chronicles. Mūnis, Āgahī, and other Khivan authors usually cite the text of only those letters and documents that they deemed important and that contain some information that fits into the fabric of their narrative. As a consequence, other historical works do not include, for example, correspondence between an expedition force and the Khivan court, while the *Jamshīdī ṭavāyifī fatḥī* incorporates the texts of nine letters that represent correspondence between Allāh-Qulī Khān and Raḥīm-Qulī. These letters are not characterized by any special artistic merit that would justify their inclusion as emblematic examples of the epistolary genre, and they contain no remarkable factual material.[91]

In short, if we assume that the existing manuscript is only part of a larger work on the history of Allāh-Qulī Khān or Raḥīm-Qulī Khān, it is extremely difficult to explain why one military expedition is described in such detail,

---

89 In two previously published studies, the number of letters was mistakenly given as 33, see Āgahī, *Jāmi' al-vāqi'āt-i sulṭānī*, XX; Toshov, "Khiva khonligi tarikhiga oid yangi manbalar," 73.

90 See, e.g: Mūnis/Āgahī, *Firdaws al-iqbāl*, text, 29–30 [notes 177, 180]; Mūnis/Āgahī, *Firdaws al-iqbāl*, translation, xxxvii-xxxviii [notes 186, 189]; Āgahī, *Riyāż al-dawla*, ff. 35b, 56a, 158b, 160a, 164a–166a, 167a–b, 219a–b, 223b–224a, 224b–225b; Āgahī, *Jāmi' al-vāqi'āt-i sulṭānī*, 150, 165; Āgahī, *Gulshan-i dawlat*, ff. 54a, 80a, 84a–b, 146a–147b, 149a–150a, 152b–154b, 185b 186a, 209b–210a, 230a–b; Bayānī, *Shajara-yi khwārazmshāhī*, ff. 441b 442a, 455b–456a, 458a, 461b–462a. In historical works written in Khorezm after the establishment of Soviet power, the use of various documents becomes almost the norm.

91 The purely formal nature of these letters is evidenced, for example, by a message from Raḥīm-Qulī to his father (f. 47a–b), in which he did not even bother to inform the *khān* about his decision to change the route and the purpose of the expedition. Such information was clearly communicated verbally via messenger.

no matter how important it may be. There were many such campaigns during the reigns of both *khāns*, and illuminating each of them in such a high level of detail, or even comparatively less thoroughly, would result in an excessive increase in the volume of the presumed text.

Nevertheless, a slightly different explanation is also possible. In an earlier work, I argued that the final resolution of the question of the genre to which *Jamshīdī ṭavāyifī fatḥī* belongs is prompted by the identification of the authors of two other short, anonymous works.[92] The first of these concerns the first year of the rule of Allāh-Qulī Khān (the year of the chicken in the 12-year cyclical calendar) and has come down to us as a single manuscript housed at the Institute of Oriental Manuscripts in St. Petersburg under the call number B 768. The second text is dedicated to the sixth year (the year of the tiger) of Allāh-Qulī Khān's reign. The unique manuscript of this work is held by the same institution under call number B 769.[93] Recently, during a research trip undertaken in April and June 2015, one more text of this same type was discovered in the Manuscript Division of the National Library of Russia in St. Petersburg (call number T.n.s. 108). It contains a description of the campaign against Khurasan carried out in 1253–1254/1838 under the leadership of the chief Khivan vizier, Muḥammad Yūsuf Mihtar (died 1255/1839), in order to render assistance to Herat, which was at that time beleaguered by Iranian troops. None of these three texts includes an author's preface, as a result of which we do not know the titles given to them by their authors; in the literature and in inventories they are known under the provisional titles *Tārīkh-i Allāh-Qulī Muḥammad Bahadur Khān*, *Tārīkh-i Allāh-Qulī Khān*, and *Vāqi'a-yi Yūsuf Mihtar*, respectively.

The author of the first two works is now known to us. He is Mīrzā Masīḥā Bukhārī, a Bukharan by birth who served the Khivan *khāns* and who was appointed to the post of *munshī* by Muḥammad Raḥīm Khān I in 1233/1818.[94] It should be noted that the attribution of the first text was facilitated by Īsh Murād Ākhūnd. The anonymous author cites two of his own chronograms dedicated to the death of Muḥammad Raḥīm Khān I and the

[92] Toshov, "Khiva kholnligi tarikhiga oid yangi manbalar," 73.

[93] For a description of the manuscripts, see Dmitrieva et al., *Opisanie tiurkskikh rukopiseĭ*, nos. 108, 109; Dmitrieva, *Katalog tiurkskikh rukopiseĭ*, nos. 69, 79. The descriptions contain a number of inaccuracies.

[94] Mūnis/Āgahī, *Firdaws al-iqbāl*, text, 1007; Mūnis/Āgahī, *Firdaws al-iqbāl*, translation, 458.

accession to the throne of his son, Allāh-Qulī Khān.[95] In his *Tārīkh-i Sayyid Muḥammad-Khānī*, Īsh Murād Ākhūnd includes the text of the first of these chronograms, naming its author (Mīrzā Muḥammad Masīḥā Bukhārī) and calling him his "mentor" (*ustād*).[96] It is highly likely that the third text is also the work of Mīrzā Masīḥā. Moreover, in the *Tārīkh-i Allāh-Qulī Khān*, the author refers to his earlier work on the events of the year of the cow, and in the *Vāqi'a-yi Yūsuf Mihtar*, to a planned text concerning Russo-Khivan relations in connection to the arrest of Khivan merchants in the Russian Empire. Based on these and other facts, we can safely conclude that it was customary in the Khanate of Khiva for the *khān*'s personal secretary to compose annual histories of his patron's rule or descriptions of significant events, and that these texts were subsequently used in the writing of well-known official chronicles such as the *Firdaws al-iqbāl*, the *Riyāż al-dawla*, and others.[97]

This begs the question: should *Jamshīdī ṭavāyifī fatḥī* be classified as this type of text? The *Jamshīdī ṭavāyifī fatḥī* and the works of Mīrzā Masīḥā have so much in common that this question may seem rhetorical. Especially, if one considers that Āgahī made use of this text while compiling his *Zubdat al-tawārīkh*. Nevertheless, something is still lacking for complete certainty. First of all, we still do not know in what capacity Īsh Murād participated in the campaign he describes. Everything would fall into place if we knew that he served as Raḥīm-Qulī's personal secretary. We can certainly admit such a possibility, even without direct evidence, but it remains a stretch. We cannot exclude the possibility that Īsh Murād was appointed to the post of *ra'is* after 1841, and that Āgahī committed a parachronism in referring to him as *ra'īs*.[98] It seems less doubtful, however, to assume that he was instructed to perform the duties of clerk or registrar of events during this campaign. But we are not sufficiently well acquainted with the Khanate's administrative system to be completely confident in our judgments. In particular, a range of questions associated with record-keeping in the Khanate of Khiva remains

---

95 [Mīrzā Masīḥā Bukhārī], *Tārīkh-i Allāh-Qulī Muḥammad Bahadur Khān*, MS IOM, inv. no. B 768, ff. 23a–24b.

96 Īsh Murād 'Alavī, *Tārīkh-i Sayyid Muḥammad-Khānī*, f. 512a.

97 See: N. Toshov, "Khiva solnomalarining yozma manbalari khususida," *Sharqshunoslik/Vostokovedenie/Oriental Studies* 4 (2015): 87–98. A more detailed analysis of these and other issues raised in this article will be undertaken in the above mentioned work, *Khorezmian Historiography (19th – 20th Centuries).*

98 Āgahī completed *Zubdat al-tavārīkh* in 1846.

completely unstudied: the social composition of the *munshīs*, their number and their distribution among various departments, their responsibilities, etc. Thus, in the absence of sufficient data, the question remains open, and we cannot exclude the possibility that Īsh Murād composed *Jamshīdī ṭavāyifī fatḥī* of his own accord, in imitation of the works of Mīrzā Masīḥā. But even if it was composed on the author's own initiative, the creation of the text was supported by Raḥīm-Qulī. Otherwise, the author would likely not have been granted access to almost all correspondence produced during the campaign.

6. The letters in the *Jamshīdī ṭavāyifī fatḥī*

In view of the exceptional importance of these letters in several respects, I will discuss them in greater detail. Below is a list of those letters that are included in *Jamshīdī ṭavāyifī fatḥī*:

No.	Addresser	Addressee	Letter title	Folios
1	Muḥammad 'Alī Khān, ruler of Kalāt	Raḥīm-Qulī	*'arża-dāsht*	25a–26a
2	Raḥīm-Qulī	Muḥammad 'Alī Khān, ruler of Kalāt	*'ināyat-nāma*	27a–b
3	Raḥīm-Qulī	Allāh-Qulī Khān	*'arża-dāsht*	37a–b
4	Raḥīm-Qulī	Shāh Kāmrān, ruler of Herat	*muḥabbat-nāma*	38a–b
5	Raḥīm-Qulī	Vālī Bīk, ruler of Tāsh Qūrghān	*'ināyat-nāma*	39a–b
6	Vālī Bīk, ruler of Tāsh Qūrghān	Raḥīm-Qulī	*'arża-dāsht*	40b–41b
7	Raḥīm-Qulī	Vālī Bīk, ruler of Tāsh Qūrghān	*'ināyat-nāma*	46a–b
8	Raḥīm-Qulī	Allāh-Qulī Khān	*'arża-dāsht*	47a–b

No.	Addresser	Addressee	Letter title	Folios
9	Yār Muḥammad, vizier to Shāh Kāmrān	Raḥīm-Qulī	*'arża-dāsht*	49a–50a
10	Raḥīm-Qulī	Yār Muḥammad, vizier to Shāh Kāmrān	*'ināyat-nāma*	50b–51a
11	Allāh-Qulī Khān	Raḥīm-Qulī	*'ināyat-nāma*	54a–b
12	Karīmdād Khān Hazāra, ruler of Qal'a-yi Naw	Raḥīm-Qulī	*'arża-dāsht*	55b–56a
13	Allāh-Qulī Khān	Raḥīm-Qulī	*'ināyat-nāma*	59a–b
14	Raḥīm-Qulī	Allāh-Qulī Khān	*'arża-dāsht*	61a–62a
15	Raḥīm-Qulī	Shāh Kāmrān, ruler of Herat	*muḥabbat-nāma*	63b–64a
16	Raḥīm-Qulī	Yār Muḥammad, vizier to Shāh Kāmrān	*'ināyat-nāma*	64b–65a
17	Vālī Bīk, ruler of Tāsh Qūrghān	Raḥīm-Qulī	*'arża-dāsht*	65a–67a
18	Miżrāb Khān, ruler of Maymana	Raḥīm-Qulī	*'arża-dāsht*	67b–68b
19	Vālī Bīk, ruler of Tāsh Qūrghān	Raḥīm-Qulī	*'arża-dāsht*	70a–73a
20	Raḥīm-Qulī	Miżrāb Khān, ruler of Maymana	*'ināyat-nāma*	73b–74b
21	Raḥīm-Qulī	Rulers of Tāsh Qūrghān, Ḥiṣār, Sar-i Pul, Shāh Mardān, Balkh and Andkhūy	*'ināyat-nāma*	75a–b

No.	Addresser	Addressee	Letter title	Folios
18	Miżrāb Khān, ruler of Maymana	Raḥīm-Qulī	*'arża-dāsht*	67b–68b
19	Vālī Bīk, ruler of Tāsh Qūrghān	Raḥīm-Qulī	*'arża-dāsht*	70a–73a
20	Raḥīm-Qulī	Miżrāb Khān, ruler of Maymana	*'ināyat-nāma*	73b–74b
21	Raḥīm-Qulī	Rulers of Tāsh Qūrghān, Ḥiṣār, Sar-i Pul, Shāh Mardān, Balkh and Andkhūy	*'ināyat-nāma*	75a–b
22	Raḥīm-Qulī	Allāh-Qulī Khān	*'arża-dāsht*	76a–77a
23	Karīmdād Khān Hazāra, ruler of Qal'a-yi Naw	Raḥīm-Qulī	*'arża-dāsht*	77a–78a
24	Raḥīm-Qulī	Karīmdād Khān Hazāra, ruler of Qal'a-yi Naw	*'ināyat-nāma*	78b–79a
25	Raḥīm-Qulī	Karīmdād Khān Hazāra, ruler of Qal'a-yi Naw	*'ināyat-nāma*	83a
26	Raḥīm-Qulī	Allāh-Qulī Khān	*'arża-dāsht*	83b–84b
27	Raḥīm-Qulī	Allāh-Qulī Khān	*'arża-dāsht*	88a–89a
28	Vālī Bīk, ruler of Tāsh Qūrghān	Raḥīm-Qulī	*'arża-dāsht*	90a–93a
29	Shāh Valī Khān, ruler of Andkhūy	Raḥīm-Qulī	*'arża-dāsht*	93a–94a
30	Karīmdād Khān Hazāra, ruler of Qal'a-yi Naw	Raḥīm-Qulī	*'arża-dāsht*	96a–97a

No.	Addresser	Addressee	Letter title	Folios
	to Shāh Kāmrān			103a
36	Allāh-Qulī Khān	Raḥīm-Qulī	*'ināyat-nāma*	104a–b
37	Raḥīm-Qulī	Maḥmūd Khān, ruler of Sar-i Pul	*'ināyat-nāma*	109a–b

In fact, the total number of letters to which the author had access was much greater. In several instances Īsh Murād presents one or two letters as a kind of sample, stating that there were other messages with the same or similar content. For example, in one case only one out of eight letters is provided (ff. 38b, 39b), and in two other cases, one out of five letters is given (ff. 67a, 109b).[99] There are also cases in which Īsh Murād mentions letters without incorporating their contents, although he sometimes provides a general overview.[100] We also observe the phenomenon when several letters were combined into one text by Īsh Murād himself (f. 75a–b). In three places Īsh Murād notes that he could not provide the text of a given letter, as he did not see the letter itself (ff. 81a, 96a, 103a). All three of these letters were written by Allāh-Qulī Khān to his son Raḥīm-Qulī, which suggests that their content was not meant for a broader audience.

Three letters addressed to Raḥīm-Qulī were clearly translated from Persian (ff. 49a, 67b, 101b); two of these were written by Yār Muḥammad, Kāmrān Shāh's vizier, and one by Miżrāb Khān, the ruler of Maymana.

Unfortunately, attempts to locate the original versions of the documents in the *Jamshīdī ṭavāyifī fatḥī* have not been successful,[101] so we have no way of knowing how Īsh Murād could use them. I stated above that in his later

99 See also: Īsh Murād 'Alavī, *Jamshīdī ṭavāyifī fatḥī*, ff. 41b, 46b, 73a, 94a, 98b.

100 See: Īsh Murad 'Alavī, *Jamshīdī ṭavāyifī fatḥī*, ff. 63a, 89b, 104b, 106a, 107b, 115a.

101 Since the project within which the current work is being published has just started, it has a long way to go in terms of completing one of its most important tasks, namely, determining what documents should have been, or at least could have been, in the Archives of the Khivan *khāns*, but are not. Once this is addressed, we can move on to the question of why these documents are not available there, while other documents of this kind have been preserved in this part of the archive. The latter also include letters used in narrative sources.

writings, Īsh Murād made changes to the texts of the documents found in his sources. In fairness it must be said, however, that his revisions did not change the meaning of the documents. We can hope that the letters included in the *Jamshīdī ṭavāyifī fatḥī* are presented, at any rate, without any significant changes that would alter their meaning, especially since there is no apparent reason for such changes. At the same time, there is no guarantee that Īsh Murād transmitted the text of the letters word for word.

7. Some remarks on the language and style of the work

In its linguistic and stylistic features, the *Jamshīdī ṭavāyifī fatḥī* does not differ significantly from other historical works composed in Turki in the Khanate of Khiva in the nineteenth century, although in general it is characterized by a lesser degree of flamboyance than the chronicles of Mūnis and Āgahī. The bulk of the text's vocabulary consists of Arabisms and Persianisms, and occasionally, mostly in verse, words from the local dialect, such as *īl* – "hand", *dīgīn* – "to", (*rangī*) *dūnūb* – "having paled", *yāghdāyīgha yārāshā* – "depending on the situation" (ff. 28b, 59a, 115b, 119b). The latter phrase is used in a letter. Simple sentences are interspersed with lush, difficult phrases. The author makes wide and relatively successful use of rhetorical figures, especially metaphor, hyperbole and comparison. Sunrise and sunset are always described using a variety of tropes.

Here it should be noted that *Jamshīdī ṭavāyifī fatḥī* shows clear signs of influence by the works of Mīrzā Masīḥā Bukhārī. A whole series of phrases employed by Īsh Murād appear in the *Tārīkh-i Allāh-Qulī Muḥammad Bahadur Khān*. Several such borrowed phrases do not seem to appear in the works of any other Khivan historians (for example, *sundus va istabraq mānandī* – "like silk and gold brocade"[102]).

The text contains many blessing formulas and constructions borrowed from the texts of the included letters. As an example we can point to the author's frequent use of the formulas *rūḥuna fidāhu* and *rūḥunā va rūḥ al-'ālamīn fidāhu* ("Let our soul and the soul of the world become a sacrifice for him!"), which are absent from the chronicles of Mūnis and Āgahī but are

---

[102] Īsh Murād 'Alavī, *Jamshīdī ṭavāyifī fatḥī*, f. 82b; Mīrzā Masīḥā Bukhārī, *Tārīkh-i Allāh-Qulī Muḥammad Bahādur Khān*, f. 7a.

often found in other letters.[103] The influence of the letters can be traced in the text's lexicon. Moreover, the importance of the letters to the structure of the text is indicated by the fact that some of their titles are written in cinnabar. No other sections or chapters are set apart, except for the title at the very beginning, which sounds exactly like the title of a chapter. Additionally, a small empty space is left before the text of the individual letters. There is even poetry devoted to the letters (ff. 39b, 81a, 106a).

Poetic inserts of various forms (*tārīkh*, *mathnavī*, etc.) and length (from one to 27 *bayt*s) are fairly common, especially at the beginning and end of the composition. In all there are 85 pieces, totaling 437 *bayt*s. Except for one poem from Firdawsī's *Shāh-nāma* (f. 53a), all of these verses were authored by Īsh Murād and were written, with the exception of one Persian chronogram (f. 42a–b),[104] in Turki. Many of these poems do not stand out in terms of elegance and were apparently composed in haste. Of the nine Qur'ānic quotations cited in the manuscript, four are in the text of letters.

Special mention is required by some stylistic errors, some of which lead to semantic absurdities. These are mostly associated with the use of conjunctions and word order. The most significant of these are given below:

اول عالیمقام داغی دولت بیله طعام تناولیدین سونک آتلانیب (for اول عالیمقام داغی طعام تناولیدین سونک دولت بیله آتلانیب) (f. 9a).

مذکور جایدین پیشین نمازین اوقوب (for پیشین نمازین اوقوب مذکور جایدین) (f. 23a).

اول حصار اهلی مونچه شکوه و کیرودار بیله‌کیم لشکر اهلین مشاهده قیلدیلار (!) (f. 58a).

ویس محرم بیله مرو ولایتی‌غه یوز تورلوک فتح و نصرت بیله صحت و سلامت مراجعت کورکوزوب نزول قیلغانلارین (for مرو ولایتی‌غه یوز تورلوک فتح و نصرت بیله صحت و سلامت مراجعت کورکوزوب نزول قیلغانلارین ویس محرم بیله) (f. 88a).

موقوف بیر نیچه کون قویدی‌لار (for بیر نیچه کون موقوف قویدی‌لار) (f. 105b).

---

[103] See, e.g.: Central State Archive of the Republic of Uzbekistan, f. I-125, op. 2, d. 161, ff. 4, 6, 7, inter alia.

[104] Khivan poets wrote chronograms primarily in Persian, see Āgahī, *Jāmi' al-vāqi'āt-i sulṭānī*, XXII.

III. The Manuscript and the Principles for Publication of the Text

1. A description of the manuscript

The manuscript consists of 124 folios. Some folios at the beginning and the end have been cut out. The manuscript is enclosed in green-colored binding with a burgundy leather spine. Both covers feature medallions with pendants. The paper is eastern and burnished. The size of the paper is 23 x 14 cm, and the size of the text is 15 x 7 cm, with 11 lines on each page. The text is written with a *nasta'līq* in black ink. The headings, some verses of the Qur'ān, and delimiters between hemistiches are cinnabar. There are two types of catchwords. The name of the transcriber and the date of transcription are unknown. Folio 123 has a hole that has damaged the text, and in some folios (ff. 17a, 44b, 46a, 111b, etc.) part of the text is blurred. Folios 9b, 24a, 67a and 124b bear the seal of the owner of the manuscript with the legend "Āq-muhr-i 'Abd al-Rasūl Bāy, 1334 [1915–1916]."

There is a strong likelihood that the manuscript is an autograph. This is evidenced by the nature of some of the additions made in the margins.[105] An even stronger indication is given by the handwriting. When comparing the manuscript with the Tashkent copy of the *Tārīkhcha-yi Muḥammad Ya'qūb Khwāja*, we see a great similarity of handwriting (see the attached photo illustrations), despite the fact that manuscript 845 is clearly a draft, while manuscript 9981 is a clean copy. Moreover, individual blurred sections give the impression that the text was subjected to editing, and folio 17a even preserves traces of such modifications: there are diacritical marks above the letter *sīn* in the word *sa'ādat*, left, apparently, when the word was changed (see illustration).

2. The orthography of the manuscript

The manuscript's orthography is relatively stable, at least in comparison with the autographs of Āgahī and Mūnis. For example, the initial *yī* is almost always conveyed by two *yās*. Nevertheless, the inconsistency characteristic

[105] See folios 4b, 7b, 8b, 24b, 42a, 69b, and especially 98b.

of Turkic-language literary monuments is also evident here. It is expressed primarily in the use of different forms of the same words and affixes (بیراز || بیر آز؛ کراک || کیراک؛ آنکا || انکا؛ غه || کا) and in the fact they are sometimes written separately and sometimes together.

Some quotations from the Qur'ān, as well as individual words, are given with vowels. In the case of Qur'ānic verses, these almost always include errors. Diacritics are not always given, although this does not create any difficulties in reading the text.

3. Guidelines for the text's publication

This edition preserves the original text as it appears in the manuscript, including fused spellings of two words. Only spelling mistakes and some stylistic errors have been fixed, and the uncorrected versions from the manuscript are noted in the footnotes. Quotations from the Qur'ān have been fully vowelized. The following mistakes and peculiarities have been corrected without any reservations:

1. The use of non-standard use or absence of the *hamza* sign in words for which dictionaries always use that sign (مأوا، تأیید، مأمور، مؤدا، توأم، رؤس، تأکید).
2. Improper vowel additions to quotations from the Qur'ān.
3. In order to avoid confusion with the Persian آرا, the Turkic word آرا || ارا is given in the form ارا.
4. The systematic spelling of the word هرآیینه has been corrected to هرآینه, and the frequent spelling قبلکاه has been corrected to قبله‌کاه.

Additions and amendments made in the margins and between lines are marked in the footnotes. Words of Turkish origin that passed into Persian (*būshqāb*, *chākmān*, etc.) are given in the form in which they are written in the text of the manuscript, although Persian dictionary can give alternative versions. Some complex words of Arabic origin are rendered in different manners: مالاکلام, but کما ینبغی.

Bibliography

Abbreviations

COM – Abu Rayhan Biruni Center for Oriental Manuscripts at the Tashkent State Institute of Oriental Studies of the Ministry of Higher and Specialized Secondary Education of the Republic of Uzbekistan, Tashkent.
IOM – Institute of Oriental Manuscripts at the Russian Academy of Sciences, St. Petersburg.
NLR – National Library of Russia, St. Petersburg.

Manuscripts

Āgahī Muḥammad Riza Mīrāb b. Īr Niyāz Bīk. *Gulshan-i dawlat*. MS COM permanent collection, inv. no. 7572.

Āgahī Muḥammad Riżā Mīrāb b. Īr Niyāz Bīk. *Riyāż al-dawla*. MS IOM, inv. no. D 123.

Āgahī Muḥammad Riżā Mīrāb b. Īr Niyāz Bīk. *Shāhid al-iqbāl*. MS IOM, inv. no. C 572.

Bayānī Muḥammad Yūsuf. *Shajara-yi khwārazmshāhī*. MS COM permanent collection, inv. no. 9596.

Central State Archive of the Republic of Uzbekistan. F. I-125, op. 2, d. 161, 526.

[Īsh Murād b. Ādīna Muḥammad]. [*Jamshīdī ṭavāyifī fatḥī*]. MS COM permanent collection, inv. no. 9981.

Īsh Murād Ākhūnd b. Ādīna Muḥammad al-ʻAlavī. *Mayāmin al-tarjumān va muʼnis al-insān tarjumasī*. MS NLR, inv. no. T.n.s. 16.

Īsh Murād Ākhūnd b. Ādīna Muḥammad al-ʻAlavī. *Sulṭān al-lughāt*. MS from the private collection of Anbara Atamuradova and Allanazar Abdurahimov.

Īsh Murād Ākhūnd b. Ādīna Muḥammad al-ʻAlavī. *Tārīkh-i Sayyid Muḥammad-Khānī*. MS IOM, inv. no. C 573.

Īsh Murād Ākhūnd b. Ādīna Muḥammad al-ʻAlavī. *Tārīkhcha-yi Muḥammad Yaʻqūb Khwāja*. MS IOM, inv. no. C 574; MS COM permanent collection, inv. no. 845.

Khān Āghā b.Yalangtūsh Khān. *Tārīkh-i Jamshīdīhā*. Institute of History, Archeology, and Ethnography at the Tajikistani Academy of Sciences, MS A. A. Semenov Library, inv. no. 68.

[Mīrzā Masīhā Bukhārī]. *Tārīkh-i Allāh-Qulī Muḥammad Bahādur Khān*. MS IOM, inv. no. B 768.

Muḥammad ʻĪsā Tūra b. Raḥīm-Qulī Khān. *Sayāḥat-nāma* (or *Ḥajj-nāma*). MS COM permanent collection, inv. no. 7695.

Mūnis Shīr Muḥammad. *Tūy-nāma*. MS NLR, inv. no. T.n.s. 88.

Sayyid Ḥāmid Tūra Kāmyāb b. Sayyid Muḥammad Khān. *Tavārīkh al-khavānīn*. MS COM permanent collection, inv. no. 7717.

Published works

Abdullaev F. A. *Ŭzbek tilining Xorazm shevalari*. Tashkent, 1961.

Āgahī Muḥammad Riżā Mīrāb. *Jāmi' al-vāqi'āt-i sulṭānī*. Edited by N. Tashev. Samarkand/Tashkent, 2012.

Āgahī Muḥammad Riżā Mīrāb. *Zubdat al-tavārīkh*. Edited by Kh. Nazirova. Tashkent/Samarkand, 2016.

Barfield Th. *Afghanistan: A Cultural and Political History*. Princeton, 2010.

Bregel' Iu. É. "Sochinenie Baiani 'Shadzhara-yi khorezmshakhi' kak istochnik po istorii turkmen." *Kratkie soobshcheniia Instituta narodov Azii* XLIV (1961): 125–157.

Bregel Yu. "The Tawārīkh-i Khōrazmshāhīya by Thanā'ī: The Historiography of Khiva and the Uzbek Literary Language." In *Aspects of Altaic Civilization II: Proceedings of the XVIII PIAC, Bloomington, June 29–July 5, 1975*, edited by L. V. Clark and P. A. Draghi. Bloomington, 1978, 17–32.

Bregel Yu. "The New Uzbek States: Bukhara, Khiva and Khoqand: c. 1750–1886." In *The Cambridge History of Inner Asia: The Chinggisid Age*, edited by N. Di Cosmo, A. J. Frank and P. B. Golden. Cambridge, 2009, 392–411.

Brockelmann C. *Geschichte der arabischen Litteratur*. Supplementband I. Leiden, 1996.

Dmitrieva L. V. *Katalog tiurkskikh rukopiseĭ Instituta vostokovedeniia Rossiĭskoĭ akademii nauk*. Moscow, 2002.

Dmitrieva L. V., Muginov A. M., and Muratov S. N. *Opisanie tiurkskikh rukopiseĭ Instituta narodov Azii*, vol. 1. Moscow, 1965.

Dmitrieva L. V. "Tiurkskie rukopisi kollektsii 'novaia seriia' sobraniia Gosudarstvennoĭ Publichnoĭ biblioteki im. M. E. Saltykova-Shchedrina." *Vostochnyĭ sbornik* 3 (1973): 76–85.

Hofman H. F. *Turkish literature: A Bio-bibliographical Survey*. Section III, pt. I, vols. 1–6. Utrecht, 1969.

Katalog khivinskikh kaziĭskikh dokumentov XIX – nachala XX vv. Edited by A. Urunbaev, T. Khorikava, T. Faĭziev, G. Dzhuraeva and K. Isogaĭ. Tashkent/Kyoto, 2001.

Khorezm v istorii gosudarstvennosti Uzbekistana. Edited by É. V. Rtveladze and D. A. Alimova. Tashkent, 2013.

Masson V. M. and Romodin V.A. *Istoriia Afganistana*, vol. II. Moscow, 1965.

Materialy po istorii turkmen i Turkmenii, II: Iranskie, bukharskie i khivinskie istochniki. Moscow/Leningrad, 1938.

Muḥammad Taqī Lisān al-Mulk Sipihr. *Nāsikh al-tavārīkh: Tārīkh-i qājārīya*. Edited by J. Kiyanfar, vol. 2. Tehran, 1377/1998.

Mūnis Shīr Muḥammad Mīrāb and Āgahī Muḥammad Riżā Mīrāb. *Firdaws al-iqbāl: History of Khorezm*. Edited by Yu. Bregel. Leiden/New York, 1988.

Mūnis Shīr Muḥammad Mīrāb and Āgahī Muḥammad Riżā Mīrāb. *Firdaws al-iqbāl: History of Khorezm*. Translated from Chaghatay and annotated by Yu. Bregel. Leiden/Boston/Köln, 1999.

Noelle-Karimi Ch. *The Pearl in its Midst: Herat and the Mapping of Khurasan (15th – 19th Centuries)*. Vienna, 2014.

Persidskie i tadzhikskie rukopisi Instituta narodov Azii AN SSSR (Kratkiĭ alfavitnyĭ katalog). Edited by N. D. Miklukho-Maklaĭ, part 1. Moscow, 1964.

Sartori P. "On Madrasas, Legitimation, and Islamic Revival in 19th-Century Khorezm: Some Preliminary Observations." *Eurasian Studies* 14 (2016): 98–134.

Semenov A. A. "Dzhemshidy i ikh strana (Po dzhemshidskoĭ rukopisi nachala XX veka." *Izvestiia Turkestanskogo otdeleniia Russkogo geograficheskogo obshchestva* XVI (1923): 161–174.

Sobranie vostochnykh rukopiseĭ Akademii nauk Respubliki Uzbekistan: Istoriia. Edited by D. Iu. Iusupova and R. P. Dzhalilova. Tashkent, 1998.

Sobranie vostochnykh rukopiseĭ Akademii nauk Uzbekskoĭ SSR, vol. I. Tashkent, 1952; vol. III. Tashkent, 1955.

The History of Afghanistan: Fayż Muḥammad Kātib Hazāra's *Sirāj al-tavārīkh*, vol. 1. Translated by R. D. McChesney. Leiden/Boston, 2013.

Toshev N. "Khorezmiĭskiĭ prints 'Isa Tora i ego novonaĭdennoe Saĭakhat-nama." In *Istoriografiia i istochnikovedenie srednevekovogo Vostoka*. Baku, 2012, 205–207.

Toshov N. "Khiva khonligi tarikhiga oid yangi manbalar: Éshmurod Alaviyning "Khuroson fathi tarikhi" asari." *Sharqshunoslik* 16 (2013): 68–75.

Toshov N., "Khiva solnomalarining yozma manbalari khususida." *Sharqshunoslik/Vostokovedenie/Oriental Studies* 4 (2015): 87–98.

Toshov N., "Povtoriaemost' imen i psevdonimov kak faktor nedorazumeniĭ: primer khorezmskogo poéta Khalisa." Forthcoming.

Veselovskiĭ N. *Ocherk istoriko-geograficheskikh svedeniĭ o Khivinskom khanstve ot drevneĭshikh vremen do nastoiashchego*. St. Petersburg, 1877.

Wood W. A. *The Sariq Turkmens of Merv and the Khanate of Khiva in the Early Nineteenth Century*. PhD diss., Indiana University, 1999.

Yapp M. E. "Kāmrān Shāh Durrānī," *EI*[2] IV: 523–524.

Yastrebova O. and Azad A. "Reflections on an Orientalist: Alexander Kuhn (1840–88), the Man and his Legacy." *Iranian Studies* 48:5 (2015): 675–694.

PLATES

MS 9981 ff 1b–2a

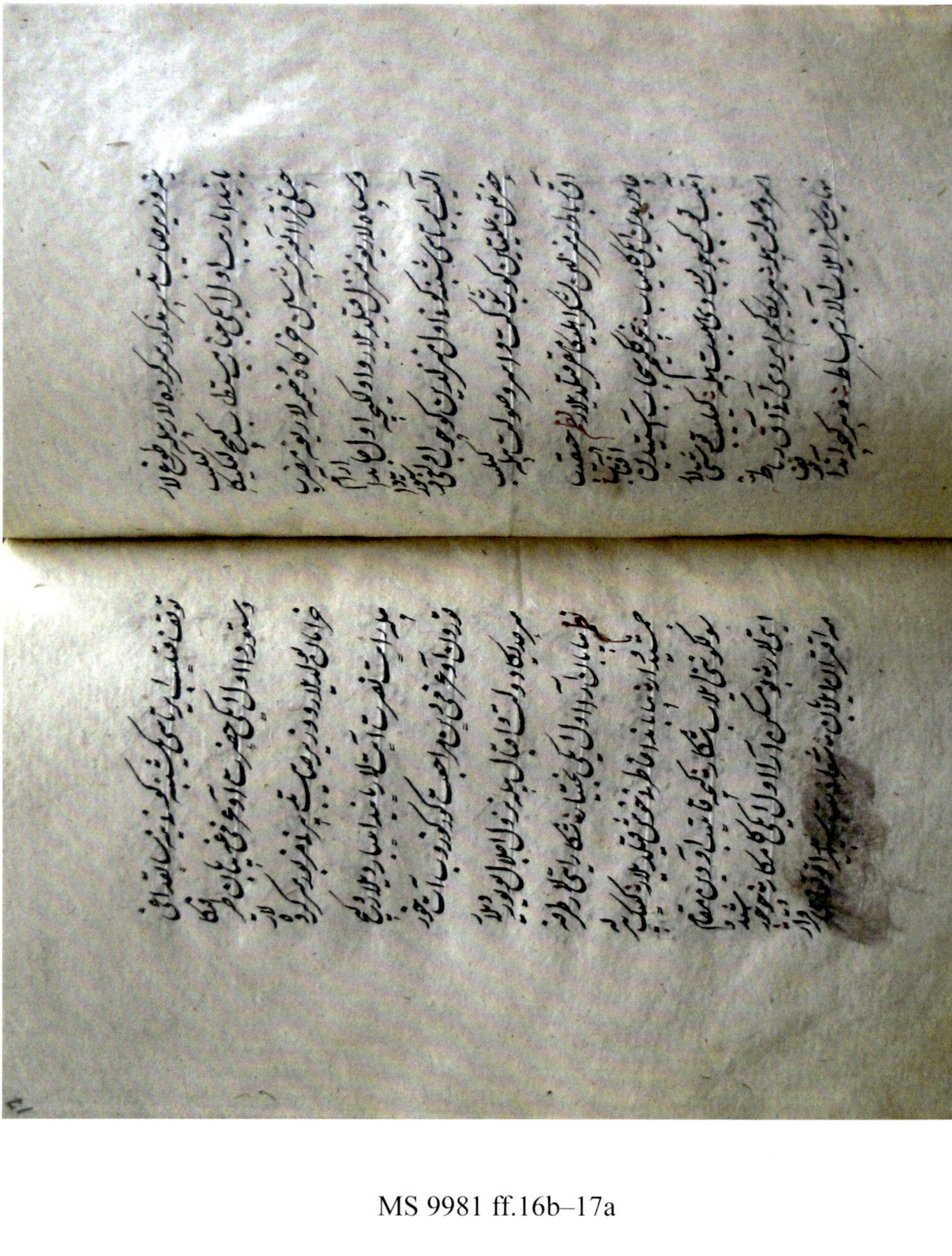

MS 9981 ff.16b–17a

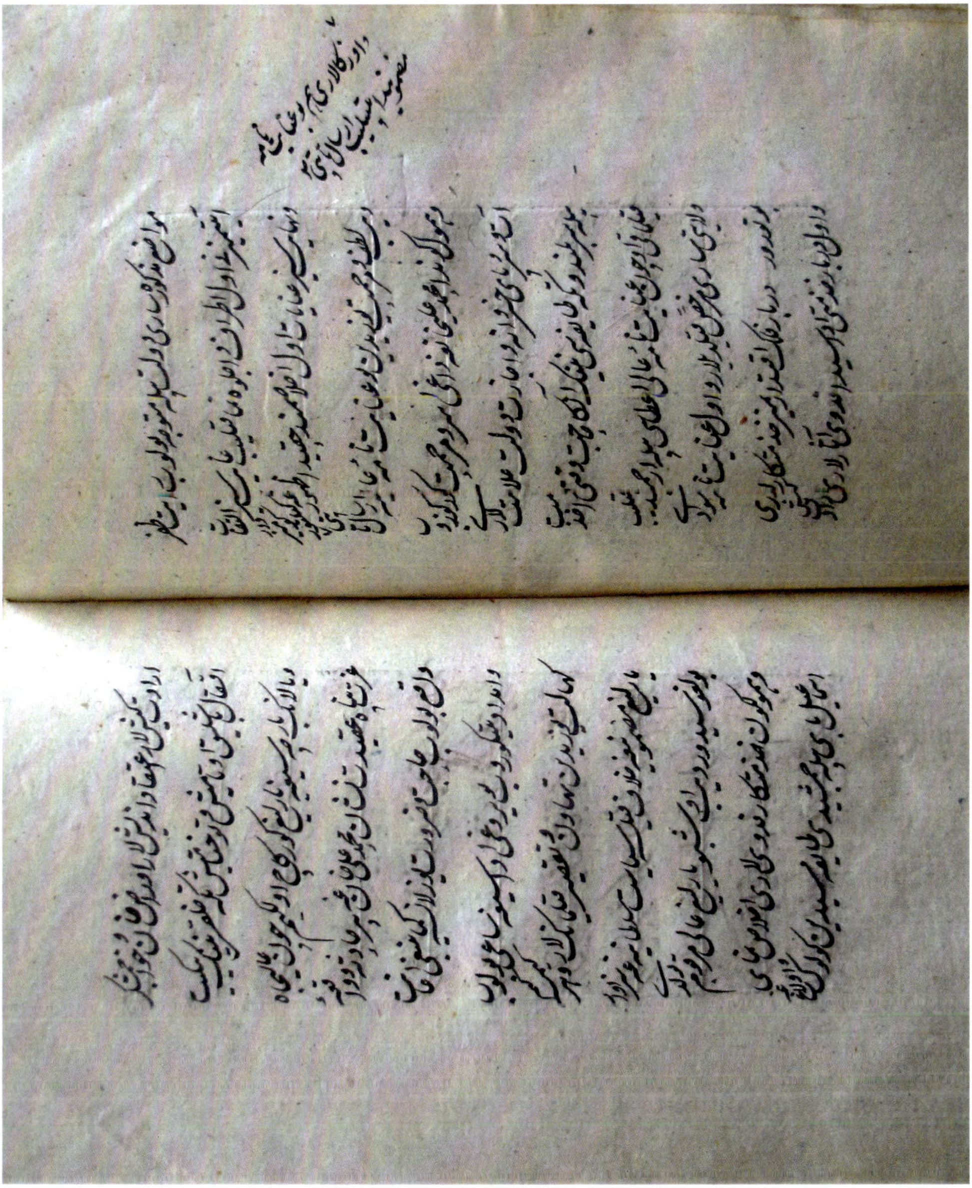

MS 9981 ff. 98b–99a

MS 9981 fol. 124b

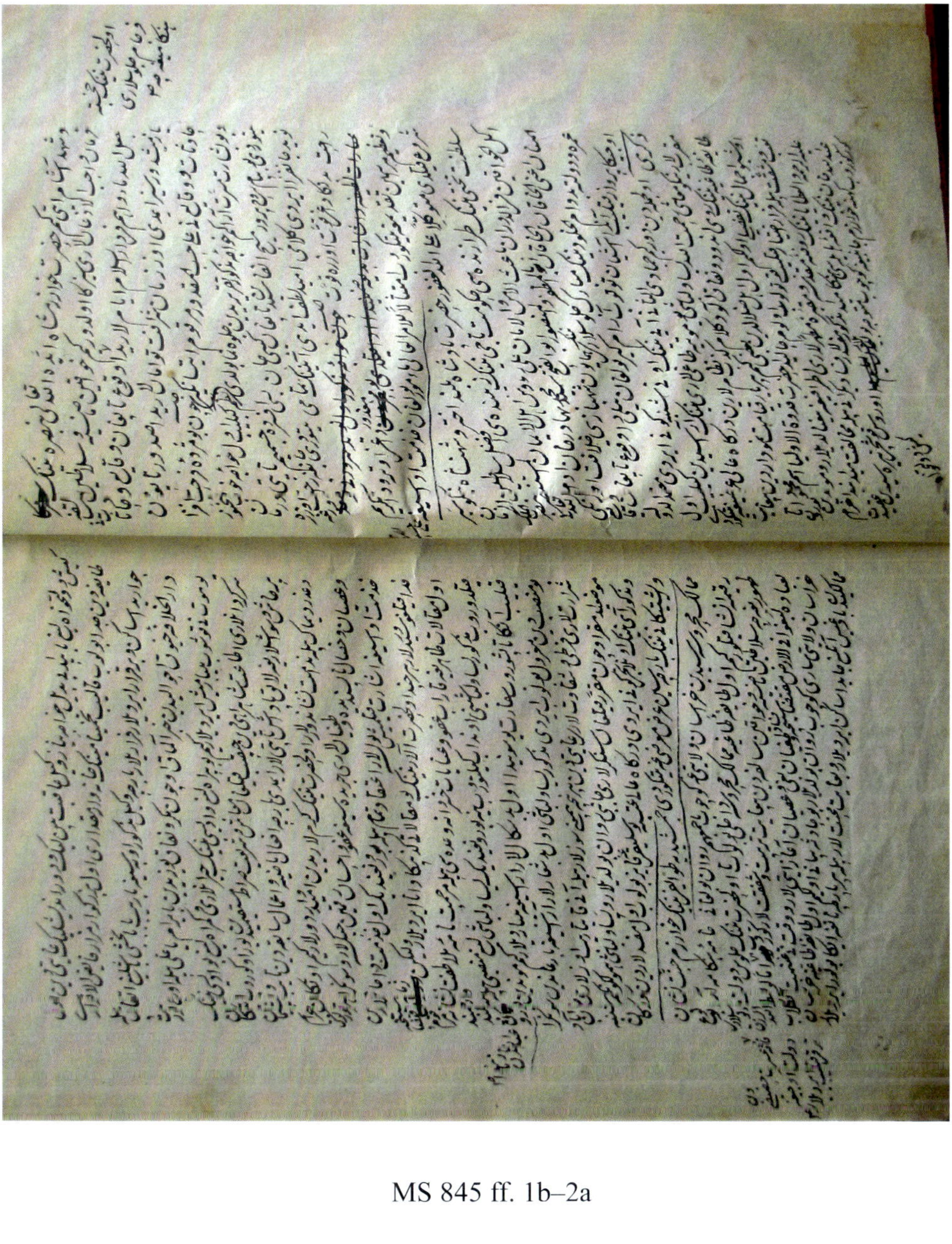

MS 845 ff. 1b–2a

TEXT

Band VII: Iranische Namen in semitischen Nebenüberlieferungen

Faszikel 1A: Iranische Personennamen in der neuassyrischen Nebenüberlieferung. Von Rüdiger Schmitt. 2009 (SBph, 792. Band/Iranische Onomastik, Nr. 6)

Faszikel 1B: Iranische Personennamen in der neu- und spätbabylonischen Nebenüberlieferung. Von Ran Zadok. 2009 (SBph, 777. Band/Iranische Onomastik, Nr. 4)

Faszikel 2: Iranische Personennamen in der hebräischen Bibel. Von Manfred Hutter. 2015 (SBph, 860. Band/Iranische Onomastik, Nr. 14)

Faszikel 5: Noms propres syriaques d'origine iranienne. Von Philippe Gignoux, Christelle Jullien, Florence Jullien. 2009 (SBph, 789. Band/Iranische Onomastik, Nr. 5)

Band VIII: Iranische Namen in ägyptischer Nebenüberlieferung

Von Rüdiger Schmitt und Günter Vittmann. 2013 (SBph, 842. Band/Iranische Onomastik, Nr. 13)

IRANISCHES PERSONENNAMENBUCH

BEGRÜNDET VON MANFRED MAYRHOFER
HERAUSGEGEBEN VON RÜDIGER SCHMITT, HEINER EICHNER,
BERT G. FRAGNER UND VELIZAR SADOVSKI

Band I: Die altiranischen Namen
Von Manfred Mayrhofer. 1979 (Sonderpublikation).

Faszikel 1, 2 und 3 in einem Band:
Faszikel 1: Die avestischen Namen.
Faszikel 2: Die altpersischen Namen.
Faszikel 3: Indices zum Gesamtband.

Band II: Mitteliranische Personennamen

Faszikel 2: Noms propres sassanides en moyen-perse épigraphique. Von Philippe Gignoux. 1986 (Sonderpublikation)

Faszikel 3: Noms propres sassanides en moyen-perse épigraphique. Supplément (1986–2001). Von Philippe Gignoux. 2003 (Sonderpublikation)

Faszikel 5: Personennamen in parthischen epigraphischen Quellen. Von Rüdiger Schmitt, 2016 (SBph, 881. Band/Iranische Onomastik, Nr. 15)

Faszikel 7: Bactrian Personal Names. Von Nicholas Sims-Williams. 2010 (SBph, 806. Band/Iranische Onomastik, Nr. 7)

Faszikel 8: Personal Names in Sogdian Texts. Von Pavel B. Lurje. 2011 (SBph, 808. Band/Iranische Onomastik, Nr. 8)

Band III: Neuiranische Personennamen

Faszikel 3: Die ossetischen Personennamen. Von Sonja Fritz. 2006 (SBph, 746. Band/Iranische Onomastik, Nr. 2)

Band IV: Materialgrundlagen zu den iranischen Personennamen auf antiken Münzen: Nomina propria Iranica in nummis

Von Michael Alram. 1986 (Sonderpublikation)

Band V: Iranische Namen in Nebenüberlieferungen indogermanischer Sprachen

Faszikel 4: Iranische Namen in den indogermanischen Sprachen Kleinasiens: Lykisch, Lydisch, Phrygisch.Von Rüdiger Schmitt. 1982 (Sonderpublikation)

Faszikel 5A: Iranische Personennamen in der griechischen Literatur vor Alexander d. Gr. Von Rüdiger Schmitt. 2011 (SBph, 823. Band/Iranische Onomastik, Nr. 9)

Faszikel 6a: Iranische Namen in den griechischen Dokumenten Ägyptens. Von Philip Huyse. 1991 (Sonderpublikation)

IRANISCHE ONOMASTIK

HERAUSGEGEBEN VON BERT G. FRAGNER UND FLORIAN SCHWARZ

(Nr. 1–10: Herausgegeben von Bert G. Fragner und Velizar Sadovski)

Nr. 1: Rüdiger Schmitt, Das Iranische Personennamenbuch: Rückschau, Vorschau, Rundschau (mit einer Bibliographie zur Iranischen Personennamenkunde). 2006 (SBph, 744. Band)

Nr. 2: Sonja Fritz, Die ossetischen Personennamen. (= Iranisches Personennamenbuch, Band III, Faszikel 3). 2006 (SBph, 746. Band)

Nr. 3: Ulla Remmer, Frauennamen im Rigveda und im Avesta. 2006 (SBph, 745. Band)

Nr. 4: Ran Zadok, Iranische Personennamen in der neu- und spätbabylonischen Nebenüberlieferung. (= Iranisches Personennamenbuch, Band VII, Faszikel 1B). 2009 (SBph, 777. Band)

Nr. 5: Philippe Gignoux, Christelle Jullien, Florence Jullien, Noms propres syriaques d'origine iranienne. (= Iranisches Personennamenbuch, Band VII, Faszikel 5). 2009 (SBph, 789. Band)

Nr. 6: Rüdiger Schmitt, Iranische Personennamen in der neuassyrischen Nebenüberlieferung. (= Iranisches Personennamenbuch, Band VII, Faszikel 1A). 2009 (SBph, 792. Band)

Nr. 7: Nicholas Sims-Williams, Bactrian Personal Names. (= Iranisches Personennamenbuch, Band II, Faszikel 7). 2010 (SBph, 806. Band)

Nr. 8: Pavel B. Lurje, Personal Names in Sogdian Texts. (= Iranisches Personennamenbuch, Band II, Faszikel 8). 2010 (SBph, 808. Band)

Nr. 9: Rüdiger Schmitt, Iranische Personennamen in der griechischen Literatur vor Alexander d. Gr. (= Iranisches Personennamenbuch, Band V, Faszikel 5A). 2011 (SBph, 823. Band)

Nr. 10: Rüdiger Schmitt, Manfred Mayrhofer: Leben und Werk. Mit vollständigem Schriftenverzeichnis. 2012 (SBph, 828. Band)

Nr. 11: Matteo De Chiara, Mauro Maggi and Giuliana Martini (Hrsg.), Buddhism Among the Iranian Peoples of Central Asia (= Multilingualism and History of Knowledge, Volume I. Hrsg. von Jens E. Braarvig, Markham J. Geller, Gebhard Selz und Velizar Sadovski). 2013 (SBph, 848. Band)

Nr. 12: Olav Hackstein and Ronald I. Kim (Hrsg.), Linguistic Developments along the Silkroad: Archaism and Innovation in Tocharian (= Multilingualism and History of Knowledge, Volume II. Hrsg. von Jens E. Braarvig, Markham J. Geller, Gebhard Selz und Velizar Sadovski). 2012 (SBph, 834. Band)

Nr. 13: Rüdiger Schmitt und Günter Vittmann, Iranische Namen in ägyptischer Nebenüberlieferung. (= Iranisches Personennamenbuch, Band VIII). 2013 (SBph, 842. Band)

Nr. 14. Manfred Hutter, Iranische Personennamen in der hebräischen Bibel. (= Iranisches Personennamenbuch, Band VII, Faszikel 2). 2015 (SBph, 860. Band)

Nr. 15: Rüdiger Schmitt, Personennamen in parthischen epigraphischen Quellen (= Iranisches Personennamenbuch, Band II, Faszikel 5). 2016 (SBph, 881. Band)

Nr. 63: Şevket Küçükhüseyin, Selbst- und Fremdwahrnehmung im Prozess kultureller Transformation. Anatolische Quellen über Muslime, Christen und Türken (13.–15. Jahrhundert). 2011 (SBph, 825. Band)

Nr. 64: Geschichte Wassaf's. Deutsch übersetzt von Hammer-Purgstall. Herausgegeben von Sibylle Wentker nach Vorarbeiten von Elisabeth und Klaus Wundsam. Band 3. 2012 (SBph, 827. Band)

Nr. 65: Antonio Panaino und Velizar Sadovski, Disputationes Iranologicae Vindobonenses, II. 2013 (SBph, 845. Band)

Nr. 66: Geschichte Wassaf's. Deutsch übersetzt von Hammer-Purgstall. Herausgegeben von Sibylle Wentker nach Vorarbeiten von Elisabeth und Klaus Wundsam. Band 4. 2016 (SBph, 878. Band)

Nr. 67: Luke Treadwell, Craftsmen and coins: signed dies in the Iranian world (third to the fifth centuries AH). 2011 (Dph, 423. Band, gleichzeitig: Veröffentlichungen der Numismatischen Kommission, Band 54)

Nr. 69: Amr Taher Ahmed, La « Révolution littéraire ». Étude de l'influence de la poésie française sur la modernisation des formes poétiques persanes au début du XXe siècle. 2012 (SBph, 829. Band)

Nr. 70: Roman Siebertz, Preise, Löhne und Lebensstandard im safavidischen Iran. Eine Untersuchung zu den Rechnungsbüchern Wollebrand Geleynssen de Jonghs (1641–1643). 2013 (SBph, 835. Band)

Nr. 71: Walter Posch, Osmanisch-safavidische Beziehungen 1545–1550: Der Fall Alḳâs Mîrzâ. Teil 1 und Teil 2. 2013 (SBph, 841. Band)

Nr. 72: Niccolò Pianciola und Paolo Sartori (Hrsg.), Islam, Society and States across the Qazaq Steppe (18th – Early 20th Centuries). 2013 (SBph, 844. Band)

Nr. 73: Desmond Durkin-Meisterernst, Grammatik des Westmitteliranischen (Parthisch und Mittelpersisch). 2014 (SBph, 850. Band/Grammatica Iranica 1, hrsg. von Velizar Sadovski)

Nr. 74: Christine Noelle-Karimi, The Pearl in its Midst. Herat and the Mapping of Khurasan (15th–19th Centuries). 2014 (Dph, 463. Band)

Nr. 75: Bert G. Fragner, Ralph Kauz und Florian Schwarz (Hrsg.): Wine Culture in Iran and Beyond. 2014 (SBph, 852. Band)

Nr. 76: Alexander Lubotsky, Alanic Marginal Notes in a Greek Liturgical Manuscript. 2015 (SBph, 859. Band/Grammatica Iranica 2, hrsg. von Velizar Sadovski)

Nr. 77: Tilmann Trausch, Formen höfischer Historiographie im 16. Jahrhundert. Geschichtsschreibung unter den frühen Safaviden: 1501–1578. 2015 (SBph, 861. Band)

Nr. 78: Jeff Eden (transl. and annot.), The Life of Muḥammad Sharīf. A Central Asian Sufi Hagiography in Chaghatay. With an appendix by Rian Thum and David Brophy. 2015 (SBph, 864. Band)

Nr. 79: Rüdiger Schmitt, Stilistik der altpersischen Inschriften. Versuch einer Annäherung. 2016 (SBph, 875. Band/Grammatica Iranica 3, hrsg. von Velizar Sadovski)

Nr. 80: Andreas Wilde, What is Beyond the River? Power, Authority, and Social Order in Transoxania, 18th-19th Centuries. 2016 (SBph, 877. Band)

Nr. 81: Chiara Barbati, The Christian Sogdian Gospel Lectionary E5 in Context. 2016 (SBph, 874. Band)

Nr. 42: Helmut Slaby, Bindenschild und Sonnenlöwe. Die Geschichte der österreichisch-iranischen Beziehungen bis zur Gegenwart. Nachdruck. 2010 (SBph, 770. Band)

Nr. 43: Tommaso Gnoli, The Interplay of Roman and Iranian Titles in the Roman East (1st–3rd Century A.D.). 2007 (SBph, 765. Band)

Nr. 44: Thamar E. Gindin, The Early Judaeo-Persian Tafsīrs of Ezekiel: Text, Translation, Commentary. Vol. II: Translation. 2007 (SBph, 766. Band)

Nr. 45: Thamar E. Gindin, The Early Judaeo-Persian Tafsīrs of Ezekiel: Text, Translation, Commentary. Vol. III: Commentary (*in Vorbereitung*)

Nr. 46: Bert G. Fragner, Ralph Kauz, Roderick Ptak und Angela Schottenhammer (Hrsg.), Pferde in Asien: Geschichte, Handel und Kultur / Horses in Asia: History, Trade and Culture. 2009 (Dph, 378. Band)

Nr. 47: Giorgio Rota, La Vita e i Tempi di Rostam Khan. Edizione e traduzione italiana del Ms. British Library Add 7,655. 2009 (SBph, 790. Band)

Nr. 48: Fridrik Thordarson, Ossetic Grammatical Studies. 2009 (SBph, 788. Band)

Nr. 49: Rüdiger Schmitt und Gerhard Brugmann (Hrsg.), Aus Karl Brugmanns Jugenderinnerungen. Eingeleitet und mit Anmerkungen versehen von Rüdiger Schmitt. 2009 (SBph, 786. Band)

Nr. 50: Velizar Sadovski, Untersuchungen zu Sprache und Stil des ältesten Indo-Iranischen (Veda und Avesta). (Stilistica Indo-Iranica, II.) (*in Vorbereitung*)

Nr. 51: Velizar Sadovski und David Stifter (Hrsg.), Iranistische und indogermanistische Beiträge in memoriam Jochem Schindler (1944–1994). 2012 (SBph, 851. Band)

Nr. 52: Ralph Kauz, Giorgio Rota und Jan Paul Niederkorn (Hrsg.), Diplomatisches Zeremoniell in Europa und im Mittleren Osten in der frühen Neuzeit. 2009 (SBph, 796. Band)

Nr. 53: Giorgio Rota, Under Two Lions. On the Knowledge of Persia in the Republic of Venice (ca. 1450–1797). 2009 (SBph, 793. Band)

Nr. 54: Manfred Mayrhofer, Indogermanistik: Über Darstellungen und Einführungen von den Anfängen bis in die Gegenwart. 2009 (SBph, 787. Band)

Nr. 55: Ela Filippone, The Fingers and their Names in the Iranian Languages. (Onomasiological Studies of Body-Part Terms, I). 2010 (SBph, 811. Band)

Nr. 56: Olav Hackstein, Apposition and Nominal Classification in Indo-European and Beyond. 2010 (SBph, 798. Band)

Nr. 57: Geschichte Wassaf's. Persisch herausgegeben und deutsch übersetzt von Hammer-Purgstall. Neu herausgegeben von Sibylle Wentker nach Vorarbeiten von Klaus Wundsam. Band 1. 2010 (SBph, 802. Band)

Nr. 58: Gisela Fock, Die iranische Moderne in der Bildenden Kunst: Der Bildhauer und Maler Parviz Tanavoli. 2011 (SBph, 815. Band)

Nr. 59: Geschichte Wassaf's. Deutsch übersetzt von Hammer-Purgstall. Herausgegeben von Sibylle Wentker nach Vorarbeiten von Elisabeth und Klaus Wundsam. Band 2. 2010 (SBph, 803. Band)

Nr. 60: Toshifumi Gotō: The Old Indo-Aryan Morphology and its Indo-Iranian Background. 2013 (SBph, 849. Band)

Nr. 61: Yuri Stoyanov, Defenders and Enemies of the True Cross. The Sasanian Conquest of Jerusalem in 614 and Byzantine Ideology of Anti-Persian Warfare. 2011 (SBph, 819. Band)

Nr. 62: Barbara Karl, Treasury – Kunstkammer – Museum: Objects from the Islamic World in the Museum Collections of Vienna. 2011 (SBph, 822. Band)

Nr. 21: Ladislav Zgusta, The Old Ossetic Inscription from the River Zelenčuk. 1987 (SBph, 486. Band)

Nr. 22: Wolfram Kleiss, Die Entwicklung von Palästen und palastartigen Wohnbauten in Iran. 1989 (SBph, 524. Band)

Nr. 23: Nosratollah Rastegar, Zur Problematik einiger handschriftlicher Quellen des neupersischen Namenbuches. 1989 (SBph, 525. Band)

Nr. 24: Dorit Schön, Laristan – eine südpersische Küstenprovinz. Ein Beitrag zu seiner Geschichte. 1990 (SBph, 553. Band)

Nr. 25: Rüdiger Schmitt, Epigraphisch-exegetische Noten zu Dareios' Bīsutūn-Inschriften. 1990 (SBph, 561. Band)

Nr. 26: Jost Gippert, Iranica Armeno-Iberica. Studien zu den iranischen Lehnwörtern im Armenischen und Georgischen. Band I–II. 1993 (SBph, 606. Band)

Nr. 27: R. E. Emmerick and P. O. Skjærvø, Studies in the Vocabulary of Khotanese III. 1997 (SBph, 651. Band)

Nr. 28: Xavier Tremblay, Pour une histoire de la Sérinde. Le manichéisme parmi les peuples et religions d'Asie Centrale d'après les sources primaires. 2001 (SBph, 690. Band)

Nr. 29: Rüdiger Schmitt, Die iranischen und Iranier-Namen in den Schriften Xenophons. (Iranica Graeca Vetustiora. II). 2002 (SBph, 692. Band)

Nr. 30: Rüdiger Schmitt, Meno-logium Bagistano-Persepolitanum. Studien zu den altpersischen Monatsnamen und ihren elamischen Wiedergaben. Unter redaktioneller Mitwirkung von Velizar Sadovski. 2003 (SBph, 705. Band)

Nr. 31: Antonio Panaino, Rite, parole et pensée dans l'Avesta ancien et récent. Quatre leçons au Collège de France (Paris, 7, 14, 21, 28 mai 2001). Edité par Velizar Sadovski, avec la collaboration rédactionnelle de Sara Circassia. 2004 (SBph, 716. Band)

Nr. 32: Roman Siebertz, Die Briefmarken Irans als Mittel der politischen Bildpropaganda. 2005 (SBph, 722. Band)

Nr. 33: Rüdiger Schmitt, Iranische Anthroponyme in den erhaltenen Resten von Ktesias' Werk. (Iranica Graeca Vetustiora. III). 2006 (SBph, 736. Band)

Nr. 34: Heiner Eichner, Bert G. Fragner, Velizar Sadovski und Rüdiger Schmitt (Hrsg.), Iranistik in Europa – gestern, heute, morgen. Unter redaktioneller Mitarbeit von Hannes Hofmann und Vera Giesen. 2006 (SBph, 739. Band)

Nr. 35: Uto v. Melzer, Farhangnevīs. Materialien zu einem Persisch-deutschen Wörter-buch. Hrsg. von Nosratollah Rastegar. Band I–IV. 2006 (Dph, 339. Band)

Nr. 36: Manfred Mayrhofer, Einiges zu den Skythen, ihrer Sprache, ihrem Nachleben. 2006 (SBph, 742. Band)

Nr. 37: Siegfried Weber, Die persische Verwaltung Kaschmirs (1842–1892). Band 1–2. 2007 (SBph, 754. Band)

Nr. 38: Farhangnevīs. Datenbank zu Uto von Melzers lexikographischen Materialien: Persisch-Deutsch/Deutsch-Persisch. Hrsg. von Nosratollah Rastegar. 2007 (CD-ROM)

Nr. 39: Rüdiger Schmitt, Pseudo-altpersische Inschriften. Inschriftenfälschungen und moderne Nachbildungen in altpersischer Keilschrift. 2007 (SBph, 762. Band)

Nr. 40: Thamar E. Gindin, The Early Judaeo-Persian Tafsīrs of Ezekiel: Text, Translation, Commentary. Vol. I: Text. 2007 (SBph, 763. Band)

Nr. 41: Antonio Panaino und Velizar Sadovski, Disputationes Iranologicae Vindobonenses, I.: Antonio Panaino, Chronologia Avestica. Velizar Sadovski, Epitheta und Götternamen im älteren Indo-Iranischen. 2007 (SBph, 764. Band)

VERÖFFENTLICHUNGEN ZUR IRANISTIK

HERAUSGEGEBEN VON BERT G. FRAGNER UND FLORIAN SCHWARZ

(Nr. 1–21: Veröffentlichungen der Iranischen Kommission,
Nr. 22–29: Veröffentlichungen der Kommission für Iranistik,
Nr. 30–31: Herausgegeben von Bert G. Fragner
Nr. 32–68: Herausgegeben von Bert G. Fragner und Velizar Sadovski)

Nr. 1: Manfred Mayrhofer, Onomastica Persepolitana. Das altiranische Namengut der Persepolis-Täfelchen. Unter Mitarbeit von János Harmatta, Walter Hinz, Rüdiger Schmitt und Jutta Seiffert. 1973 (SBph, 286. Band)
Nr. 2: Karl Jahn, Die Geschichte der Kinder Israels des Rašīd ad-Dīn. 1973 (Dph, 114. Band)
Nr. 3: Manfred Mayrhofer, Zum Namengut des Avesta. 1977 (SBph, 308. Band, 5. Abhandlung)
Nr. 4: Karl Jahn, Die Frankengeschichte des Rašīd ad-Dīn. Einleitung, Übersetzung und Kommentar. 1977 (Dph, 129. Band)
Nr. 5: Ronald Zwanziger, Zum Namen der Mutter Zarathustras. (Sonderdruck aus Anzeiger, 114/1977)
Nr. 6: Rüdiger Schmitt, Die Iranier-Namen bei Aischylos. (Iranica Graeca Vetustiora, I). 1978 (SBph, 337. Band)
Nr. 7: Manfred Mayrhofer, Supplement zur Sammlung der altpersischen Inschriften. 1978 (SBph, 338. Band)
Nr. 8: Karl Jahn, Die Indiengeschichte des Rašīd ad-Dīn. Einleitung, vollständige Übersetzung, Kommentar und 80 Texttafeln. 1980 (Dph, 144. Band)
Nr. 9: Oswald Szemerényi, Four Old Iranian Ethnic Names: Scythian – Skudra – Sogdian – Saka. 1980 (SBph, 371. Band)
Nr. 10: Rüdiger Schmitt, Altpersische Siegelinschriften. 1981 (SBph, 381. Band)
Nr. 11: Kaikhusroo M. JamaspAsa, Aogəmadaēcā. A Zoroastrian Liturgy. 1982 (SBph, 397. Band)
Nr. 12: R. E. Emmerick and P. O. Skjærvø, Studies in the Vocabulary of Khotanese I. 1982 (SBph, 401. Band)
Nr. 13: Manfred Mayrhofer, Lassen sich Vorstufen des Uriranischen nachweisen? (Sonderdruck aus Anzeiger, 120/1983)
Nr. 14: Reinhard Pohanka, Zu einigen Architekturstücken von Tell-e Zohak bei Fasa, Südiran. (Sonderdruck aus Anzeiger, 120/1983)
Nr. 15: Wilhelm Eilers, Iranische Ortsnamenstudien. 1987 (SBph, 465. Band)
Nr. 16: Reinhard Pohanka, Die Masdjed-e Djoume in Darab, Südiran. (Sonderdruck aus Anzeiger, 121/1984)
Nr. 17: R. E. Emmerick and P. O. Skjærvø, Studies in the Vocabulary of Khotanese II. 1987 (SBph, 458. Band)
Nr. 18: Wolfgang Felix, Antike literarische Quellen zur Außenpolitik des Sāsāniden-staates. Erster Band (224–309). 1985 (SBph, 456. Band)
Nr. 19: Reinhard Pohanka, Burgen und Heiligtümer in Laristan, Südiran. Ein Surveybericht. 1986 (SBph, 466. Band)
Nr. 20: N. Rastegar und W. Slaje, Uto von Melzer (1881–1961). Werk und Nachlaß eines österreichischen Iranisten. 1987 (SBph, 477. Band)

ایش مراد بن آدینه محمد العلوی

جمشیدی طوایفی فتحی

نشرگه تیارلاوچی

نوریاغدی تاشوف

وین – ۲۰۱۸

|1b| جمشیدی طوایفی فتحی تأییدات ربانی و تقویت سبحانی اعانتی بیله شهزادهٔ سپهرمرتبت داراشوکت فریدون‌حشمت اسکندرجاه سلیمان‌جایکاه نصرت‌پناه ظفرهمراه ناصر الملة و الدین معین الدین المتین باعث الامن و الامان شفیق اهل الایمان ابو الفتح و الظفر شهزاده رحیمقلی بهادر سلطان جعله الله تعالی مظفَّراً و منصوراً الی انقراض الزمان‌غه بی‌صعوبت و مشقت میسَّر بولغانی‌نینک ذکری

حضرت پادشاه انجم‌سپاه قبلة الخواقین المعظم کعبة السلاطین المکرم |2a| اسکندرنشان فریدون‌مکان دارادربان سلیمانجاه جمشیددستکاه نظم

قایسی شهکیم شهنشه دوران مالک انسُ جان مدار جهان
شاه‌لار سرورُ سرافرازی شاه الله قلی ابو الغازی
یوز سکندرچه بار آنکا چاکر چاکری هر بیری چو اسکندر
مفتخِر قوللوغیغه خاقان‌لار درکهی قول‌لاری کیلیب خانلار
عز و جاهی بلند آنینک چون مهر خاک درکاهی بو رفیع سپهر
مظهر جودُ مصدر احسان یوقتور احسانیغه حدُ پایان
شوکتی صیتی خود جهاننی توتوب بلکه بو توقوز آسماننی توتوب
نی قالیب ملک مشرقُ مغرب نی قالیب ملک ابطح یثرب
نی خراسانُ ملک هندستان نی عراقُ نی کشور ایران
شاه‌نینک قوللوغیغه باغلاب بیل |2b| خذمت امری اوچون چو سایر ایل
قهری اوتیغه بیرسه چونکه شمال بالکل اولغوسی کول جهان فی الحال
قیلا آلماس اول اوتنی هیچ زبون غیر لطفی که بیرکای آنکا سکون

لطفی دریاسی کر اورار ایسه موج همه شاداب اولور حضیض ایله اوج
همتی قصری ایلادور عالی کوه زر آنکا کاه تمثالی
هر قایان دولت ایله عازم اولوب فتح و نصرت ایکی ملازم اولوب
ای خدا شاه‌نی قیلیب مسرور دایما ایت مظفر و منصور
شاه‌لار اورتاسیدا ممتاز ایت تا قیامت سر و سرافراز ایت

چون اولحضرت‌کیم ذات بابرکات‌لاری ایمان اهلیکا امن و امان باعثی‌دور خوارزمشاه‌لیق اورنکی اوزره جلوس |3a| بویوروب اون یتی ییل انقضا تاپتی تأریخ هجری مینک تقی ایکی یوز ایلیک یتی‌دا سیغیر ییلی‌نینک نصف اخیری اثناسی ایردیکیم اوز کوزلاری‌نینک نوری کونکول‌لاری‌نینک سروری شجاعت‌پناه جلادت‌دستکاه خلافت تختی‌نینک زیب و فری سلطنت تاجی‌نینک عالی کوهری پادشاه‌لیق سپهری‌نینک[1] مهر تابانی شهنشاه‌لیق بحری‌نینک دُرّ درخشانی نظم

آفتاب فلک دولت و دین
ماهتاب اُفق جاه و جلال
معدلت قصری تاپیب آندین بود
مکرمت مسندی هم زیبُ جمال
در یکدانهٔ درج شوکت

1 نینک above the line.

مـه رخشـندهٔ بـرج اقبـال
خاطـری بحری محیط احسـان
زرفشـانلیقدا کفـی ابـر نـوال
معـدن حلـمُ وقـارُ تمکیـن
|3b| مرکـز دایـرهٔ فضل و کمال
قُـوَّت خاطـر اهـل عالـم
راحـت روح شـه فرخفـال
عظمت کشـوریدا چون جمشید
منزلـت ملکیـدا داراتمثـال
شـیر آجـام شـجاعت‌کیم ایرور
چـون مَـرَل الّیـدا اعـدا پامال
کول بولور قهری اوتی اورسه علم
دهرنینک خرمن بودی فی الحال
آب لطفی آنکا بیرکوسـی سکون
یوقسه پست اولماغیدور امر محال
عدلیدیـن عالـم ارا ایـلا فـراغ
قوی قورت همرهـی‌دور فارغ‌بال
خلقی‌دین بارچه اولوس خرمُ شاد
رافتی‌دین باری عالم خوشـحال
بـاری ایـل وِردُ دعاسـی بوکیـم
تاپماغـای هیچ خور عمری زوال

همـــه دم فتح و ظفـــر بولغای یار
هر قایان قویسه یوز اول نیک خصال
نوش قیلغای همه دم صاف سرور
|4a| یتماکای خاطریغه دُرد ملال
تا قیامت آنکا لطف ایتکای حق
قـــدح عیـــش و طـــرب مالامال
درکهـــی خذمتیغـــه باغلا کمر
ای مرادی ســـنکا یوق اوزکا مآل

ثریامکان اعنی شهزاده رحیمقلی بهادر سلطان زاد الله تعالی یوما فیوماً دولته و نصرته الی انقراض الزمانغه لشکر ظفراثرلاری افواجیدین نیچه کروه نصرت‌پژوه‌لارین نیچه سرکرده‌لار بیله‌کیم هر بیری شجاعت بیشه‌سی‌نینک شیری مبارزت معرکه‌سی‌نینک دلیریدور قوشوب ایران و خراسان اعادیسی‌نینک[1] محاربه و مقاتله‌سی اوچون بویوروب ییباردیلار و مأمور بولغان سپهبدلار جمله‌سیدین سیادت‌پناه نجابت‌دستکاه عالیمقام عوض خواجه شیخ الاسلام |4b| و عمدة الامرا خلاصة الوزرا ضمیر صافی بارچه اموردا عقده‌کشاد[2] اتا مراد قوشبیکی زاد الله رواجه و مبارز نامدار شجاع روزکار خدای یار بی و جلادت‌مظهر سید نظر بی و ملازم‌لار نیکومعاشی خذمتکار جان‌سپار یخشیمراد یوزباشی و محمد امین سینک‌باشی و شجاعت‌پیشه‌لار یولداشی عبد الله یساولباشی و

---

1 نینک above the line.

2 Read عقده‌کشای.

رحمت الله یساولباشی [1]و محمد مراد بای محرم[1] و بولارغه اوخشاش ینه نیچه سرکرده‌لارکیم بارچه‌سی اسامی‌سی‌نینک ذکری کلام تطویلیغه باعث بولورکیم ملال موجبی‌دور اولوجه‌دین مذکور سپهبدلار اواسمی ذکریکا اکتفا قیلیلدی

نظم

سپهبد هر بیریسی جلد و چالاک آنینکدیک کیم عدو کر بولسه افلاک
قیلور بیر حمله‌سی بیرله آنی پست ایتار اول لحظه اوق یر بیرله |5a| همدست
باریسی نامدار و نام‌آور اوروش هنکامیدا آنداق دلاور
عدو شیر اولسه خود ور فیل محمود قیلور بیر ضربه بیرله آنی نابود

چون رمضان المبارک آیی اوتوب شوال آیی‌نینک آلتینجی جمعه کونی جمعه نمازی اداسیدین سونکرا بیر ساعت بیله تورت دقیقه اوتوب اوقات اشرفی ساعات اسعدی ایردیکیم شهزادهٔ عالیجناب خورشیدانتساب فرمان واجب الاذعان موجبینچه مذکور سرکرده‌لار و بویورولغان سپاه نصرت‌پناه‌لاری بیله انجم شاهی نجوم سپاهی بیله ظهور قیلیب فلک عرصه‌سی سیریغه یوز قویغاندیک آفتاب‌وار خیوق صانها الله تعالی عن الحرق و الغرق افقیدین طلوع قیلیب |5b| فَإِذَا عَزَمْتَ فَتَوَكَّلْ عَلَى ٱللَّهِ[2] مؤداسینچه اعتقادلارین ناصر حقیقی درکاهی‌غه رُست و توکل‌لارین دُرُست قیلیب مذکور امر اداسی‌غه عزیمت کورکوزوب مقصد ساری روانه بولدیلار و علما اهلی و امرا خیلی و نیچه

[1-1] In margin.

[2] Qur'ān III: 159.

شهزاده و بیک‌زاده‌لارکیم سلطان صاحبقران سپهرمکاننی اوزاتیب چیقمیش ایردیلار اجازت شرافت‌آیت‌لاری بیله بعضی‌سی کندمکاندین و بعضی‌سی زره میدانیدین و بعضی‌سی صیاد موضعی‌دین کوب دعای خیرلار قیلیب مراجعت کورکوزدیلار نظم

چیقیب صولت بیله اول عالم‌آرای سالیب دوران اراکوب هوی ایله های
توبُ کرنای اونی دوراندین آشیب نه دوران کنبذ کرداندین آشـیب
اعادی |6a| جسمی‌غه سالیب تزلزل آنینکدیک کیم باری عالم‌غه غُلغل

چون سلطان صاحبقران ایَّد الله بنصره‌کیم وجود مسعودلاری زمان قراری و جهان مداری‌دور علما و امرا و باقی طوایف مذکوره بیله وداع‌لاشیب یول قطعیغه یوز قویدیلار بیراز مسافت یول یوروب کوب شوکت و اسرو صولت بیله کیلیب یانکی آریق حولی‌لاری‌کاکیم اباً عنجد موروثی وطن و هامن‌لاریدور نزول اجلال بویوردیلار نظم

دولـت بیلـه اول شـجاع کامل اول حولینـی چونکه قیلدی منزل
اول حیـدر بیشـهٔ شـجاعت اوشـبو کیچـه آنـدا ایتی راحت

چون ایرتاسی آفتاب عالمتاب ضیا و سنا عسکری بیله اسلام اهلی لشکریدیک فلک قصریدین |6b| طلوع و ظهور قیلیب کفر سپاهی‌دیک ظلمت جنودی دستکاهی‌غه شکست بیردی سرکرده‌لار باشلیق سپاه اهلیکا ضیافت قیلیب

مطعومات و مشروبات ایصالی بیله بارچه‌سین خوشحال قیلدیلار و اولکون کیم شنبه کونی ایردی مذکور ایش‌دین و طعام اکلیدین فارغ بولغان‌لاریدین سونکرا چاشت وقتی آتلانیب دولت بیله بیر نیچه مسافت‌نی قطع قیلیب عاص حولی‌لاریکیم بی‌نظیر هامن و دلپذیر نشیمن‌لاریدور آنکا تشریف بویوروب اندک توقف قیلیب سپاه اهلیکا جشن عام بیریب اولموضعدین کوچوب یکشنبه کیچه‌سی هیبت تمام و صولت مالاکلام بیله کیلیب هزاراسب اهلی‌نینک دیده‌لاریکا تکاورلاری |7a| اقدامی‌نینک غباریدین توتیا بیتکوردیلار نظم

تجمُّل بیرلـه اول کیتی‌مـدارا — هزاراسـب قلعه‌سـینی قیلدی مأوا
قدومـی بیرلـه اول دریـای رأفت — بـو قلعه ایچرا بیتکوردی شـرافت
دعـا قیلماق اوچـون اول کامرانغه — بـار اهلی بـاردی عالی آسـتانغه
بویانکلیغ بولدی اول ایل نینک دعاسی — قایو ایش بولسـه سلطان مدعاسی
خداییم بی‌مشقّت حاصل ایتکای — مرادی هر نی بولسه واصل ایتکای
خصوصـاً بو سـفر بولغای مبارک — مبـارک ایلاکای تینکـری تبارک

چون سلطان صاحبقران کیم قلعهٔ مذکوره‌دا قرار توتتی‌لار اوچ کیچه اول قلعه‌دا آرام آلیب قالغان بعضی ضروریات انجامی‌غه قیام کورکوزدیلار و سه‌شنبه کونی قلعهٔ مذکوره‌دا علما و امرا اهلیکا ضیافت کوناکون قیلیب اطعمه و |7b| اشربهٔ ملذّذ و فواکه رنکارنک تارتیب دعای خیرلارین آلدیلار و [1]علما و اُمَرا[1] طعام و

[1-1] In margin.

شراب تناولیدین فراغت تاپغاندین سونکرا بو نوع دعا قیلدیلارکیم نظم

خضر و الیـاس رهبرینک بولغای
انبیـا یـارُ یاورینـک بولغـای
کامران‌لار مطیـع امرینک اولوب
دهـر ملکی مُسـخَّرینک بولغای

چون خدیو کامکار و سلطان نامدار ضیافت تکلفاتیدین فراغت تاپتی‌لار زرین‌لجام کمیت‌لاریکا راکب بولوب خورشید انور بوز برجدی منظردین اشراق قیلیب آفاق اهلیکا ضیابخش بولغاندیک قلعهٔ مذکوره‌دین توب آتدوروب[1] و کرنای چالدوروب غایت‌سیز شوکت و نهایت‌سیز صولت بیله چیقیب مقصد ساری نهضت قیلدیلار نظم

|8a| کوب تجمل کوب شکوه ایله خدیو کامکار
اشـهب زرین‌لجامی‌غـه بولـوب اولـدم سـوار
بی‌نهایـت کوکبـه بیرلـه چیقیـب اول قلعه‌دین
قویـدی یول قطعی‌غه یوز دولـت بیله اول بختیار
رعدیـک توب‌لار اونـی دوران‌غه سـالیب زلزله
کوییـا عالـم ارا برلـدی قیامـت آشـکار

[1] آتدورب.

توب دخانی کثرتیدین بیر بیرینی کورماییین
عالم اهلی بولدیلار جان‌سیز بدندیک بیمدار

چون سلطان صاحبقران بو نوع اساسه و بو طریقه دبدبه بیله یول قطعی‌غه عازم بولدیلار یول قطعی اثناسیدا بیر بیچاره و غریبی آلدلاریکا چیقیب دعا قیلمیش بولسه انعام و احسان مالاکلاملاریدین کونکلی‌کا سرور بیتکوروب نیچه |8b| مرحله‌نی قطع قیلیب یکه چیقیر موضعین سرادق عظمت‌نمونه‌لاریغه مقر قیلدیلار و هزاراسب علمالاری‌کیم سلطان صاحبقراننی اوزاتیب چیقمیش ایردیلار مذکور موضع‌دین اجازت‌لاری دولتین تاپیب [1]دعای خیر قیلیب[1] مراجعت کورکوزدیلار نظم

یکه چیقیر سرحدین شوکت بیحد بیله
اول دُر بحر کرم ایلادی آرامکاه
اولکیچه راحت آلیب آندا توقف قیلیب
لشکر بیعدیغه قیلدی آنی جلوه‌کاه
جمله اولوس‌کا دعا بو که آنکا لطف ایتیب
یاور و یار ایلاکای فتح و ظفرنی آله

چون ایرتاسی چهارشنبه کونی‌کیم مهرنینک اشهب زرین‌لجامی بو فلک

[1-1] In margin.

فیروزه‌فام‌دین طلوع قیلیب سپهر میدانی قطعی‌غه خرام کورکوزدی |9a| اول عالیمقام داغی دولت بیله طعام تناولیدین سونک آتلانیب توب آتدوروب و کرنای چالدوروب دبدبهٔ سلطانیه بیله اول موضع‌دین کوچوب یر و کوک اجزاسیغه زلزله سالیب فتناک قلعه‌سی اورتاسیدین کذر قیلیب ساری حاجی مرحله‌سی محاذی‌سیغه بیتوشکان چاغدا امیر الأُمرا خلاصة الوزرا دستور آصف‌نهاد اتا مراد قوشبیکی سلمه الله تعالی‌نی‌کیم نظم

قویاشدیک خاطری صاف و مجلا بولوب رأی منیری عالم‌آرا
مصفا رأییدین کشورلار آباد باری کشور ایلی تدبیریدین شاد

بیر نیچه سرکرده‌لار بیله عسکر اهلیکا باش قیلیب رأیت ظفرآیت‌لار بیرله بیباریب اوزلاری بیر نیچه مخصوص جانسپارلاری بیله |9b| شکار قیلماق اوچون قیرغه چیقیب عقاب‌وار ایتالکولارنی سالیب شهلا کوزلیک غزاله‌لارنی آلیب خاطر عاطرلارین خوش قیلیب قوش ساری مراجعت کورکوزوب شیخ آریقی موضعین آرامگاه قیلدیلار نظم

صید ایتیب مشکین کییک‌لارنی کونکول مرآتیغه
بیتکوروب بیحد و غایت اوشبو صیقلدین جلا
شیخ آریقی سرحدیکا مقدمی تشریفیدین
قایتیب آودین کیچه بیتکوردی شرف بیرله صفا

چون پنجشنبه[1] صبحی‌نینک[2] خاور شهی نور عسکرین ظلمت جنودی اوستیکا ییباریب سواد نهادیدین دِمار چیقاریب بودُ نابودین تارُ مار قیلدی سلطان صاحبقران ینه توب آتدوروب و کرنایلاتیب حشمت تمام و شوکت مالاکلام بیله اول سرحددین ارتحال بویوروب |10a| دولت بیله آتلانیب مقصد ساری توجُّه کورکوزدیلار و تیوه بویون کیلکان چاغدا ینه اوتکان کونداکی یوسوندا وزیر معظم و دستور مکرم قوشبیکی بیک‌نی مذکور سرکرده‌لار بیرله طوغ قمرفروغ‌لار یانیدا ییباریب اوزلاری شکار قیلماق اوچون بیر نیچه خصوصیت‌کیش خذمتکارلاری بیرله قیر اوستیکا صعود قیلیب نامعدود تذرو بیرله رعنا کییک‌لارنی آلیب کونکول‌لاری سپهریغه اوشبو تماشالار کواکبی بیله زیب و آرا ییتکوروب کیچ‌قورون بولغاندا قوش جانبی‌غه معاودت کورکوزوب اوچ تیفه آتلیغ جاینی لشکرکاه قیلدیلار نظم

صیدکه[3] جانبی‌دین فرحت ایله چون سلطان
کیلدیُ اوچ تیفه‌نی لشکریکا قیلدی مکان
|10b| کیچه کوندوز آنینک حقیدا تیلاک بو که منکا
ساقلاغای لطف ایتیبان جمله بلادین سبحان

و اول منزلدا ایکی کیچه اویوب شنبه کونی نهاری قیلیب صولت خسروانه بیله

[1] پنجشنبه above the line.

[2] نینک above the line; صبحی altered from صبح.

[3] که above the line.

آتلانیب یول‌نینک میمنه ومیسره‌سیکا نکاه قیلیب بارور چاغدا ناکاه اوترولاریدا میدان اورتاسیدا هزبری[1] نمایان بولدی‌کیم هیبتی‌دین شیر ژیان و ببر دمان پیکریکا تزلزل توشکودیک ایردی چون مبارک نظرلاری اول فیل‌صورت حیوانغه توشکاچ بی‌محابا[2] آنینک جانبی‌غه آت قویدی‌لار و چون سلطان صاحبقراندین اوشبو اطوار و رفتارنی‌کیم مشاهده قیلیلدی بیر نیچه جلد و چالاک ییکیت‌لارکیم افلاک غضنفرین بیر حمله‌دا توتوب عدم بیشه‌سیکا ییبارکودیک |11a| ایردیلار توش توشدین آت قویوب شمشیر آبدارلاری آبی بیله اول میدان لباسین مذکور ناپاک وجودی لوثیدین پاک قیلدیلار نظم

ایدیلار حاضر اولچاغ نوجوان‌لار چو رستم ایش چاغیدا پهلوان‌لار
باریسی شیر زور و فیل‌پیکر عدو اوترودا کر بولسون غضنفر
عدو بلکیم کر اولسه شیر افلاک قیلیچی بیرله ایلاب سینه‌سین چاک
آنینکدیک ایلاکایلار آنی معدوم وجودی کویی ایرماس ایردی معلوم
مع القصه که بو خیل دلآور کوروب میداندا اول ناپاک‌مظهر
قویوب‌آت‌توش‌توشیدین‌ایلاب[3] اهلاک وجودیدین جهاننی قیلدیلار پاک

و اوشبو امر تفأل‌اثر وقوعیدین سونکرا ایام ماضیه یوسونیدا بنه امیر الامرا

[1] .حزیری؟ حزبری؟

[2] .بی‌مهابا

[3] ایلاب above the line.

خلاصة الوزرا قوشبیکی بیک |11b| سلمه الله عن البلایانی مزبور[1] سپهبدلار بیله لوای نصرت‌انتمالار یانیدا ییباریب اوزلاری شکار قیلماق اوچون بیابان ساری مسطور مخصوص‌لار بیله خرامان بولدیلار و کیچکا یقین بولغاندا تفرج‌کارلیق و تحسین‌شکارلیق مصقلی بیله کونکول‌لاری کوزکوسیغه صیقل و جلا بیریب بیش یاغاچ موضعین عسکرلاریغه قرارکاه قیلدیلار و یکشنبه کونی مذکور موضع‌دا لشکر اهلی[2] مکث کورکوزوب اوزلاری بیر نیچه اعتقادهمدم اخلاص‌توأم محرم‌لار بیله آو عزمیغه جازم بولوب صیدکاه جانبی‌غه دولت بیله آتلانیب کیتی‌لار چون نماز شام بولوب کون خاقانی مغرب شادروانیغه کیریب پرده‌پوش بولوب ایردی حضرت پادشاه دوران و شهنشاه انسُ جان کامرانلیق کوهری‌نینک بحری |12a| حکمرانلیق اختری‌نینک سپهری نظم

شاه‌لار شـاهی سلاطین قبله‌سی   بختیـارُ کامـران‌لار کعبه‌سـی
حکمرانلیق کوهری‌نینک دُرجی اول   کامرانلیق اختری‌نینک برجی اول
ذات پاکـی منزلـت آرایشـی   عدلیدیـن بیچـاره‌لار آسایشـی
صولتی‌دین کوه‌لار تاپیب شکست   شـوکتی‌دین آسـمان الیدا پست
لطفـی بیرلـه سـرفراز ایلاب آله   قیلمیش آنی دهر ارا خوارزمشـاه
دایما حق شـادُ مسرور ایلاکای   تـا قیامت آنی منصـور ایلاکای

چرخ‌درکاه دارادستکاه ابو المظفر و المنصور ابو الغازی خوارزمشاه طول الله

---

[1] مذبور.

[2] اهلی above the line.

ایام عمره و دولته هیبت تمام و صولت مالاکلام بیله بحر و بر اجزاسیغه زلزله و تاغُ دشت اعضاسیغه ولوله سالیب مذکور جایغه نزول‌لاری |12b| شرفی بیله شرافت بیتکوروب ایکی کوکب سعد بیر بُرجدا قران قیلغاندیک اول مکاننی آرامگاه قیلدیلار و چون شهزادهٔ سپهردرگاه کیوان‌بارگاه آودین مراجعت و معاودت کورکوزوب قوش‌غه نزول بویوروب اولحضرت‌نینک تشریف بویورغانلاریغه و وزیر صایب‌تدبیرنینک مذکور سرکرده‌لار بیله ادب ساقلاب اولجناب‌سیز حضرت ملازمت‌لاریغه بارماغان‌لاریغه وقوف پیدا قیلغاندین سونکرا مذکور وزیر بیله سرکرده‌لارکا اعلام بیتکوروب بارچه‌لارین ملازمت‌لاری دولتی بیاه عالیمقام قیلیب قمر شاهی انجم‌نینک جنود نامعدودی بیله قویاش ملازمتی‌غه یوز قویوب ضیا کسب قیلغاندیک اولحضرت‌نینک کیمیاخاصیت |13a| خذمت‌لاریغه عازم بولدیلار و چون اولجناب مذکور وزیر و سرکرده‌لار بیله حضرت پادشاه‌نینک حضور باهر السرورلاری شرفیکا مشرف بولدیلار کیمیااثر نظرلاریدین تربیت تاپیب بهجت تمام بیله مراجعت کورکوزوب همول قوش‌نی مقام قیلدیلار نظم

چو دولت بیله شاهُ سلطان ایکاو
بو منزلنی‌کیم ایلادی‌لار مکان

آنینکدیک که مهرْ درخشنده ماه
شرف برجیدا ایلاکای‌لار قران

چون اولکیچه داغی مذکور مقامدا آرام آلیب ایرتاسی دوشنبه کونی آفتاب

عالمتاب چرخ اخضردین طلوع قیلغاندیک چادر اخضردین شهزادهٔ شیرهمت بیرصولت طلوع قیلیب اشهب‌لاریکا راکب بولوب اوز کعبه‌لاری |13b| زیارتی اوچون بارکاه‌لاری جانبی‌غه یوروش قیلیب یقین بیتکان وقتدا حضرت پادشاه جهان و مالک رقاب زمینُ زمان دام عمره و دولته داغی دولت بیله آتلانیب میدان اورتاسیدا ایکی بحر زخار[1] التقا پیدا قیلغاندیک بیراو بیراولاریکا ملاقی بولوب روح و رواندیک قاریشتی‌لار چون بیر آز مسافت یول[2] یوردیلار اولحضرت داغی اوَّلغی دستوردا وزیر صایب‌تدبیرنی سابق‌داغی سرکرده‌لار بیله لشکر اهلیکا سر و سروَر قیلیب رأیت نصرت‌علامت‌لار یانیدا بویوروب ییباردیلار و اول ایکی جناب مستطاب‌کیم بیری خلافت مهری‌نینک سپهری و ینه بیری سلطنت سپهری‌نینک مهریدور شکار قیلماق اوچون قیر اوستیکا روان بولوب |14a| تا کیچکا تیکرو مشکبو غزاله‌لارنی صید قیلیب بو نوع تماشالار زلالی بیله کونکول‌لاری نهالی‌غه نشوُ نما بیتکوروب کیچ بولغاندا حضرتین علیتین آودین معاودت قیلیب صدبر مرحله‌سین لشکر اهلیکا مقر قیلدیلار نظم

تاجدار عصر کردون بارکاه
داور داراشکوه خوارزمشاه
قایتیب آودین مینک تومان فرحت بیله
قیلدی صدبر سرحدین آرامکاه
توتتی آندا چرخ‌آسا درکهین

[1] ذخار.
[2] یول above the line.

داغــی ســلطان فریدون دســتکاه
چون شه و سلطان آنکا قیلغاچ نزول
آندا باریب توشتی لار جمع سپاه

و اوشبو منزلدا اولکیچه استراحت قیلدیلار چون ایرتاسی سه‌شنبه کونی مهر شاهدی منوَّر چهره‌سیدین |14b| تون‌نینک قرا بُرقعین رفع قیلیب خوارزمشاه عدالتی‌نینک عینی‌دیک جمال باکمالی انواری‌نینک لمعاتیدین حضیض و بلند و حقیر[1] ارجمند اوزه یکسان یاغدو سالدی دارای زمان بیله شهزادهٔ دوران ادام الله دولتهما اسرو شوکت بیله آتلانیب آو قصدیغه بیابان طرفیکا عزیمت کورکوزوب وزیر مذکورنی مزبور سپهبدلار بیله طوغ‌لار یانیدا ییباریب کیچ بولغاندا[2] کلکون سولکون بیله زیبا غزاله‌لارنی آلیب تورلوک تماشالار کل‌لاری بیله کونکول‌لاری کلشنیکا زیب و آرا بیریب سودوک سرمنزلیکا ادهم و اشهب‌لاری ایزی‌نینک نقشی بیله صفا بیتکوروب ارم‌نما قیلدیلار نظم

چو قایتیب صیدکه‌دین شادُ خرَّم	شــهُ شــهزاده اول ایکــی مکرم
|15a| قیلیب مقدم‌لاریدین جنّت‌آسا	ســودوک‌نی ایلادیــلار طرفه مأوا
بو کیچه اول ایکی صاحب کرامت	بو ســرحد ایچرا توتتی‌لار اقامت

چون ایرتاسی چهارشنبه کونی نور عسکری ظلمت دستکاهی‌غه تُرکتاز قیلیب

---

[1] Hereafter read و.

[2] بولغاند.

خانمانین تارُ مار قیلدی اول سرمنزلدین سابق‌داغی یوسوندا ینه وزیر معظّم ناظم مصالح بنی آدم قوشبیکی بیک‌نی رأیت ظفرآیت‌لار بیله ارسال قیلیب حضرت خوارزمشاه بیله سلطان صاحبقران ایّدهما الله بنصره آو عزمی‌غه بیابان طرفیکا خرامان بولوب بیر نیچه آهو و جیرن‌نی صید و قید قیلیب مسرت تمام بیله مراجعت کورکوزوب اقشام دهن شیر بیشه‌سین لشکرلاری شیرلاریکا مقام قیلدی‌لار نظم

|15b| چونکه شه‌قویدی‌دشت‌ساری‌یوز   کشت ایتیب اولکون ایچرا تاغُ توز
سالیبان صقر و بازدین تویغون   آلدی بیحدکییک بیله سویغون
خاطر پاکین ایتی حدسیز خوش   قایتی اول ساریکیم ایردی قوش
کیچ کیلیب اول انام نیکوسی   دهن شیر بولدی پابوسی
کوهر تاج خسرو عالم   قرة العین داور اکرم
اولداغی دشت‌دین خرام ایتی   تون بو منزل ارا مقام ایتی
لشکر اهلی‌کیم ایردی شیرآسا   توتتی‌لار اوشبو بیشه‌دا مأوا

و اوشبو منزلدا بخارا خانی امیر نصر الله‌نینک ایلچی‌سی کیلیب ییبارکان پیشکش و تحفه‌لاری بیله محبت‌نامه‌سین خوارزمشاه روحنا و روح العالمین فداه[1] حضرت‌لاریکا ملازم‌لار واسطه‌سی بیله ییتکوردی و اولکیچه مذکور بیشه‌دا آرام آلیب ایرتاسی پنجشنبه کونی |16a| سابقداغی دستور بیله صفالی

[1] فداه above the line.

مرحله‌سیکا کمیت سیمین‌ستام‌لاری توینا‌غی‌نینک زیب و آرایشی بیله صفا بیتکوردیلار نظم

بو ایکی تاجدارُ نام‌آور	امام عادلُ سلطان صفدر
کیلیب اولکیچه‌سی بو ایکی عادل	صفالی سرحدینی قیلدی منزل
تاپیب مقدم‌لاریدین طرفه حالی	صفالی بولدی‌موندین سونک‌صفالی

چون ایرتاسی جمعه کونی مهر سلطانی‌نینک سپهر افقیدین تجمل تمام بیله طلوعی انجم و اخترنینک نامعدود جنودی انهزامی‌غه باعث بولدی حضرت پادشاه دوران بیله سلطان صاحبقران نصرهما الله بتأییده آو عزمی‌غه سمند دوندلاریکا راکب بولوب دشت جانبی‌غه روان بولدیلار و ایام سالفه دستورینچه |16b| ینه وزیر صایب‌تدبیر مذکور سرکرده‌لار بیله طوغ‌لار یانیدا باریب اول ایکی جناب مستطاب کیچ‌لیکیکا کیلیب چیشلی قرا آیغیر بیشه‌سین خرکاه و خیمه‌لاریغه مضرب و سپاه‌لاریغه منزل قیلدیلار و اولکیچه اول جایدا آرام آلیب ایرتاسی شنبه کونی اول منزلدین کوچوب اولغی دستوردا حضرتین علیتین کوب شوکت و اسرو صولت بیله کیلیب آق رباط سرمنزلین لشکر اهلیکا مقر قیلدیلار نظم

چیقیب چادریدین ایکی کامیاب	نیچوککیم سحاب آستیدین آفتاب
آتیب توب کوچوب یوردی هیبت بیله	کیلیب توشتی‌لار اسرو صولت بیله
یریکاکیم ایردی آتی آق رباط	نهایت‌سیز ایلاب آلار انبساط

و بیر کیچه آندا |17a| توقف قیلیب ایرتاسی یکشنبه کونی ینه سابقداغی دستوردا اول ایکی حضرت آو عزمی‌غه بیابان طرفیکا خرامان بولدیلار و وزیر صایب‌تدبیرنی مزبور سرکرده‌لار بیله رأیت نصرت‌آیت‌لار یانیدا ییباردیلار و کیچ‌قورون آو عزمی‌دین مراجعت کورکوزوب آت‌خور سرحدیکا دولت و اقبال بیله نزول اجلال بویوردیلار نظم

بیابـــان ارا اول ایکـــی بختیـــار
شـــکار ایتی‌لار طرفه جمشیدوار
بیاباندا خاطرنـــی خوش قیلدیلار
کییک بیرله سولکوننی ایلاب شکار
کیچه قایتیب آودین مقام ایتی‌لار
بو مســـکن ارا اول ایکی کامکار
چو خورشـــید و مه اقتران ایلابان
ســـعادت ســـپهریدا توتغـــای قرار

|17b| و بو منزلدا سکیز کون توقف کورکوزوب هر کوندا لشکر اهلین فوج فوج طایفه طایفه سان کوروب نهایتی‌غه بیتا آلمادیلار نیدین‌کیم سپاه اهلی حددین افزون و عدددین بیرون ایردی نظم

سپه خیلی چرخ انجمی‌دین فزون عـدددا بیابـان قومی‌دیـن فزون
بو سوز صدقیغه باوردور[1] اوشبو سند حسـابیداکیم عاجز اولدی خرد

چون سکیزینجی یکشنبه کونی مهر شهریاری سپهرنینک ماوی‌رنک بارکاهی‌دین ظهور قیلیب تورتونجی تخت اوزره نشست کورکوزوب شعاع فراشیغه بویوروب انوار طبق‌لاری بیله قمر قرصین و کردون بوشقابی‌غه انجم فاکهه‌لارین سالیب خوارزمشاه حضرت‌لاری بیله سلطان صاحبقران |18a| سلمهما الرحمن عن بلیات الزمان بارکاه‌لاری ملازم‌لاریغه فدا و صدقه قیلدوردی حضرت خوارزمشاه مد ظله العالی داغی علما و امرا خیلی باشلیق سپاه اهلیغه توی بیریب بارچه‌لارین عرش‌اشتباه درکاه‌لاریغه اونداتتی‌لار چون طوایف مذکوره‌کیم آستان‌بوسلیق شرفیغه مشرّف بولوب جبهه‌سالیق دولتین داغی تاپتی‌لار اولجماعه‌غه ملذّذ طعام‌لار و مُلوَّن فواکه‌لار تارتتی‌لارکیم هر بیری لَذّتدا جنت طعامیدیک خوشکوار و فردوس ثماریدین نمودار ایردی و اول معرکهٔ عالیه‌دا فرنکی قند بیرله مصری نبات تاشدیک بیمقدار و کیساکدیک بی‌اعتبار ایردی نظم

بولوب جنت‌طعامیدیک |18b| طعامی ملـذّذ چون عسـل نعمت تمامی
مُربّـا و نشـالا بیرلـه شـربت ایرور جان شیره‌سیدیک کان لذّت
آلاردین نفع آلور کیم جسمُ جانی تاپـار آندبـن حیـات جاودانـی

[1] Altered from بارەدور (?).

چون علما و امرا طعام و شراب تناولیدین فراغت تاپیب دعای خیر قیلیب اجازت‌لاری دولتی بیله سرافراز بولوب قوش‌لاری ساری مراجعت کورکوزدیلار خوارزمشاه بیله سلطان صاحبقران ایکی حضرت دام فرحتهما صولت خاقانیه و شوکت سلطانیه بیله آتلانیب آت‌چاپارکاه جانبی‌غه باریب برق‌رفتار و چرخ‌نمودار آت‌لارنی چاپتوروب غضنفرهیئت فیل‌صورت پهلوانلارنی کوراش توتتوروب هر بیریکا بایراق بیریب جیب |19a| و ایتاکین زر و نقره‌دین تولدوردیلار نظم

بیر نیچه سمند برق‌رفتار	سرعت ارا چون سپهر دوار
چاپماقغه بویوردیلار آلارنی	جزم ایتی آلار داغی چاپارنی
بیر نیچه‌سی کیلدی برقدیک تیز	چاپماق ارا برقدیک اوروب خیز
بیر نیچه ایدی شجاع‌پیشه	باری‌نینک ایشی کوراش همیشه
میدان ارا چیقتی بیر دلیری	چون بیشه ایچیدا نرّه‌شیری
چیقتی ینه بیری چون غضنفر	دیوهیأت ایدی و فیل‌پیکر
چون توتتی ایکاو بیریسی ییقتی	کیم سونکرا ینه بیریسی چیقتی
هر بیر بو صفت تلاش قیلدی	تنکه بیله تونی چاش قیلدی
هم تاپتی فرح بسی سایس‌لار	جیب بیله[1] ایتاک‌لاری |19b| تولوب زر

چون خاقان جهان بیله سلطان صاحبقران دام دولتهما غایت‌سیز تماشالارنینک فرحت‌شمایم نسایمی‌دین بو نوع خرم‌لیق ریاحینین کونکول‌لاری کلستانیدا

[1] بیله above the line.

آچتی‌لار دولت بیله اول یردین مراجعت کورکوزوب ینه اول منزلکا نزول بویوروب کیچه داغی مذکور منزلدا آرام آلیب استراحت قیلدیلار چون ایرتاسی دوشنبه صبحی آی سلطانی ستاره‌نینک بی‌کناره لشکری بیله خورشید انور ملازمتی‌دین وداع قیلیب مفارقت و مهاجرت بادیه‌سی قطعی‌غه یوز قویدی سلطان صاحبقران باشلیق وزیر صایب‌تدبیر و مأمور بولغان سرکرده‌لار خوارزمشاه دام دولته‌نینک مبارک فاتحه‌لارین آلیب وداع‌لاشیب دولت بیله آتلانیب |20a| مقصد ساری عزیمت کورکوزوب کوب شوکت اسرو صولت بیله کیلیب کوکارجین‌لی توغایین قدوم‌لاری شرفی بیله چین شهریدیک دلنشین قیلدیلار نظم

شکوه ایله سلطان صاحبقران کوکارجین‌لی‌نی ایلادی چون مکان
قدومی بیله بولدی کویا که چین بولوب شهر چین‌دیک عجب دلنشین

چون [1]سه‌شنبه کونی[1] مهرنینک نیکوچهر سلطانی تجمل تمام بیله کردون توسنیغه مینیب سپهر میدانی قطعی‌غه خرام کورکوزدی سلطان صاحبقران ایّد الله بنصره شوکت مالاکلام بیله رخش برق‌خرام‌لاریغه راکب بولوب بیر نیچه میدان مسافتین قطع قیلیب دایه خاتون قلعه‌سی‌نینک محاذی‌سیدا شمالی طرفیدا واقع بولغان بیشه‌دا نصرت‌برچم علم‌لارین جلوه‌نما قیلدیلار |20b| نظم

نیچه میدان قطع ایتیب سلطان کردون احتشام

[1-1] Above the line.

دایه خاتون بیشه‌سین دولت بیله قیلدی مقام
مقدمیدین اوشبو بیشه آنچه‌کیم تاپتی شرف
واجب اولدی سونکرا موندین جنت‌آسا احترام

و اول کیچه مذکور محل‌دا بی‌خلل راحت آلیب ایرتاسی چهارشنبه کونی خورشید انور بوز برجدی منظردین طالع بولوب عالم اکناف و اطرافیغه انواریدین لامع بولدی سلطان صاحبقران نصره الله بتأییده دولت بیله آتلانیب یول اوستیدا قلعهٔ مذکوره ایچیدا جنت‌مکان عبد الله خان‌نینک کاروان استراحتی اوچون بنا قیلغان سرایین تماشا قیلیب قیر اوستیکا چیقغان وقتدا ینه وزیر صایب‌تدبیر |21a| قوشبیکی بیک دام صدقه و اخلاصه‌نی طوغ‌لار یانیدا ییباریب اوزلاری بیر نیچه خصوصیت‌کیش چاووش و چاکرلاری بیله مرل و جیرن صیدی اوچون بادیه جانبی‌غه عزم قیلیب کوب آهو و قویان و کلکون سولکون و سویغوننی صید و قید قیلیب بو نوع تماشالار صیقلی بیله کونکول‌لاری مرآتیغه صفا بیتکوروب کیچ بولغاندا کیلیب قاباقلی بیشه‌سین مأوا قیلدیلار نظم

شکوه ایله اول داور کامکار
بیابان ارا ایلادی کوب شکار
مسرت بیله قایتیب آودین کیچه
قاباقلی ساری باریب اول بختیار
تومان مینک شکوه و تجمل بیله
نزول ایلابان آندا توتتی قرار

چون یوح بیضا داوری |21b| غایت‌سیز فتوح بیله مشرق بحاری کناریدین انوار سویین کردون بختی‌لاریغه لمعات مشک‌لاری بیله یوکلاب سپهر ریکزاری قطعی‌غه رفتار کورکوزدی سلطان نامدار و خدیو کامکار داغی فلک جمّازه‌سیدیک توانا و قوّت‌لیغ تیوه‌لارکا کردون طبقه‌سی یانکلیغ مشک‌لار بیله لشکر اهلی اوچون سو یوکلاتیب هفت ریک خوارزم قطعی‌غه‌کیم قیش فصلیدا تفسان و آتش‌فشانلیقی مشهور و معروف جهان‌دور [1]توکل بیله[1] عزیمت کورکوزوب بیر نیچه مسافت‌نی طی قیلیب مغفرت‌نشان عبد الله خان‌نینک بنا قیلغان سردابه‌سی قریبی‌دا بیر ریکزار اوستیکا دولت بیله کیلیب نزول بویوردیلارکیم حالا اول سردابه حوض خانغه مشهوردور |22a| نظم

بو یانکلیغ چول ایچرا دخول ایلادی	باریب بیر قوم اوزره نزول ایلادی
قومی ایردی اول حوض خانغه قریب	مساحت‌دا تخمینی ایلیک جریب

و اوشبو منزلدا تا یاریم کیچه‌کا تیکرو راحت آلیب یاریم کیچه‌دین سونکرا شبکیر اوروب تانک نمازین یولدا ادا قیلیب جمعه کونی چاشت وقتی سلیمانوار آرام اوچون تخت‌نی مقام قیلدیلار نظم

اول سلیمانجاهُ اسکندرنظام	تخت‌نی آرام اوچون قیلدی مقام
کوب تجمل بیرله اول فرخنده‌بخت	قیلدی منزلکاهینی اولکوندا تخت

[1-1] In margin.

چون ایرتاسی شنبه کونی خورشید سلطانی غایت‌سیز طُمطُراق و کیرودار بیله مشرق تختی اوزره رخ‌نما بولوب آفاق دشتی قطعی‌غه عزیمت کورکوزدی |22b| سلطان صاحبقران غایت‌سیز شوکت بیله آتلانیب بیر نیچه مسافت‌نی طی قیلیب بیر بلند قوم اوستیکا باریب هبوط بویوردیلار نظم

چو نهضت ایتیب قطع منزل قیلیب — شتاب ایله طی مراحل قیلیب
شکوه ایله اول داور نامور — باریب ایلادی بیر قوم اوستین مقر

و اولکیچه مذکور موضع‌دا یاریم کیچه‌کا تیکرو توقف کورکوزوب کیچه نصفی‌دین سونکرا شبکیر قیلیب بامداد نمازین یولدا ادا قیلیب یکشنبه کونی چاشت وقتی بیر ریک‌زار اوستیکا توشوب اندک راحت ایتیب پیشین نمازی اداسیدین سونکرا ینه حشمت بیله آتلانیب بیر نیچه مسافت یول یوروب عصر چاغی سرطلانلی سرحدیدین اوتوب ینه بیر قوم اوزره نزول و هبوط بویوردیلار |23a| نظم

یول یوروب شوکت بیله سلطان افریدون‌سیَر
عسکر بیحد بیله سرطلانلی‌دین ایلاب کذر
بی‌نهایت صولت ایله نیچه منزل قطع ایتیب
عصر چاغی ینه بیر قوم اوستینی قیلدی مقر

و اولکیچه مذکور مقام‌دا سحرکا تیکرو آرام آلیب سحر وقتی اسرو دبدبه بیله

آتلانیب مقصد ساری عازم بولدیلار و ایرتانک نمازین یول قطعی اثناسیدا ادا قیلیب دوشنبه کونی بیر نیچه مسافت قطعی‌دین سونک چاشت وقتی باریب بیر ریکزار اوستیکا توشوب اندک راحت قیلدیلار و مذکور جایدین[1] پیشین نمازین اوقوب دولت تمام بیله رخش خوشخرام‌لاریغه راکب بولوب دبدبهٔ تمام بیله عصردین اول‌راق یانتاقلی |23b| سرحدین خرکاه اخضرلاری بیله عسکر اهلیکا قرارکاه قیلدیلار نظم

اول کوهر قلزم تکرُّم	تعجیل ایله قطع ایتیب نیچه قوم
لشکر داغی بحردیک اوروب موج	موجی قوم اوزه توتوب ولی اوج
بو نوع سپاه بیرله سلطان	قطع ایتی نیچه قومُ بیابان
یر رسم اطاعت ایلادی کرم	قوم بیرله ایتیب طریقینی نرم
قوم یوقکه فرس تکاثریدین	توپناغ اثری توافریدین
قوم شکلیکا آیلانیب بمرَّه	یر پیکری بولدی ذرَّه ذرَّه
بو کوکبه بیرله اولکرامی	یانتاقلینی ایلادی مقامی
بیتکوردی قدومیدین طراوت	تاپتی بو هم اوزکاچه نضارت
بو مرحله بولدی روضه‌آیین	هم رشک بر ممالک چین

چون سلطان |24a| صاحبقران اول سرحدنی نزول شرافت‌وصول‌لاری بیله فردوس‌آیین و غیرت خلد برین قیلدیلار[2] همولکیچه مذکور موضع‌دا مکث قیلیب

[1] Read جایدا.

[2] Hereafter و.

خفتن نمازی اداسیدین سونکرا التفات‌لاری جامه‌خانه‌سیدین خلاع زراندود انعام و احسانی بیله امرا زمره‌سی فرقین فرقدان فرقیدین آشوروب بارچه‌سین طلّاپوش قیلیب خاطرلاریدین یول قطعی محنتین بالکل فراموش قیلدیلار چون ایرتاسی سه‌شنبه صبحی بنات النعش ساریق‌لاری سپهر مروی‌نینک آق آت و بوز آتی بیله قمرنینک سیمین‌پیکر غلامین سلطان بیضا بارکاهی‌غه تحفه و پیشکش یوسونیدا چیکیب اوزلارین |24b| خفاش‌وار [1]اول درکاه ملازمتیدین[1] عاجز و تحایف و تنسوقاتین نالایق و ناچیز تاپتی‌لار مرو اولتوروملی ساریق جماعه‌سی‌نینک کدخدالاری حاکم‌لاری نیاز محمد بای باشلیق رکاب‌بوسلیق شرفیکا مشرف بولوب بیر نیچه خورشیدطلعت غلام‌لار بیله برق‌سرعت براق‌صورت آت‌لارنی تحفه و پیشکش رسمیدا سلطان صاحبقران حضرت‌لاریکا اوتکاردی‌لار و عالیشان رفیع‌مکان کلات حکمرانی محمد علیخان‌نینک‌کیم بو خاندان دولت‌بنیان‌نینک قدیمی اخلاص‌نشانیدور عرضه‌داشتین محمد قلی بیک‌کیم آنینک معتبر مقرب‌لاریدین‌دور نظر اقدس‌لاریغه ملازم‌لار واسطه‌سی بیله همول یردا فایز قیلدی و اول عرضه‌داشت سوادی |25a| بو تورور

سلطنت دودمانی‌نینک خلاصه‌سی خلافت خاندانی‌نینک سلاله‌سی عارج معارج شوکت و اجلال مرتقی مدارج عزت و اقبال حکمرانلیغ چمنی‌نینک هوای دلکشاسی کامرانلیغ کلشنی‌نینک بهجت‌شمیم نسیم روح‌افزاسی لازال اغصان العمر و الدولة مُورّقةً[2] بسحاب نصرت

[1-1] In margin.

[2] مُورّقةً in margin.

الرحمان‌نینک جهان‌مدار دربارلاری ملازم‌لاری‌نینک رأی اقدس اعلالاریغه عرض ییتکورورکیم اولجناب والانینک مرو ولایتی‌غه تشریف بویورماق‌لاری مسموع بولونوب غایت‌سیز فرحت و نهایت‌سیز مسرت بو بندۀ سرافکنده‌کا حاصل بولدی و چون بو اخلاصمند اول کیتی‌مدار دربارنینک عُروة الوثقی‌سیغه متمسک بولوب |25b| اول دولت علیا دامنین محکم توتوب کوب مُدَّتدورکیم اعتقاد ایلیکین اوزکا یاندین چیکیب اُمیدنی اول آستانۀ سپهرنشانه‌غه یکجهت قیلیب خدمت اموری‌نینک مستعدی‌دور ایمدی [1]توقع اولکیم[1] بو مخلص‌نی التفات‌لاری بیله[2] سربلند قیلیب مرو ولایتی‌غه تشریف بویورغان‌لارین اعلام قیلسه‌لار هرآینه فرج الله‌نی ناقابل پیشکشی بیله درکاه جهان‌پناه‌لاری ساری یوللاب باقی فرمایشات و خدمات اداسیغه کما ینبغی ساعی بولغوم‌دور و اکر طژن موضعین قدوم شرافت‌لزوم‌لاری بیله کلشن قیلسه‌لار اوزوم[3] بارکاه عرش‌اشتباه‌لاری عتبه‌بوسلیقی‌نینک رُتبه‌سین تاپیب خدمت مراسمین تقدیم‌غه ییتکورکوم‌دور و محمد قلی بیک‌نی داغی بو عرضه‌داشت |26a| حاملی قیلیب اول جانب دولت‌جوانب‌غه یوللادیم تاکیم تشریف‌لاری حقیقتین معلوم قیلیب مراجعت کورکوزکای باقی هر کونه بویروغ‌لاری بولسه فرمان‌بردارورمن

[1-1] In margin.

[2] بیله above the line.

[3] اوزوم above the line.

چون سلطان صاحبقران بو عرضه‌داشت سطورین منظورلاری قیلیب مطالعه‌لاری شرفی بیله خورشید انور ورقیدیک نورافزا قیلدیلار اسکندرانه شوکت و جمشیدانه صولت بیله صباسیرلاریغه رکوب قیلیب بیر نیچه مسافت راه قطعین تقدیمغه سپاه رزمخواه‌لاری بیله ییتکوروب[1] ترخان قودوقیدین عبور قیلیب نزول اجلال بویوردیلار نظم

کرامی‌منزلت سلطان جمجاه — توتوب آندا عجب خرکاه دلخواه
ییتوردی مقدمیدین کوب سعادت — |26b| مذلّت چاهی تاپتی جاه‌عزّت
همولچاه اوشبو ساعت جاه تاپتی — فلک اوجیدا منزلگاه تاپتی
یتیب اول یرکا سلطان نکوچهر — بو چشمه بولدی کویا چشمهٔ مهر
سویی بولدی آنینک چون آبحیوان — اولوک کرایچسه‌آندین تاپغوسی جان
نحوستدین بولوب ترخان الآن — که موندین سونکرا بولدی آتی ترخان

چون سلطان صاحبقران شرافت‌وصول نزول‌لاری بیله اول منزلنی روضه‌آیین و بهشت‌تزیین قیلدیلار سالور خلقی حاکم‌لاری محمد امین[2] بیک باشلیق درکاه کیهان‌پناه عتبه‌سیغه جبهه‌سالیق درجه‌سین تاپیب تحفه و تنسوقات‌لارین دربار کیتی‌مدار بنده‌لاری‌نینک ایلیکیکا تسلیم قیلدیلار |27a| و محمد قلی بیک مذکورنی مزبور جایدا لباس شاهانه بیله سربلند و عنایت‌نامهٔ مرحمت‌ختامه اعطاسی بیله‌کیم اعتقاد طریقیدا ایراد قیلغان عرضه‌داشت جوابیدور ارجمند

[1] ییتکوروب in margin.

[2] .آمین

قیلیب اجازت‌لاری دولتی‌نینک پیرایه‌سی بیله بلندپایه قیلدیلار و اول عنایت‌نامه تسویدی بو تورور

عالیجاه معلی‌جایکاه اخلاص و اعتقادنشان رفیع المکان محمد علی خان دام اخلاصه‌غه یارلیغ کورکاچ اولکیم محمد قلی بیک بیله اخلاص اظهاری اوچون مکتوب قیلیب ییبارکان عرضه‌داشتینک آستانهٔ سپهرنشانه‌دا تورغان ملازم‌لار واسطه‌سی بیله ییتوشوب مضمونی کما ینبغی معلوم و مفهوم بولدی ایمدی کراکدورکیم اخلاص بابیدا قیلغان |27b| لافینک‌غه لایق درکاه آسمانجاهی‌میز عتبه‌بوسلیقی رتبه‌سین تاپیب ملازم‌لار سلکیکا انتظام یوسونیدا انخراط تاپیب اخلاص کمرین اعتقادینک بیلیکا استحکام بیله باغلاب خدمت قیلسانک هرآینه رفعت اوجی اوزه ترقی قیلیب غایت‌سیز مرحمت و نهایت‌سیز عنایت‌لار کورکونک‌دور دیب التفات یوزیدین بو عنایت‌نامهٔ عالیه ارسال تاپتی

و اول محل‌دا سحرکا تیکرو مکث کورکوزوب آندین سونکرا شبدیز برق‌خیزلاریغه عنایت آلهی و هدایت نامتناهی بیله رکوب قیلیب اعتقاد بی‌انتها بیله بامداد نمازین یولدا ادا قیلیب بیر نیچه مرحله قطعین تقدیمغه ییتکوروب چهارشنبه کونی چاشت وقتی کِشمان میدانین خیمه |28a| و خرکاه‌لاریغه مکان قیلیب رشک کلزار جنان قیلدیلار و اول رفیع‌مکان مذکور میداندا پیشین‌کا تیکرو

راحت آلیب پیشین نمازی اداسیدین سونکرا جمشیدانه اساس و اساسهٔ بیقیاس بیله رخش راحت‌بخش‌لاریغه سوار بولوب مقصد ساری توجه کورکوزدیلار و لشکر صفوفین آنداق راست قیلدیلارکیم باوجود لشکر طولاً و عرضاً بیر فرسخ مسافتی مقداریدین زیاد ایردی ادهم‌لار اقدامی بیراو بیراولاریدین نه ایلکاریراق روان و نه کیین ساری میلانی بار ایردی و بو اثنادا بیر نیچه شمشیرباز بهادُرلار و قادرانداز[1] متهوّرلارکیم جلد و چالاکلیک بیرله موصوف و معروف ایردیلار نیزه‌بازلیق و تفنک‌اندازلیق[2] |28b| بیله طَرید[3] آغاز قیلیب خلایقغه تماشالار کورکوزوب چرخ وغابازغه داغی تحیر و تحسُّر بارماغین تیشلاتتی‌لار نظم

بهـادرلار اولنـوغ چـالاک ایرور — شتاب ایچرا مانندی افلاک ایرور
عدو بولسـه کـر دیـو مازندران — و کر بولسه خود فیل و ببر دمان
کیشی های دیکونچه یتیب یانیغه — قیلـور لاله‌کـون یر یوزیـن قانیغه
آلارکیم بو میدان‌دا جولان قیلیب — طَرید[3] امرینی آنچه امکان قیلیب
چیقیب بیر کروه‌کیم ایدی پهلوان — آلیب ایل‌لاریکا درخشـان سنان
ینه بعضی ایلکیکا آلیب تفنک[4] — ایرور کوییا اوشـبو هنکام جنک

---

1 قادرآنداز.
2 توفنک‌آندازلیق.
3 طُرید.
4 توفنک.

تفنک[1] یوقکه آتش‌فشان اژدری | و لیکن عجب کیم تیمور پیکری
ینه بعضی |29a| شمشیر بُرّان آلیب | مقابل‌غه بیمُ هراست سالیب
قیلیب حمله‌لار بیر بیریکا عیان | حواله قیلیب نیزهٔ جان‌ستان
حواله قیلیب بعضی‌سی کیم تفنک[1] | ینه بیری جانب آتیب بی‌درنک
بو میدان ارا هر طرف آت سالیب | سوران رسمی بیرله علالا قیلیب
طرقای سُمّ سمند دوند | فلک سمعیغه بیتکوروب کوب کزند
اویون ایلادیلار عیان اولکروه | فلک بولدی آندین تحیرپژوه
بو یانکلیغ شکوهُ تجمل بیله | روان بولدیلار اسرو غلغل بیله
خدایا بو سلطان صاحبقران | اکر هر طرف عزمین ایسه عیان
کرم بیرله لطفینک‌نی بار ایت آنکا | ظفر بیرله نصرتنی یار ایت آنکا

|29b| چون بو نوع شکوه و کیرودار بیله نهضت قیلدیلار چشمه‌لار انفجاریدین جویبارلار منشعب بولوب بحر کناریدین داخل بولوب آنکا انضمام پیدا قیلغاندیک مرو ولایتی اطراف و جوانبی‌دا اولتوروملی تورکمانیه و آیماقیه نواکری فوج فوج اول اثنادا یتیب سلطان صاحبقران ایَّد الله بنصره حضرت‌لاری‌غه باش ایندوروب تعظیم رسمین تقدیمغه بیتکوروب دریای لشکر ظفراثر قطراتی‌نینک سلکیکا انتظام تاپتی‌لار بو طریقه تفرج صیقلی بیله کونکول‌لاری کوزکوسیغه صفا بیتکوروب آفتاب غروبی‌نینک قُبَیلی‌دا کیلیب کاوبُر سرمنزلین مأوا قیلدیلارکیم اولمنزل خوارزم طرفیدین کیلکانکا هفت ریک خوارزم نهایتی و

[1] توفنک.

مرو آبشاری‌نینک |30a| بدایتی‌دور نظم

کاوبرنـــی ایلادی سـلطان مکان مقدمیدین قیلدی چون باغ جنان
ظاهر اولدی کوزکودیک روشن زلال عالـم اهلیغه سـویی کوثـر مثال
آبشـاری هر طرف بی‌وهم و ظن آبحیـوان یانکلیغ هر یان موج‌زن
کورسه هر کیم آنی خود بی‌قالُ قیل روضه‌دا قیلغای تخیُّل سلسـبیل
تشنه‌لیک‌نینک خوفیدین تاپیب امان لشکر اهلی بولدی باری شادمان

چون پنجشنبه صبحی اخلاص‌آثار زوارنینک[1] کونکول‌لاریدیک روشن و مصفّا بولوب خورشید سلطانی مینک تومان شکوه بیله چهره کورکوزوب سپهرنینک دیرینه قلعه‌سی خلوت‌نشین‌لاری‌نینک طواف و زیارتی اوچون انوار لشکری ایچرا تحرک سالیب عزیمت |30b| کورکوزدی سلطان صاحبقران جعل الله غالباً علی اعدائه کرنایلاتیب و توب آتدوروب[2] دبدبهٔ سلطانیه بیله یر و کوک اجزاسیغه زلزله سالیب آتلانیب لشکر بیحد و مرلاری بیله کذرلاری مرو شاهجان‌نینک کهنه قلعه‌سی اورتاسیدین واقع بولوب اوّل قبلة العارفین کعبة السالکین صاحب الخدمات الصمدانی خواجه یوسف همدانی نور الله مرقده‌نینک سراسرخاصیت زیارت‌لاریدین مستفیض بولدی‌لار نظم

[1] نینک above the line.

[2] آتدروب.

طریقت اهلی خاص الخاصی دور اول حقیقت بحری نینک غوّاصی دور اول
وحید اهل عرفانُ تجرُّد فرید ملک ارکان تفرُّد
دیان دوران ارا اهل تَعرُّف مبارک اسمین آنینک خواجه یوسُف
چو اخلاص ایله بولدی آنکا زایر |31a| که حاصل ایتی آندین فیض وافر

ایکینجی سلطان الاولیا برهان الاتقیا احدیت بارکاهی رازی نینک امینی قاضی حقیقی قضاسی غه راضی سلطان سنجر ماضی قدس الله اسراره نینک زیارت کبریت علامت لاریدین داغی فیض کیر بولدیلار نظم

معارف اهلی نینک سلطانُ خانی ولایت کشوری نینک حکمرانی
هدایت افسری نینک زیوری اول کرامت تختی نینک زیبُ فری اول
حقیقت عالمین قیلغان مسخَّر مبارک اسمی دور سلطان سنجر
آنینک هم مرقدین ایلاب زیارت کونکول نینک قصرینی ایتی عمارت
زیارت امریدین سلطان کامل فیوض بی نهایت ایتی حاصل
الّهی مدعاسی بولسه هر ایش همیشه قیل اول ایشدا فیض بخشش

|31b| اوچونجی ولایت مآب هدایت انتساب معرفت میدانیدا دلیرانه قدم اورغوچی پهلوان احمد زمچی برَّد الله مضجعه نینک متبرک مزار فیض آثارین داغی زیارت ایتیب صفوت و مسرَّت علی سبیل الکمال استحصال ایتی لار

نظم

آستانی مرجع اهل کمال / جبهه‌سای اولیای ذی الجلال
سرمه‌سان توفراغی آنینک نور عین / تاپیب آندین اتقیا مینک زیب و زین
هم فنا وادی‌لارین قیلغان تمام / هم بقا[1] ملکی[2] ارا توتغان مقام
هم حقیقت ساریغه یول باشلاغان / اوزلوکی بار کرانین تاشلاغان
قدس اربابی بیله بولغان انیس / انس اصحابی بیله یار و جلیس
لی مع الله خلوتی نینک محرمی / قربت اوجیدا ملایک همدمی
بیشهٔ عرفان ارا |32a| غرنده شیر / معرفت میدانیدا بیر دلیر
احمد زمچی آنکا اسمُ لقب / کوب خوارق ظاهر ایتکان بو العجب
پهلوانلیق بیرله تاپغان اشتهار / ایلابان دوران ارا کوب کارُ زار
صدق ایله خاطرنی ایلاب پاکُ صاف / ایلادی سلطان آنی داغی طواف
اول زیارت‌دین یتیب بیحد مدد / خاطری تاپتی صفای بیعدد

تورتونجی ینه بیر بزرکوار عالیمقدارنی زیارت ایتیب فتوحات بی‌منتها و فیوضات لایُعَد[3] و لایحصی‌سیدین بهره‌مند و ارجمند بولدیلارکیم کوب تفحص و تفتیش بسیاردین سونکرا آنداق معلوم بولدی و مجاورلاریدین مونینکدیک مسموع بولدیکیم |32b| اول بزرکوار غیاث المستغیثین قدوة المتقین زبدهٔ آل طهٰ و یاسین عمدهٔ اولاد سید المرسلین معرفت الله طریقیدا رایی موافق امام جعفر صادق زاد الله فیوضاته و فتوحاته علی الزایرین و الطایفین ایرکانلار نظم

[1] بقا above the line.

[2] Altered from ملک.

[3] لایَعُد.

امـام المتقیـن و قطـب عالـم غیاث المسـتغیثین غـوث اعظم
طریقت قصری‌نینک بنیادی آندین حقیقت اهلی‌نینک ارشادی آندین
ولایـت اهلی‌نینـک عالیمقامـی هدایت رسمی‌نینک صاحب‌نظامی
نقـود معرفت‌نینـک مخزنـی اول تعرُّف کل‌لاری‌نینک کلشـنی اول
مشـایخ اهلیـکا آوازه آندیـن سـلوک اوراقیغـه شـیرازه آندیـن
سـیادت باغی جان‌پرور هواسـی بو کلشن‌نینک‌نسیم|33a|دلکشاسی
دمی عیسـی دمیدیـک روح‌پرور سـوزی صادق و لیکن[1] آتی جعفر
طواف ایلاب مونی هم شاد و مسرور بیتوشـتی خاطریغـه فیـض موفور
آلهی عزمین هر یان قیلسـه تعیین بو سلطان کونکلیکا فیض ایلا تلقین

چون سلطان صاحبقران بو بزرکوار عالیمقدارلارنی بیر بیر زیارت قیلیب جوار فیض‌آثارلاریداغی مجاورلارغه صدقات و نذورات بیحد اعطاسی بیله بارچه‌لاری فرقین فرقدان فرقیدین آشوروب ارواح مقدسه‌لاریدین اعانت توقع قیلیب ینه خجنک بُراق‌رنک‌لاریکا رکوب کورکوزوب خسروانه صولت بیله یول قطعی‌غه روانه بولدیلار غایت‌سیز شکوه و کیرودار بیله اول جمشیداطوار ظفراثر عسکرلاریغه |33b| مرو دریاسی‌نینک کناریدا کل پَر موضعین مقر قیلدیلار و اول جایدا کیچه‌سی راحت کرین بولوب ایرتاسی کیم جمعه کونی ایردی خورشید سلطانی نهایت‌سیز تجمل بیله فلک اطلسی اوزه سمند سوروب سپهر قورغانی ساری توجه کورکوزدی و قمر خادمی تومان مینک نیازمندلیک بیله انجم

[1] لیکین.

دراهمی بیله بودُ نابودین اول سلطان نیکواطوار نثاری قیلدی سلطان صاحبقران جعل الله[1] منصوراً و مسروراً بالوفور الی انقطاع الدوران شوکت تمام و حشمت مالاکلام بیله رخش خوشخرام‌لاریغه رکوب قیلیب توب آتدوروب و کرنایلاتیب عالم اکنافیغه غلغل و آفاق سوادی ایچرا تزلزل سالیب رأیت نصرت‌آیت‌لار شقه‌لاریغه کشاد و مهجه‌لاری |34a| کوزکوسیغه صیقل و جلا قویاش مرآتیدین زیاد بیتکوروب و قیلاودار یالاولارنی جلوه‌غه کیرکوزوب لشکر صف‌آرالیقی اوچون میمنه و میسره‌دا ایکی جارچی‌کیم اونی غوغاسی توقوز فلک‌نی صداغه کیرکوزور ایردی جار اوروب مقصد ساری حرکت قیلدیلار اول اثنادا عالیجاه نیاز محمد بای سابق الذکرکیم بو خاندان عظام و دودمان کرام‌نینک جان‌سپار و جان‌نثار خذمتکاری ایردی خذمتکارلیق قواعدی و جان‌نثارلیق مراسمی‌نینک اظهاری اوچون آلدلاریغه یاریم فرسخ یردین جان پرنیانی‌دیک حریر اطلس‌لارنی پای‌انداز یوسونیدا توشاب مبارک تارک‌لاریغه بیحد درم نثار قیلدی و لشکر داغی |34b| اولمقدار جمع بولوب صف توزوب ایردیلارکیم بیابان قومی و آسمان انجمی حسابیدین افزون ایردی نظم

تجمل بیله بولدی سلطان روان	بولوب همرهی لشکر بیکران
توب آتیب زمینُ زمان کولدوراب	چالیب کرنایُ آسمان کولدوراب
قیلیب جارچی‌لار ایکی یاندین ندا	صف‌آرالیق امرین قیلورلار ادا
اونیدین جهانغه علالا توشوب	فلک جوفیکا اسرو غوغا توشوب

[1] الله above the line.

بیریب طوغ‌لار شُقّه‌سیغه کشاد   ایسیب بارچه‌سیغه نسیم مراد
کیلیب پرچمی لیلة القدردیک   بولوب مهچه‌لار اوستیدا بدردیک
درخشان لوا جلوه‌کر بیعدد   آلارغه بولوب نی نهایت نی حد
زر و سیم‌دین کیلدی پیکرلاری   آی و کون کیبی زیبُ زیورلاری
|35a| بولوب نیزه‌لار هر طرف جلوه‌کر   ایسیب توش توشیدین نسیم ظفر
سنان‌لار ایتیب ایلا کثرت عیان   ایرور بیر قالین نیستانی روان
یالاو هر بیری مهر تابنده‌دیک   سنان‌لار شهاب درخشنده‌دیک
ایرور هر بیری ایلاکیم تند و تیز   عدو باغری‌غه بیتکای آندین ستیز
جزایرلار آنداق کورورداب کیتیب   فلک کنبذی‌کا صداسی یتیب
سالیب تاغ و چول ایچرا غُلغل بسی   توشوب یر و کوککا تزلزل بسی
مسلَّح باری لشکر ره‌نورد   کییب جوشن آنداقکه روز نبرد
خیال ایلاکیم اول صفت بو فریق   باریسی تیمور بحری ایچرا غریق
سپه قلزمی‌غه توشوب ایلا جوش   توقف‌سیز اوتتی فلک‌دین خروش
|35b| پدیدار اولوب کویی غوغای حشر   بو کون بولدی پیدا علالای حشر
سپاهی که توتمیش ایدی یر یوزین   قیلیب خیره کردی فلک نینک کوزین
یتیب آنداکیم بای فرمان‌پذیر   توشاب ایردی جان پارچه‌سیدیک حریر
ایدی پارچه‌لار سندس دلنشین   همه اطلسُ خز و دیبای چمن
سوروب اوستیدین رخشین ایتی خرام   خدیو فلک‌قدر دارانظام
ینه ایلادی بای خدمت‌شعار   مبارک باشیغه جواهر نثار
قدم بر قدم صُرَّه اغزین آچیب   زر و نُقره‌نی اولچه امکان ساچیب
بو نوع شوکتُ بزرک آیین بیله   روان بولدی‌لار اسرو تزیین بیله

آلهی بو سلطان کشورستان اقالیم ارا بولغای اول حکمران
سلاطین ارا کامران بولغای اول |36a| ممالک‌دا صاحبقران بولغای‌اول

بو نوع اساسه و دبدبه و بو طریقه شعشعه بیله کیلیب مذکور بای‌نینک بنا قیلغان قلعه‌سیغه قدوم شرافت‌لزوم‌لاری بیله آبادلیق و فقرالاریغه دیدار فیض‌آثارلاریدین شادلیق بیتکوردیلار نظم

بولوب مقدمی‌دین بسی شادلیق یتیب قلعه‌غه اسرو آبادلیق
بو قورغان اراکیم خدیو جهان سپهر ایچرا چون مهر توتتی مکان
بولوب اهلیدین قایغو بالکل عدم آنکا بولدی رشکین ریاض ارم

چون سلطان صاحبقران ایّد الله بنصره دخول شرافت‌لزوم سعادت‌وصول‌لاری بیله قلعهٔ مذکوره‌نی رشک خلد برین قیلدیلار بای مذکور ضیافت شاهانه ترتیب بیریب مه‌رخسار |36b| خورشیددیدار زلف‌دار غلام‌لار برق‌رفتار و بُراق‌نمودار اشهب زرین‌لجام‌لارنی تحفه و پیشکش رسمی بیله چیکیب درکاه جهان‌پناه ملازم‌لاری‌نینک قول‌لاریغه تفویض قیلدی و تورت کیچه قلعهٔ مذکوره‌دا راحت‌کزین بولوب سه‌شنبه کونی خذمتکار جان‌سپارلاری اخلاص‌نمای یوموت نظر باینی صحت و سلامت مرو ولایتی‌غه تشریف بویورغان‌لارین عرضه‌داشت قیلیب سکندرجاه دارادستکاه اوز کعبه‌لاری خوارزمشاه ادام الله ظلال عاطفته علی خلق الله حضرت آسمان‌بسطت‌لاری ساری یوللادی‌لار و

اول عرضه‌داشت الفاظ و عباراتی جواهری‌نینک کتابت رشته‌سیکا انتظامی بو یوسوندا وقوع و صدور تاپتی

|37a| حضرت پادشاه انجم‌سپاه و شهنشاه فلک‌بارکاه قبلة السلاطین العظام کعبة الخواقین الکرام سلطنت مهری‌نینک سپهر رفعت‌آثاری خلافت کوهری‌نینک بحر وسعت‌نموداری حکمرانلیغ جواهری‌نینک مخزن فرحت‌بخشاسی کامرانلیغ زواهری‌نینک کلشن جهان‌آراسی شفقت کانی مرحمت عُمّانی حکومت‌پناه منزلت‌دستکاه جناب مستطاب قبله‌کاهیمیز خوارزمشاه ادام الله ظلال عاطفته علی خلق الله‌نینک درکاه جهان‌پناه‌لاریغه ادعیهٔ متوافره و اثنیهٔ متکاثره تحایف و هدایاسی ارسالیدین سونکرا بو مخلص‌نینک عرضه‌داشتی اولکیم لله الشکر و المنه هادی ازلی هدایتی‌نینک |37b| برکتی و دعوت اجابت‌آیت‌لاری خاصیتی‌دین صحت و سلامت مرو ولایتی داخلی بولوب مقاصدات شواهدی‌نینک واصلی‌دورمیز و سرور علی سبیل الوفور حصول و وصول آغاز قیلیب ترقی‌پردازدور و نظر باینی بو عرایض اظهاری اوچون بو عریضة الاخلاص حاملی قیلیب سراسرخاصیت خدمت‌لاریغه ییباردوک و موندین سونکرا فرمایش عالی‌نمایش‌لاری نی نوع بولمیش بولسه جان و دل بیله آنینک اداسیغه ساعی بولغومیزدور دیب اخلاص و اعتقاد یوزیدین بو عرضه‌داشت ارسال تاپتی

و همولکوندا اخلاص‌نشان میرزا خان خلیفه‌نی هرات خانی شاه کامرانغه‌کیم بو دولت‌خانه‌نینک قدیمی دوستی‌دور ایلچی یوسونیدا |38a| محبت‌نامه‌لارین تاپشوروب ییباردی‌لار و اول محبت‌نامه سوادی بو تورور

بسالت و ایالت‌پناه حکومت و منزلت‌دستکاه محبت‌نشان مصادقت و مخالصت‌امتنان رفیع المکان شاه کامران دام محبته‌نینک ضمیر منیر موالفت‌تخمیریغه واضح و لایح بولسونکیم چون قدیم الایام‌دین اباً عنجد اتحاد و محبت سلسله‌سی‌نینک رابطه‌سی ایکی دولت اورتاسیدا استحکام تاپیب هیچ بیر واقعه و حادثه مقراضی بیله بو چاغغه تیکرو انقطاع تاپغان ایرماس ایرکان اولجهت‌دین رابطهٔ قدیمه تجدید و تأییدی اوچون اخلاص‌نشان خذمتکار جان‌سپاریمیز میرزا خان خلیفه‌نی |38b| بو محبت‌نامه حاملی قیلیب اول دوست قدیمی احوالاتی‌نینک صحت و عافیت‌غه مقرون ایرکانین بیلیب مراجعت کورکوزکای دیب بو محبت‌نامه ارسال تاپتی

و موندین ایکی کون سونکرا پنجشنبه کونی میمنه حاکمی مضراب خانغه اخلاص‌توأم قوتوش محرم‌نی و قلعهٔ نودا هزاره حاکمی کریمداد خانغه بیردی محمد خاننی و تاش قورغان حاکمی والی بیک‌کا و سرپل حاکمی محمود خانغه و انت‌خوی حکمرانی شاه ولی خانغه و شیبرغان کامرانی رستم خانغه و شاهمردان خانی شجاع الدین خانغه یوموت بیردی بیک‌نی و کوشکدا جمشیدی طایفه‌سی‌نینک حکومت‌نشانی میر احمد خانغه یوموت توردی قیلیچ

سردارنی تعیین قیلیب هر بیرلارین بیر عنایت‌نامه تفویضی بیله |39a| سرافراز قیلیب ییباردیلار و تاش قورغان حاکمی والی بیککا ارسال تاپغان عنایت‌نامه الفاظی بو تورور

عالیجاه رفیع‌جایگاه ارادت‌آثار عقیدت‌اطوار عالیشان اخلاص‌نشان والی بیککا یارلیغ کورکاچ اولکیم چون سین همیشة الاوقات جناب مستطاب قبله‌گاهی‌میز خوارزمشاه سلمه الله تعالی حضرت‌لاریغه مترادفةً و متوالیةً عرضه‌داشت‌لار ارسالی بیله اخلاص و اعتقادینک‌نی اظهار قیلور ایردینک و چون رأیت ظفرآیتیمیز مرو ولایتی‌دا شُقه‌کشا بولوب بو اطراف اولتورملی رعایا حمایتیمیز چتری‌نینک سایه‌سیدا راحت‌گزین بولوب سیراب مدعا بولدیلار ایمدی کراکدورکیم اول اخلاصینک اظهاریغه لایق و اعتقادینک تکراریغه موافق |39b| خدمت اداسیغه جدُ جهد بیله کما ینبغی ساعی بولسانک اوترودا التفات بیغایت و مرحمت بی‌نهایت کورکونک‌دور دیب تلطف یوزیدین بو یارلیغ عالی ارسال تاپتی

و چون اوزکا عنایت‌نامه‌لار مضمونی بو عنایت‌نامه مؤداسیغه قریب بلکه کوبراکی بیر ایردی، اولوجه‌دین اوشبو عنایت‌نامه‌غه اکتفا ایتیب خامهٔ عاجزی‌ختامه اوزگالار ترقیم و تحریریغه جُرأت کورکورمادی نظم

عنایت‌نامه‌لارکیم تاپتی ارسال
ایدی هر بیریسی توقیع اقبال

قویاش بیرله قمـر اوراقی یانکلیغ
ایرور هـر بیر نوید عـز و اجلال
عباراتی مسـیح انفاسی یانکلیغ
حیـات جاودانـی جانبـی دال

و چون موندین سونک |40a| بیش کون انقضا تاپیب آلتینجی سه‌شنبه کونی ایردی‌کیم پنجده اولتورملی فقرالاریدین قاضی محمد نیاز و قاضی نور محمد و انّه نیاز ایناق و آدینه محمد بیک و بابا خان فرمانه‌جی باشلیق ایرساری و چارشنکی جماعه‌سی پیشکش و تحفه‌لاری بیله کیلیب عتبهٔ علیه‌لاری توفراقیغه جبهه‌سالیق درجه‌سین تاپیب ملاقات دولت‌علامات‌لاریدین داغی[1] سربلند بولدیلار و عمر و دولت‌لاری ازدیادی‌نینک دعاسین قیلماق بیله ارجمند و ایرتاسی چهارشنبه کونی تاش قورغان حاکمی والی بیک‌نینک عرضه‌داشتین علیمردان یوزباشی‌کیم مذکور بیک‌نینک مخصوص خدمتکاری‌دور آستانهٔ دولت‌نشانه ملازم‌لاری‌نینک واسطه‌سی بیله |40b| مطالعه‌لاری[2] شرفیغه مشرف قیلدی و اول عرضه‌داشت سوادی بو تورور

تا آفتاب عالمتاب آفاق سوادیغه پرتوافکن بولوب جهان شبستانین روشن قیلور همواره اول سلطنت باغی‌نینک نهال نوخروجی و خلافت درجاتی‌نینک صاحب‌کمال باعروجی قطب فلک ابهت و رفعت مرکز دایرهٔ مکرمت

---

[1] داغی above the line.

[2] Altered from مطالعه‌لاریغه.

و مرتبت اعنی خانزادهٔ بلندهمت کردون‌منزلتیمیز زمان نواییبی و دوران حوادثیدین قادر منان حفظ و حمایتی‌دا محفوظ و امان بولغای‌لار ادعیهٔ متوافره هدایاسی ارسالیدین سونکرا جناب مستطاب سپهرانتساب‌لاریغه بو شوقمند مونداق معروض توتارکیم بو آوان شرافت‌اقتران‌دا بو طریقه مسموع بولدی‌کیم |41a| حضرت پادشاه ظل الله اعنی خوارزمشاه روحنا و روح العالمین فداه بو اخلاصمندلار رفاهیتی و خاطرخواهلیقی اوچون اول بلنداقبال‌نی چهار[1] ولایت ممالکی ساری بویوروب سانسیز قوشون بیله ارسال ایتمیش‌دورلار اوشبو خبر فرحت‌اثر بیتوشوب بو اطراف اولتوروملی فقرا و رعایاغه طراوت تازه و نضارت بی‌اندازه بغیشلاب بهجت و مسرت علی سبیل الکمال حاصل بولدی و اکر مذکور ممالک ساری تشریف بویورسه‌لار بو اطراف حاکم‌لاری همه جان‌فشانلیق مراسمین تقدیمغه بیتکوروب اولوغ سودین بو یان بارچه اوز فقرالاری بولوب تینچ‌لیق بیرله دعای دولت ابدمدّت‌لاریغه اشتغال کورکوزکوسیدورلار |41b| و علیمردان یوزباشی‌نی خدمت اکسیرخاصیت‌لاری‌غه ییباردوک تاکیم تشریف‌لاری حقیقتین معلوم ایتیب مراجعت کورکوزکای باقی هر نیچوک بویروغ‌لاری بولسه فرمان‌بردارد‌ورمیز دیب اخلاص و اعتقاد یوزیدین بو عرضه‌داشت بیتلدی

[1] .جهار

و همولکوندا انت‌خوی حاکمی شاه ولی خان عرضه‌داشتین مخصوص خذمتکارلاری حضرتقلی یوزباشی بیله محمد بیردی یوزباشی درکاه فلک‌جایکاه عتبهٔ علیّه ساکن‌لاری‌نینک دلالتی بیله نظر اقدس اعلی‌لاریغه منظور قیلیب خورشید صفحه‌سیدیک پرنور قیلدی و چون بو عرضه‌داشت والی بیک‌نینک عرضه‌داشتی مضمونی‌غه محتوی و الفاظ و عباراتیغه داغی مشتمل ایردی اولوجه‌دین قلم چابک‌رقم ادهمی[1] نکارشی[2] میدانیغه |42a| قدم قویمادی و همولکیچه‌کیم پنجشنبه کیچه‌سی ایردی بو فقیر الحقیر اوشبو فرخ‌لوا سفر اوچون تاریخ ملاحظه ایتیب مذکور لفظنی‌کیم جُمَل حسابی بیله مینک ایکی یوز ایلیک یتی بولغوسیدورکیم تاریخ علمی‌نینک دقایق‌شناس‌لاریغه مخفی ایرماستور تضمین ایتیب نظر اقدس‌لاریغه منظور قیلدی ایرسه [3]فی الجمله قبول توشوب[3] التفات بیغایت و مرحمت بلانهایت‌لاری بیله بو خاکسار بیمقدارغه سربلندلیک و تا مراجعت هنکامی‌غه تیکرو مفتی‌لیق‌نینک اعلی منصبی بیله ارجمندلیق بیتکوردیلار و اول تاریخ تضمینی بو تورور تاریخ نظم

خوارزمشه که ذاتش چون بر سپهر خورشید
تخت شهنشـــهی را زیب اســـتُ زینت‌افزا
آن ســـرور ســـلاطین ســـردفتر خواقیـــن
|42b| با پور ارشـــد خـــود روزی نمود ایما

[1] ادهمی above the line.

[2] نکاریشی.

[3-3] In margin.

کان کوهر یکانه شهزادهٔ زمانه
عزم سفر نماید سوی جهاد انشاء
در کلاه عزّت نور چراغ شوکت
چشم جهان ندیدش مانند و مثل اصلا
سلطان رحیم قلی شد اسم مبارک او
فتح و ظفر دهد رو کر رو نهد بهر جا
شد ممتثل بفرمان بهر رضای یزدان
با کرّ و فرّ روان شد سلطان جم‌مدارا
از بهر سال تاریخ پرخرد بکوشم
وقت سحر ندا کرد فرخ‌لوا سفر را

و چون بو اوچوردا آنداق مسموع بولدیکیم شاه کامران بیله وزیری یار محمد خان اورتاسیدا مخالفت و منازعت واقع بولوب قتال نایره‌سی‌نینک اشتعالی کون بکون تزاید تاپیب اول یرکا یتمیش‌دورکیم |43a| وزیر شاه‌نی هرات دار السلطنه‌سی ارکیکا قاباب اشاقدین توب‌زن‌لیک و نقب‌کن‌لیک ایشیکا علی سبیل الکمال اشتغالی بار تورور بو نامرضیه افعال‌کیم اطاعت طریقی سلوکیدین مستبعددورکیم واجب تعالی امری‌نینک امتثالی‌دور مزاج شریف‌لاریغه پسندیده توشمادی، و بنه استماع قیلیلدیکیم جمشیدی، طوایفی همواره قیزیلباش بدمعاش طرفیکا مراسلات و مکاتبات ییباریب آنداق التجا قیلورلارکیم بیزلارنی بادغیس موضعی‌دین آلیب مشهد مقدس قریبی‌دین یر و یورت بیرسه قاچار دولتی‌نینک دامنین توتوب اطاعتی طوقین کردنیمیزغه سالیب اوزکا دین و آیین‌دین مراجعت

آشکار ایتیب |43b| قاچار پادشاهی‌غه چاکر و فرمان‌بردار بولغای ایردوک و آصف الدوله‌کیم مشهد حاکمی[1] محمد شاه قاچارنینک دایی‌سیدور مراسلات مذکوره جوابیدا متوالیةً و مترادفةً مونداق نکارش[2] قیلمیشدورکیم مشهد مقدس توابعاتیدین زیره آباد قلعه‌سین یر و سویی بیله آلارغه بغیشلادیم‌کیم تینکریتعالی آلارنی ضلالت وادی‌سیدین توز یول ساری هدایت ایتمیش‌دور چون سلطان صاحبقران بو ایکی حادثهٔ نامرضیه‌نی‌کیم استماع ایتی‌لار اولطرف عزیمتین اوزلاریکا لازم[3] و لشکر ظفراثر سلسله‌سی‌نینک اولطرف تحریکیکا جازم بولدیلارکیم شاید تینکریتعالی لطفی یار و انبیا ارواحی مددکار بولوب شاه کامران بیله وزیر اورتاسیدا |44a| وَالصُّلْحُ خَيْرٌ[4] مؤداسینچه صلح‌نینک خیریت‌مدار بنیادی طرحین سالیب جماعهٔ مذکوره‌نی کفر ظلماتیدین توفیق خضری‌نینک هدایتی بیله اسلام ولایتی ساری باشقاریب ایمان قویاشی‌نینک انواریغه فایز قیلا آلغایلار نیدین‌کیم بو ایش غزات درجه‌سی و جهاد مرتبه‌سیدین ثواب یوزیدین اکمل و افضل‌دور چون پنجشنبه صبحی‌کیم سلطان صاحبقران ایّد الله بنصره‌نینک بو قلعه‌غه شرافت‌وصول دخول‌لاری‌نینک اون تورتونجی کونی ایردی خورشید سلطانی غایت‌سیز تجمل بیله سپهر قورغانیدین طلوع قیلیب انوار لشکری ایچرا تحرک سالیب اسلام لشکری‌نینک کفر سپاهی‌غه غلباتیدیک ظلمت دستکاهی‌غه شکست بیردی |44b| سلطان صاحبقران

---

[1] Hereafter read و.

[2] نکاریش.

[3] Hereafter read بیلدیلار.

[4] Qur’ān IV: 128.

اسرو کروفر و شکوه قیامت‌اثر بیله خجنک بُراق‌رنک‌لاریغه رکوب قیلیب مذکور حصاردین چیقیب مقصد ساری متوجه بولدیلار توب و کرنای آوازی‌نینک صداسی بو کنبذ خضرادین اوتوب مسیحا سمعیغه یتیب اول مکان معلّا ساکن‌لاری ایچرا علالا و ارض غبرا متمکن‌لاری اورتاسیغه غوغا سالدیکیم کوییا محشر کبری آشکارا بولدی نظم

تجمــل بیلــه نامــدار جهــان | چیقیب قلعه‌دین یولغه بولدی روان
توب آتیب داغی چالدوروب کرّنای | سالیب عالم ایچرا عجب هویُ های
صداسی فلک‌دین خود ایلاب عبور | ملایک ارا سـالدی، غوغا و شور
آلار آیلادیـلار آنینکدیک کمان | |45a| همانا بو چاغ بولدی آخرزمان
تزلزل توشـوب یـرکا آنداقکه آب | اولوس ایچرا غوغای یوم الحساب
بو یانکلیغ شـکوه ایله اول نامور | روان بولــدی و قیلدی عزم سـفر
الٓهـی بـو سـلطان کیتی‌سـتان | قایان دولت ایله کر اولسـه روان
عنانیغه قای ساری‌کیم بیرسه تاب | ظفر بیرلـه نصرتنی قیل همرکاب

چون سلطان صاحبقران اعان الله بنصرته بو نوع اساسه و بو طریقه کوکبه بیله بیر نیچه مسافت راه قطعین سپاه ظفرهمراه‌لاری بیله تقدیمغه ییتکوروب برهان الاولیا سلطان الاتقیا طالقان بابا علیه الرحمه‌نینک فایض الانوار جوارلاریغه نزول بویوردیلار نظم

یـول اوزره ایـدی بزرکیـکا مزار | که‌جنت کیبی‌آنکا|45b|دلکش‌جوار
مـزاری ملایـک مـزاری کیلیب | ینه عرش یانکلیغ مداری کیلیب
آتـی صاحـب اشـتهار جهـان | عـروس جهـان طالقـی طالقان
بـو بزرک جواریغـه تاپیب وصول | عقیدت بیله قیلدی سلطان نزول
بـو نـام‌آور دهـرُ کیتی‌مـدار | همولکیچـه بـو یردا توتتـی قرار

چون ایرتاسی جمعه کونی‌نینک صبحی مجاورلار کونکلی آیینه‌سیدیک صدق و صفا آشکار قیلیب خورشید کامکاری غایت‌سیز کیرودار بیله فلک دوار خرکاهیدین طلوع قیلیب شعاع صاحب‌ارتفاع سفارت‌پیشه‌لارین نورنامه‌لار تفویضی بیله سربلند قیلیب عالم اطراف و اکنافیغه ارسال ایتیب سماوات میدانی‌نینک قطعیغه توجه کورکوزدی سلطان صاحبقران همولمنزلدا مذکور خان‌لارنینک ییبارکان ایلچی‌لاریکا |46a| خذمتکار اخلاص‌آثارلاری یموت بابا سردارنی قوشوب هر بیریکا مذکور عرضه‌داشت‌لار جوابیدا بیر عنایت‌نامه تاپشوروب سروپای شاهانه اعطاسی بیله ارجمند و اجازت ذی‌سعادت‌لاری بیله سربلند ایتی‌لار والی بیک عرضه‌داشتی‌نینک جوابیدا ارسال تاپغان عنایت‌نامه سوادی بو تورور

ارادت بیشه‌سی‌نینک شیری عقیدت معرکه‌سی‌نینک دلیری اخلاص و اعتقادی غایت‌سیز خوب و نیک والی بیک دام اعتقاده‌غه یارلیغ کورکاچ

اولکیم[1] علیمردان یوزباشی بیله ییبارکان عرضه‌داشتینک‌کیم اخلاص و اعتقادینک وفوریغه متضمن ایردی آستانهٔ معلی ملازم‌لاری‌نینک واسطه‌سی بیله ییتوشوب |46b| مضمونی کما هو حقه معلوم و مفهوم بولدی ایمدی کراکدورکیم اولمقدار اعتقادینک اظهاریغه لایق خذمت جاییغه اوزینک کیلیب خذمت قیلسانک و یا اوغلینک کیلیب خذمت مراسمین تقدیمغه ییتکورسه هرآینه درجهٔ رفیعه و مرتبهٔ منیعه اوزه ترقی قیلیب غایت‌سیز عنایات و نهایت‌سیز التفات کورکونک‌دور و اولچه[2] تیل سوزی بولسه اخلاص‌آثار بابا سردار تقریر عند الملاقات قیلغوسیدور دیب بو یارلیغ عالی بیتلدی

و شاه ولی خان عرضه‌داشتی‌نینک جوابین داغی بو طریقه‌دا یازیب ارسال قیلدیلار و همول یردا بو جانب عزیمت قیلغان‌لارین عرضه‌داشت ایتیب اوز کعبه‌لاری خوارزمشاه روحنا فداه‌نینک سراسرخاصیت خذمت‌لاریغه ییباردیلار |47a| اول عرضه‌داشت تسویدی بو یوسوندا تأیید تاپتی

حضرت قبله‌کاه عالم و امیدکاه بنی آدم پادشاه جهان و شهنشاه جهانیان سپهرمکان دارادربان قیصرپاسبان دولت و عظمت اربابی‌نینک ملاذی شوکت و حکومت اصحابی‌نینک معاذی عطوفت جواهری‌نینک کانی ملاطفت زواهری‌نینک کلشن بهشت‌نشانی شرافت‌دستکاهی‌میز جناب

---

1 Hereafter crossed-out اولکیم.

2 Altered from اخلاص.

عرش‌انتساب قبله‌کاهی‌میز خوارزمشاه ادام الله تعالی ظلال التفاته علی مفارق المفارقین و الحاضرین‌نینک عتبۀ علیه و سُدّۀ سنیه‌لاریکا اثنیۀ متوافره تحایفی ارسالیدین سونکرا بو مخلص‌نینک عرضه‌داشتی اولکیم لله الشکر و المنه حضرت خالق اکبر موهبتی‌نینک برکتی و اولحضرت |47b| دعای اجابت‌اثرلاری خاصیتی‌دین مرادات آفتابی صحت و کامرانلیغ افقیدین لامع بهجت و شادمانلیغ مشرقیدین طالع‌دور و پنجده و مرچاق آب و هواسی‌نینک تماشاسی تمناسی[1] کونکول مرآتیدا جلوه‌نما بولوب مرو ولایتی‌دین چیقیب اولجانب عزیمت کورکوزدوک و باقی هر نیچوک بویورمیش بولسه‌لار سعی مشکور و جهد موفور بیله آنکا ساعی و داعی بولغومیزدور و قالغان لسان عرایضین اخلاص‌نهاد قوتلوقمراد بارکاه‌لاری خاکیکا جبهه‌سالیق درجه‌سین تاپغان چاغدا معروض توتغوسیدور دیب بو عرضه‌داشت بیتلدی

چون بو عرضه‌داشت‌نی‌کیم ارسال قیلدیلار اول مرجع جاه و جلال عظمت و شوکت مالامال بیله آتلانیب لشکر |48a| قیامت‌اثرلاری بیله بیر نیچه بلند و پست یول قطعین تقدیمغه بیتکوروب قیزیل مست آتلیغ ریکزار اوستیدا نشست کورکوزدیلار نظم

مینیب رخشیغه چون خرام ایلادی باریب بو قوم اوستین مقام ایلادی

[1] تمناسی above the line.

مبـارک قدومی یتیب اوشـبو دم کوروـنـدی بو قـوم کوییاکیم ارَم

چون اولکیچه مذکور جایدا استراحت قیلدیلار ایرتاسی شنبه کونی اشهب برق‌خرام‌لاریغه راکب بولوب صولت تمام بیله کیلیب چاپیق خواجه کاوی دیکان موضع‌نی آرامکاه قیلدی‌لار نظم

یوروب یول خدیو عدالت‌شـمول چاپیق خواجه کاویغه قیلدی نزول
تاپیب مقدمی‌دین شرف اول مکان بولوب دلکش آنداقکه باغ جنان

و اول منزلدا ایکی کیچه |48b| لشکر اجتماعی اوچون توقف کورکوزوب دوشنبه کونی دولت تمام و هیبت مالاکلام بیله رخش خوشخرام‌لاریغه راکب بولوب خواجه کاوی آتلیغ جاینی خیمه و خرکاه‌لاری بیله سپاه ظفرهمراه‌لاریغه مقام قیلدی‌لار نظم

قطـع ایتیـب یولنـی داور پردل خواجـه کاوینـی ایـلادی منزل
مقدمیدین بولوب خوش آب و هوا بولدی جنـت کیبـی حیات‌افزا

و اولکیچه آندا استراحت ایتب ایرتاسی سه‌شنبه کونی اول خورشید فلک دولت و اقبال مینک تومان شوکت و اجلال بیله مذکور موضع‌دین ارتحال بویوروب بیر نیچه میدان قطعین تقدیمغه ییتکوروب چوبلی تیفه آتلیغ جاینی

شرافت‌ایصال قدوم‌لاری بیله[1] بهشت‌مثال قیلدی‌لار |49a| نظم

اول حکمرانی‌کیم زهـــی کیواندین آرتوق[2] درکهی
بـــو کون یوروب بولدی آنینک چوبلی تیفه منزلکهی
ییتکاچ قدومی‌دین شرف بولدی بو منزل ایچراکیم
بـــاردور کیه بیرله شـــجر ریحان بیله ســـرو ســـهی

و همول منزلدا یار محمد وزیرنینک عرضه‌داشتین شاه پسند یوزباشی بیله الله داد ایشیک اقاسی‌کیم وزیر مذکورنینک مخصوص چاووش[3] و چاکرلاریدور بارکاه جهان‌پناه هواخواه‌لاری‌نینک دلالت و وساطتی بیله نظر اقدس اعلی‌لاریغه منظور قیلدی[4] و اول عرضه‌داشت ترجمه‌سی بو تورور

فلک‌جناب قمررکاب جلالت و شوکت‌انتساب سلطنت و تاجدارلیق دودمانی‌نینک سُلاله‌سی خلافت و شهریارلیق خاندانی‌نینک |49b| نقاوه‌سی دام شوکته‌نینک مرحمت‌دستور حضوری مقیم‌لاری‌نینک رأی امجد اعلی‌لاری عرضی‌غه موننکدیک ییتکورورکیم چون موندین بورون فضیلت‌شعار صدر العلما خسرو دین‌پناه حضرت خوارزمشاه روحنا

---

1 بیله above the line.

2 آرتوق above the line.

3 Altered from چاوش.

4 Read قیلدی‌لار.

فداه‌نینک فلک‌اقتدار دربارلاریدین مرخَّص بولوب هرات واردی بولدی مبارک یارلیغ‌لاری‌کیم بو دولتخواه سرافرازلیقی اوچون اصدار شرفین بو مضمون بیله تاپیب ایردی‌کیم نواب ایناق مرو ولایتی‌غه تشریف‌فرما بولغوسیدورلار بو چاغ‌غه تیکرو کوزلار نواب والانینک تشریف‌لاری یولیغه منتظر ایردی بو زمان خجسته‌اقتراندا مرو ولایتی‌غه تشریف‌لاری احوالین ایشیتیب حددین زیاد |50a| مستظهر و مستبشر بولدی اولجهت‌دین‌کیم بو دولتخواه اوزین هر بابدا حضرت ظل الله‌نینک صداقت‌مناص و راسخ الاخلاص چاکرلاری زمره‌سیدین منظور قیلور و خدمتکارلیق طریقه‌سی‌نینک عرضی جهتیدین بو عریضه‌نی نکارش بیردی انشاء الله تعالی بو ایکی اوچ کوندا اوز عمکی‌لاری اولادیدین بیراونی فلک‌رفعت خدمت‌لاریغه روانه قیلغوسیدورکیم بو دولتخواه‌نینک اولچه معروضاتی بولسه تفصیل بیله[1] عرض قیلغوسیدور ایمدی امید اولکیم هر نه فرمایش‌لاری بولسه بو دولتخواه‌نی سرافراز قیلیب بویورسه‌لار اهمال و انفصال قیلمای کوشش قیلغوسیدور

و همولمنزلدا اولکیچه مکث قیلیب ایرتاسی چهارشنبه کونی |50b| وزیر مذکورنینک مربور ایکی کیشی‌سین اجازت ذی‌شرافت‌لاری بیله سربلند و خلعت شاهانه انعامی بیله ارجمند قیلیب ایراد قیلغان عرضه‌داشت‌لاری[2]

---

[1] بیله above the line.

[2] عریضه‌داشت‌لاری.

جوابیدا بیر عنایت‌نامه بیتیب آلارغه تفویض ایتیب ییباردیلار و اول عنایت‌نامه تسویدی بو تورور

اخلاص سپهری‌نینک ضیاآثار اختری اعتقاد بحری‌نینک صفابار کوهری عالیشان وزارت‌نشان یار محمد خان‌غه یارلیغ کورکاچ اولکیم اخلاص و اعتقادینک اظهاری اوچون ییبارکان عرضه‌داشتینک[1] درکاه آسمانجاهیمیز ساکن‌لاری‌نینک واسطه‌سی بیله نظر اقدسیمیز منظوری بولوب مضمونی کما ینبغی مفهوم بولدی ایمدی کیراکدورکیم سرادق سپهرنمونه‌میز |51a| ساری توجه کورکوزوب خاکبوسلیقی درجه‌سین تاپیب یا اوغلینک‌نی ارسال ایتیب خدمت مراسمین تقدیمغه ییتکوروب اعتقادینک صدقین اظهار قیلسانک هرآینه مرحمت بیغایت و التفات بی‌نهایت کورکونک‌دور دیب بو عنایت‌نامه ارسال تاپتی

چون سلطان صاحبقران نصر الله بتأییده اوشبو امور اهتمامی‌دین فراغ تمام حاصل ایتی‌لار اسکندرانه صولت بیله رکوب قیلیب بیر نیچه میدان قطعین تقدیمغه ییتکوروب زبدة العارفین قدوة الکاشفین نیکومعاش امام بکتاش علیه الرحمه‌نینک مرقد شریف‌لاریدین عبور قیلیب نزول بویوردیلار نظم

ولایـت اهلیـکا سـردفتر و باش　　امامت کوهـری غوّاصی بکتاش

[1] عریضه‌داشتینک.

|51b| ایدی یول نینک کناریدا مزاری جهت بو یول کناری فیض باری
خدیو پاک خلقُ پاک طینت بو مشهددین عبور ایلاب بسُرعت
عجب جاییغه کیم قیلدی تنزُّل ارم دیک روح پرور بولدی بالکل

و اول کیچه مذکور منزلدا آرام آلیب ایرتاسی پنجشنبه کونی اسرو شکوه بیله آتلانیب بیر نیچه یول یوروب قوشلی قایه آتلیغ یرکا رخش لاری قدمی نینک اثری شرفی بیله پایه بیتکوردیلار و نزول سعادت وصول لاری بیله پیرایه نظم

ایتیب مقدمی بیرله پیرایه سین آشوردی فلک دین آنینک پایه سین

و اول اقشام اول منزلدا راحت کزین بولوب ایرتاسی جمعه کونی سمند کردون خرام لاریغه رکوب قیلیب یول قطعی غه حرکت کورکوزوب شوکت تمام بیله کیلیب |52a| اوروش توشکان آتلیغ مکان نی آرامکاه قیلدیلار و اولکیچه کیم شنبه کیچه سی ایردی خفتن نمازی اداسیدین سونکرا شوکت پناه لار جلادت دستکاه لار مبارزت آثار شجاعت شعار لار خدای یار بی و ساریق حاکمی نیاز محمد بای و سالور جماعه سی نینک والی سی محمد امین بیک و اوتامیش و توختامیش تکه طایفه سی نینک سرهنک و یوزباشی لاری خدای بیرکان یوزباشی و نیاز محمد یوزباشینی کوکلان و باقی طوایف[1] مذکوره غه باش قیلیب جمشیدی طایفه سی اوستیکا کیم احوال نامرضیه و افعال ناپسندیده لاری دین یوقاریدا شمّه

[1] Altered from طوایفی.

ذکر تاپیب ایردی بویوروب ییباردیلار و مونداغ فرمان قیلدیلارکیم اکر اول طایفه سیز جماعه‌نی |52b| کوروب بی‌منازعت و مخالفت اوترونکیزکا باله و چاغه‌سی مال و مواشی‌سی بیله کوچوب چیقا بیرسه‌لار امتعه و اقمشهٔ نضیه و غیر نضیه‌لاریکا مداخلت قیلمای کوچ‌لارین ایلایینکیزکا سالیب مراجعت کورکوزونک‌لار و اکر اول طایفه مخاصمت طریقین ایلکاری توتوب قتال و کُشش قیلماقچی بولسه‌لار سیزلار داغی مذکور امورغه تقصیر قیلمای اشتغال کورکوزوب کما ینبغی کوشش قیلغای‌سیزلار و مأمور بولغان سرکرده‌لار بیله سپاه بلااشتباه هر بیری آنداق دلاورکیم پرخاش هنکامیدا مینک فیل دمان و شیر ژیان اوتروسیدین نمایان بولسه بیر حمله‌سیکا تاب و طاقت کیلتورا آلمای عدم بیشه‌سیکا کریزان بولغوسیدور نظم

سپاهی که هر بیری |53a| فیل دمان   قولیدا باری‌نینک عمود کران
ینه بکتر و خودُ خفتان کییب   ینه جُبَّه جوشن درخشان کییب
آلیب کرز و خنجر سنان بریق   عدونی بو اوت بیرله قیلغای حریق
اوروش چاغیدا باری شرزنده[1] شیر   عدوکیرلیکدا هزبر دلیر

و فردوسی داغی اوشبو مضموندا دیب‌دور نظم

سپاهی چو آشفته فیلان مست   همه نیزه و کُرز و خنجر بدست

[1] Read شرزه.

چو با تیغ آهنک خون آورند ز سنک آبُ آتش برون آورند
چو تیر از کمان در کمین آورند سر آسمان بر زمین آورند

و چون بو صفت سپاه رزمخواه بو امر دولت‌اثر ندای فرحت‌بخشاسین استماع قیلدیلار یوم البعث‌دیک آرالاریغه قوزغالان توشوب درکاه جهان‌پناه |53b| ساری توجه کورکوزوب فَتَأْتُونَ أَفْوَاجاً[1] مؤداسی آشکارا بولوب فوج فوج و طایفه طایفه کیلیب تعظیم رسمین تقدیم‌غه بیتکوروب مبارک فاتحه‌لاری بیله یوللوق‌لارین آلیب مقصد ساری حرکت قیلدیلار و مذکور کیچه اولموضع‌دا توقف قیلیب ایرتاسی شنبه کونی هم اول یردا اقامت‌کزین بولدیلار و خدمتکار جان‌سپار خانک سردار حضرت پادشاه والاجاه دارادستکاه قبله‌کاه‌لاری خوارزمشاه روحنا فداه‌نینک سراسرخاصیت خدمت‌لاریدین[2] کیلیب اولحضرت و باقی شهزاده‌لار و بیک‌لارنینک سلامتلیک‌لاری بشارتین و مبارک یارلیغ‌لارین مذکور کوندا همولمنزلدا بیتکوردی و اول یارلیغ الفاظ و عباراتی جواهری‌نینک انتظامی |54a| بو نوع وقوع تاپمیش‌دور

حکومت و سلطنت محیطی‌نینک درخشان کوهری شوکت و عظمت سپهری اوجی‌نینک تابان اختری رفعت و اجلال بوستانی‌نینک سرو آزادی عزّت و اقبال عالمی‌نینک رفعت‌نهادی جلادت و شجاعت میدانی‌نینک یکه‌تازی مبارزت و مناعت بیداسی یکه‌تازلاری‌نینک ممتاز و سرافرازی

---

1 Qur'ān LXXVIII: 18.

2 خذمت above the line.

اعنی [1]قُرَّة العینی[1] و نور دیده‌میز عالیجاه رفیعجایکاه رحیم قلی توره‌غه یارلیغ همایون عالی کورکاچ اولکیم لله الحمد و المنه ذات کامل الصفات اعلی‌میز باشلیق بارچه دولتیمیز ارکانی و حشمتیمیز اعیانی مع التعلقات صغاراً و کباراً سلامتلیک مسندیدا مقیم و عافیتمندلیک سریریدا مستقیم بولوب اللهم انصر من نصر الدین دعاسی‌غه اشتغال کورکوزورمیز و اول |54b| مکتوب سراسراسلوب‌کیم صحت و سلامت مرو شاهجان اولکاسیکا وارد و شرف نزول بویورغانیغه مشتمل بولوب اخلاص‌آثار نظر سردار بیله ارسال قیلینیب ایردی یتیشیب مضمون دُرَرْمشحونیدین کونکلی‌میزغه بی‌نهایت فروح و خاطریمیزغه حددین آرتوق فتوح یوزلاندی و ذو القعده آیی‌نینک اواسطی و سه‌شنبه کونیدا ارادت‌دثار خانک سردارنی اولطرفکا مأمور قیلدوق و تا ملاقات شاهدی جلوه‌کر بولغونچه نی نوع واقعه واقع و نی حادثه وقوعی شایع بولسه اعلام قیلماق بیله خاطر رأفت‌ذخایریمیزغه سرور و حضور بیتکورا تورسون دیب بو عنایت‌نامه عالی بیتلدی

و سلطان صاحبقران سونکغی کیچه داغی اول منزلدا توقف قیلیب ایرتاسی یکشنبه کونی |55a| تانک نمازی اداسیدین سونکرا مذکور سرکرده‌لار امدادی اوچون ایزلاریدین سیادت‌پناه نجابت‌دستکاه عالیمقام عوض خواجه شیخ الاسلام و خذمتکار جان‌سپار مخصوص ملازم‌لار یولداشی عبد الله یساولباشی

1-1 قُرَّة عینی.

ایکاولارین نوکرلاری بیله بویوروب ییباردیلار و بیر ساعت اوتکاندین سونکرا سمند دوندلاریکا رکوب قیلیب صولت تمام و شوکت عظمت‌انجام بیله کیلیب ییلغین‌لی بیله موری کوپروکی اورتاسیدا بوز بورون آتلیغ جاینی لشکر اهلیکا منزلکاه قیلدیلار و سه‌شنبه کونی اول منزلدا یموت بیردی خان بیله‌کیم هزاره کریمداد خانغه ایلچی یوسونیدا مرسول بولوب ایردی مذکور خان‌نینک اینی‌سی عبد العزیز خان کیلیب |55b| خان مشار الیه‌نینک عرضه‌داشتی بیله ییبارکان تحایف و هدایاسین هواخواه‌لار اشارتی بیله منظورلاری قیلیب آستانهٔ دولت‌نشانه‌غه جبهه‌سالیق درجه‌سین تاپتی و اول عرضه‌داشت سوادی مضمونی[1] بو تورور

حکومت درجی‌نینک تابنده کوهری عظمت بُرجی‌نینک درخشنده اختری شجاعت و نامدارلیق کانی‌نینک لعل سیرابی مبارزت و کامکارلیق عُمّانی‌نینک دُرّ نایابی شهزاده بلنداقبال دام شوکته درکاهی بنده‌لاری‌نینک رای امجد اعلی‌لاریغه بو شوقمندنینک بنده‌لیک یوزیدین عرضی اولکیم عنایت‌نامهٔ التفات‌ختامه‌کیم بیردی خان بیله بو شوقمندنی نامزد قیلیب مرسول توتوب ایردیلار ساعات اسعدی |56a| و اوقات اشرفیدا وارد بولوب غایت‌سیز افتخار و نهایت‌سیز استبشار باعثی بولدی و چون بو سرافکنده‌کا کیتی‌مدار دربارلاری چاکرلیک و جان بارینچه نوکرلیک‌لاریدین اوزکا بیر شی خاطری مرآتیدا جلوه‌نما ایرماستور لهذا

---

[1] مضمونی above the line.

نور چشمی عبد العزیز خان‌نی پیشکشی بیله بارکاه آسمانجاه خذمتی اوچون بیردی خان مشار الیه‌کا قوشوب ییباردی امید اولکیم قبول مرتبه‌سین تاپیب تا خواهش‌لاری هنکامیغه‌چه خذمت مراسمین تقدیمغه ییتکورکای و ینه نی نوع فرمان بولسه آنینک استحصالیغه کما ینبغی اشتغال کورکوزکوسیدور باقی امرکم الاشرف مطاع

و مذکور کوندا خفتن نمازی اداسیدین سونکرا جمشیدی طایفه‌سی اوستیکا ییباریلکان |56b| سرکرده‌لار بیله لشکر اهلی‌نینک فتح و نصرتی بشارتی فَقَدْ[1] جَآءَكُمُ ٱلْفَتْحُ[2] مؤداسینچه ییتوشیب فرحت اوزره فرحت و بهجت اوزره بهجت لشکر اهلیکا حاصل بولدی نظم

ییتوشــتی عجب روح‌پـرور خبر	کــه باشــدین ایاغی نویــد ظفر
سپه خیلی آندین تاپیب کوب سرور	تاپیب روح‌لاری اوزکا یانکلیغ حضور
بولوب لشکر ایچرا بسی[3] شادلیق	کونکول قصری تاپتی کوب آبادلیق

و ایزینچه طایفۀ مذکوره خوانین و بیک‌لاریدین و علمالاریدین عبد الجبار خان و اوغلی اکرم خان و احمد سلطان و عنایت الله بیک و خواجه محمد صالح و ایشان قاضی اسماعیل و خلیفه اسحاق باشلیق نیچه کیشینی توتوب کیتی‌مدار دربارلاریغه کیلتوردیلار |57a| و سلطان صاحبقران داغی آلار جریمه‌سیدین

---

[1] وقد.

[2] Qur'ān VIII: 19.

[3] بسی above the line.

اوتوب بارچه‌سیغه التفات‌لاری بیله سربلندلیق بیتکوروب آت و سروپای شاهانه انعامی‌دین بهره‌مند قیلدی‌لار و اول فتح و نصرت کیفیتی آنداقدورکیم چون عسکر ظفراثرکیم سرکرده‌لار بیله مبارک فاتحه‌لارین آلیب مقصد ساری نهضت قیلدی‌لار ایکی کیچه و کوندوز یول یوروب [1]فَٱلْمُغِيرَاتِ صُبْحاً[1] مضمونینچه دوشنبه کونی صبح وقتی قرا تیفه اولوسیغه لشکر بیحد و مر فوج فوج و طایفه طایفه متعاقبةً و متوالیةً ظاهر و نمایان بولدیلارکیم شکوه و صولت‌لاریدین البُرز کوهی داغی مقابل بولسه شکست تاپغودیک و سپهر بدمهر هم اوترولاریدا دغدغه کورکوزسه یرکا همدست بولغودیک ایردی |57b| نظم

قولیغـه آلیب[2] هر بیـری ذو الفقار — نهـاد عدودیـن چیقارغـای دمار
غضب بیرله هر بیری کر قیلسه جنک — عدو بیحد اولسـون قیرار بیدرنک
سوغورسه قیلیچ خالی ایلاب غلاف — تاپار لـرزه آندین بسـی کوه قاف
کروهی کیـم اول نیزه کـردان ایرور — بـلای جهـان و همه جـان ایرور
ینـه بیـر کروهـی قولیـدا کمان — که اعداغه آندین بولوب وهم جان
آلیـب بعضی‌سـی خنجـر آبدار — ایتـار یـر یوزین قـان بیلـه لاله‌زار
آلیب ایلکیـکا بیر کروهی تفنک[3] — عدو جانبی آتغـای هنکام جنک
سهیا مونینکدیک نیچه مینک کروه — بـاری رزمجـویُ جلادت‌پژوه
بـاری لشـکرآرا و لشکرشـکن — بـاری فیـل زورُ غضنفرفکـن

[1-1] Qur'ān C: 3.

[2] آلیب above the line.

[3] توفنک.

بــاری نامــور بــاری آوازه‌دار کیلیــب هــر بیری صفــدر روزکار
آلیب بو صفت بیرله دور حصار |58a| توتوب صف چو مژکان نیچه مینک قطار

چون بو لشکر نصرت‌اثر بو نوع شکوه قیامت‌اثر بیله کیم قرا تیفه حصاری‌نینک دوره‌سیدا نیچه صف بولوب مژکانوار قطار توردیلار اول حصار اهلی مونچه شکوه و کیرودار بیله کیم لشکر اهلین مشاهده قیلدیلار بارچه‌سی جان‌سیز بدندیک بیمدار بولوب عقل و هوش‌لاری هیچ بیر امر ادراکیکا یارمندلیک بیرمادی اول اثنادا بیر فوج سپاه نصرت‌پناه‌دین کیلیب بیکباره مذکور حصار دروازه‌سی ساری آت قویوب قلعه ایچرا دخول کورکوزوب بُرج بارولاریغه اوزلاریدین کیشی چیقارتیب تحت تصرّف‌لاریغه کیپوردیلار بیر ساعت توروب قلعه ضبطی اهتمامین قیلیب عبد الجبار خان باشلیق جماعهٔ مذکوره‌نی توتوب |58b| معتمد و معتبر بدرقه‌لار بیله درکاه کیهان‌پناه ساری یوللادیلار و چهارشنبه کونی اول منزلدین مینک تومان شوکت و اجلال بیله ارتحال بویوروب آقچه قایه آتلیغ جاینی قدوم ظفرلزوم‌لاری پیرایه‌سی بیله[1] بلندپایه قیلدیلار و ایرتاسی پنجشنبه کونی مبارزت‌پناه جلادت‌دستکاه آستانهٔ معلی ملازم‌لاری‌نینک نیکومعاشی رحمت الله یساولباشینی کوماک اوچون مذکور سرکرده‌لار عقبی‌دین یوموت اهلی‌نینک شجاعت‌پیشه‌لاری بیله بویوروب ییباردیلار و ایرتاسی شنبه کیچه‌سی خفتن نمازی اداسیدین سونکرا اخلاص‌کیش خیریت‌اندیش خلیفه بیکیش حضرت پادشاه کیوان‌بارکاه اوز کعبه‌لاری خوارزمشاه روحنا فداه‌نینک مبارک

[1] بیله above the line.

یارلیغ‌لارین یوح بیضا غیم اورتاسیدین چهره کورکوزوب |59a| غم بنیادین بوزغاندیک بییتکوروب مفارقت غمی انهدامی‌غه باعث بولوب غایت‌سیز فروح و نهایت‌سیز فتوح یوزلاندی و اول یارلیغ الفاظی جواهری تحریر سلکیکا بو نوع انتظام تاپمیش‌دور

جلالت و اجلال محیطی‌نینک تابنده کوهری عظمت و اقبال سپهری‌نینک درخشنده اختری یعنی رفعت و شوکت‌نشان شاهزاده رحیم قلی سلطان‌غه یارلیغ همایون عالی کورکاچ اولکیم لله الحمد و المنه ذات عطوفت‌سمات عالیمیز باشلیق بارچه متعلقات کباراً و صغاراً کما هو المشاهد ساغلیغ مسندی اوزره قیام تام و عافیتمندلیغ اوجیدا استقرار تمام کورکوزوب دعای خیرغه مشغولدورمیز ثانیاً اولکیم اولطرف‌نینک یاغداییغه یاراشا کوب‌نینک مصلحت و صوابدیدی بیله |59b| قایسی ایش‌دا بهبود بولسه و نی نوع حرکت کوب‌نینک کینکاشی بیله منفعت کورونسه همول ایش ساری متوجه بولسون و تا ملاقات کلشنیدین موانست کلی‌نینک روایحی کونکول مشامی‌غه بییتکونچه اولطرف‌نینک واقعات و رویدادین درکاه عالمپناهیمیز ملازم‌لاری‌غه عرضه‌داشت طریقه‌سی بیله اعلام قیلا تورسون تاکیم اطمینان دل و حضور خاطر حاصل قیلمیش بولغایمیز دیب عنایت‌نامه بیتلدی

و چون قرا تیغه اهلی‌نینک فتحی و سلطان صاحبقران نصر الله بتأییده‌نینک آلار

باره‌سیدا قیلغان احسان‌لاری خبری اول اطراف[1] قلعجاتیغه‌کیم چون شهر خلیل و چار دره و قوش آسیا و سر چشمه و اوزکا ینه نیچه قلعه‌لارکیم قرا تیفه لواحق و توابعی‌دور انتشار تاپیب بارچه اهالی و اکابرلاری |60a| رغبت تمام بیله سپهبدلار خدمت‌لاریغه کیلیب سرکرده‌لار هم کیلکانین درکاه جهان‌پناه ساری یوللاب بو یوسوندا نیچه کونکا تیکرو هر کون طایفهٔ مذکوره اکابرلاریدین فوج فوج کیلیب عتبهٔ علیه تقبیلی‌غه مشرف بولوب آت و سروپای خسروانه اعطاسی بیله ارجمند بولور ایردیلار و چون اول جماعه‌کیم اوز باره‌لاریدا سلطان صاحبقراندین مونچه التفات‌نی مشاهده قیلدیلار اسلام ولایتی ساری کوچماککاکیم فرمان واجب الاذعان‌لاری آنکا عز صدور تاپمیش ایردی میلان و رغبت اظهار قیلدیلار و سلطان صاحبقران داغی باله و چاغه‌لارین کوچوروب کیلماک اوچون بارچه‌سین اجازت ذی‌سعادت‌لاری بیله سرافراز قیلیب ییباردیلار و موندین سونک |60b| دوشنبه کونی قرا تیفه و قوش آسیا و سر چشمه و شهر خلیل و چار دره‌دا اولتوروملی جمشیدی طایفه‌سی‌نینک عبد الجبار بیک باشلیق کلاً صغاراً و کباراً باله و چاغه‌سین کوچوروب عتبهٔ علیه خاکبوسلیقی‌غه مشرف قیلیب لشکرگاه‌دین اوتکاریب توشوردی‌لار و همولکوندا اخلاص‌نشان میرزا خان خلیفه‌کیم هرات جانبی‌غه سفارت طریقه‌سیدا ییباریلیب ایردی درکاه آسمانجاه‌لاری عتبه‌بوسلیقی رتبه‌سین تاپیب شاه کامران بیله وزیر مخالفت و منازعت‌لاری کیفیتین عرض معرضی‌غه ییتکوردی و ایزیدین میرزا ابو القاسم‌نینک وزیر جانبی‌دین نی یوسوندا کیلورین داغی اظهار قیلدی و

[1] Altered from طرف.

موندین ایکی کون اوتوب چهارشنبه کونی سالور خلقی‌نینک حکمرانی محمد امین بیک‌نی مذکور خلق بیله کوچ جلاویدا |61a| و میرزا خان خلیفه‌نی نوکرلاری بیله ایزیدا یورسون دیب حکم همایون عز صدور تاپیب و یمین و یساریدا داغی معتبر و معتمد کیشی‌لارنی تعیین قیلیب جماعۀ مذکوره‌نی مرو شاهجان جانبی‌غه یوللادیلار و همولکون لشکر اهلی بیله جناب‌لاری باشلیق مونچه فتح و ظفر و آبرولاری خبرین پادشاه باتخت و جاه اوز قبله‌کاه‌لاری خوارزمشاه روحنا فداه حضرت‌لاریغه خذمتکار جان‌سپارلاری پهلوانیاز بیله‌کیم کاکللی لفظی بیله مُلقَّب‌دور عرضه‌داشت قیلیب ییباردیلار و اول عرضه‌داشت تسویدی بو تورور

حضرت قبلۀ حقیقی‌میز و کعبۀ تحقیقی‌میز پادشاه صاحب‌تخت و جاه سیامک‌رزم افراسیاب‌عزم کشتاسب‌دستکاه ناصر الملة و الدین معین الدین المتین |61b| هادم بنیاد الظلم و العدوان ماحی آثار البغی و الطغیان باعث الامن و الامان علی رؤس اهل الایمان خسرو دین‌پناه جناب شرافت‌ایاب[1] قبله‌کاهی‌میز خوارزمشاه زاد الله عمره و دولته و مملکته‌نینک بارکاه عرش‌اشتباه‌لاریغه اثنیۀ متوافره و ادعیۀ متکاثره هدایاسی ارسالیدین سونکرا بو اخلاصمندنینک عرضه‌داشتی اولکیم الحمد لله تعالی حضرت واهب النصرت فضلی برکتی و اولحضرت‌نینک دعوت اجابت‌آیت‌لاری خاصیتی‌دین آمالیمیز شجره‌سی دولت و اقبال

[1] شرافت‌آیاب.

ثمره‌سیدین بارور و امانیمیز[1] روضه‌سی صحت و عافیتمندلیغ روایحی
فوایحی‌دین معطر بولوب نصرت اوزره نصرت شاهدی وصالیغه واصل
و کونکول‌لاریمیز خزاینی‌غه[2] فرحت اوزره فرحت نقودی حاصل بولوب
|62a| بی‌تشویش جمشیدی طوایفی فتحی کُلّاً میسر بولوب اون بیش
مینک بلکه آندین زیاده خانوارنی کوچوروب بعضی‌سین مرو شاهجان
جانبی‌غه یوللادوق و اوزیمیز کوچ اتمامی‌نینک ایزیغه قاراب آقچه قایه
آتلیغ جایدا وقوف لازم بیلیب توروب‌میز و انشاء الله تعالی کوچ ایزی
صاف بولغاندین سونکرا بارچه‌سی‌نینک کوچین ولایت مذکوره ساری
یوللاغومیزدور و موندین سونک نی نوع حکم همایون‌لاری صدور تاپسه
اداسیغه کما ینبغی سعی کورکوزکومیزدور و قالغان لسان عرایضی مراتبین
عرضه‌داشت حاملی آستانهٔ دولت‌نشانه‌لاری خاکبوسلیقی‌غه مشرف
بولغان چاغدا عرض قیلغوسیدور دیب اخلاص غایتی و اعتقاد نهایتی‌دین
بو عرضه‌داشت بیتلدی التقصیر[3]

|62b| و چون بو امورلار اهتمامی‌دین سونک اوچ کیچه انقضا تاپیب شنبه
کونی ایردیکیم عزّت‌پناه شوکت‌دستکاه عبد الله بیک کیم کوشک قلعه‌سی‌نینک
حاکم رستم‌نشانیدور کیلیب دربار فلک‌اقتدارلاری عتبه‌بوسلیقی درجه‌سین تاپتی
و ایرتاسی یکشنبه کونی خذمتی‌داغی چاووش و چاکرلاری بیرله مذکور بیک‌نی

---

[1] آمانیمیز.

[2] خزابنی‌غه.

[3] التقصیر above the line.

آت و سروپای شاهانه انعامی‌دین اوز اقران و امثالی اورتاسیدا سرافراز و ممتاز قیلیب جمشیدی طوایفی‌غه کُلّاً بیک‌لاریکی قیلیب یارلیغ همایون عالی و منشور مبارک و متعالی توقیعی بیله فرقین فرقدان فرقیدین آشوردیلار و همولکون اسلام شیخ مریدلاریدین بیر نمدپوش صوفی‌کیم اسمی و نسبی معلوم ایرماس ایردی شاه کامران محبت‌نامه‌سین |63a| کیلتوروب منظورلاری قیلدی حاصل مضمونی بو ایردیکیم هرات جانبی تشریف‌لاریغه مقتضی ایردی و ایرتاسی دوشنبه کونی میرزا ابو القاسم‌کیم اسلام شیخ مذکورنینک اوغلی‌دور یار محمد خان وزیرنینک عرضه‌داشتین آستانهٔ معلی ملازم‌لاری‌نینک واسطه‌سی بیله نظر انورلاریغه منظور قیلدیکیم مضمونی مصالحه بنیادی طرحین شاه بیله آنینک اورتاسیدا سالیب بیر معتبر کیشی ییباریب آرالاریداغی منازعت و مخالفت رسومین برطرف قیلغایلار و مذکور میرزانینک تیل سوزی داغی آنکا موافق ایردی اولوجه‌دین عالیجاه رفیعجایگاه فضیلت‌پناه مبادرت‌دستگاه ملا دولتنظر بی‌نی هرات دار السلطنه‌سی سفارتی‌نینک |63b| تعیینی بیله سربلند قیلیب موندین ایکی کون سونک چهارشنبه کونی شاه کامران اوچون محبت‌نامه‌لارین وزیر[1] اوچون عنایت‌نامه‌لارین تاپشوروب میرزای مذکورغه[2] قوشوب ییباریب هر بیرین خلعت شاهانه بیله ارجمند قیلدیلار و شاه کامران ساری ارسال تاپغان محبت‌نامه سوادی بو تورور

بسالت و ایالت‌پناه حکومت و منزلت‌دستگاه محبت و مودت‌آگاه مصادقت

---

[1] Hereafter crossed-out کا .

[2] غه instead of crossed-out کا .

و مخالصت‌نشان شاه کامران دام محبته‌نینک خاطر محبت‌ذخایریغه واضح و لایح بولسونکیم لله الشکر و المنه بو داعی احوالی صحت و عافیت‌غه مقرون بولوب حضرت واهب بیچون عطیّه‌سی برکتی‌دین فرحت و نصرت کون بکون افزوندور و چون یار محمد خان |64a| وزیرکیم اولکرامی‌نینک مشقّت زمانی و صعوبت آوانیدا درکار و ضرور امورلار اداسیغه صاحب‌اقتدار خذمتکاریدور لهذا فضیلت‌پناه ملا دولتنظر بی‌نی اولجانب مأمور قیلدوق‌کیم بیز طرفدین باریب[1] وزیر کناهی عفوین التماس قیلغوسی‌دور ایمدی مناسب اولکیم [2]وَٱلْعَافِينَ عَنِ ٱلنَّاسِ[2] مؤداسینچه هر نیچوک کناهی لوثی بولمیش بولسه عفو آب پاکی بیله شُستُ شو بیرسه‌لار هرآینه [3]وَٱللّٰهُ يُحِبُّ ٱلْمُحْسِنِينَ[3] مقتضاسینچه مُحسِن و نیکوکارلار زمره‌سیکا انخراط تاپیب تینکریتعالی محبوب‌لاری‌دین محسوب بولغوسیدور و قالغان لسانی مراتبین مذکور بی عند الحضور تقریر قیلغوسیدور دیب دوست‌لیق غایتی‌دین بو محبت‌نامه ارسال تاپتی

|64b| و وزیر اوچون مفوّض بولغان عنایت‌نامه سوادی بو تورور

عالیجاه وزارت‌پناه اخلاص‌نشان یار محمد خانغه یارلیغ کورکاچ اولکیم مظهر القواعد و المراسم میرزا ابو القاسم بیله بیبارکان عرضه‌داشتینک درکاه

---

[1] باریب above the line.

[2-2] Qur'ān III: 134.

[3-3] Qur'ān III: 134, 148; V: 93.

آسمانجاهیمیز هواخواه‌لاری‌نینک وساطتی بیله نظر اقدسیمیز منظوری بولوب[1] مضمونی کما هو حقه مفهوم بولدی ایمدی کراکدورکیم [2]یَاأَيُّهَا ٱلَّذِينَ آمَنُوا أَطِيعُوا ٱللّٰهَ وَأَطِيعُوا ٱلرَّسُولَ وَأُولِي ٱلأَمْرِ مِنْكُمْ[2] مدلولینچه مخالفت قواعدین کیم تینکریتعالی امری‌نینک خلافی‌دور ترک توتوب اطاعت طریقین ایلکاری توتغیل کیم دارین مقاصد و مراداتی حصولی باعثی‌دور و عالیجاه ملا دولتنظر بی‌نی اول صوب‌غه مأمور قیلدوق تاکیم سیز |65a| ایکاوینکیز اورتانکیزدا صلح‌نینک خیریت‌مدار بنیادی طرحین سالیب مراجعت کورکوزکای دیب بو عنایت‌نامۀ عالیه ارسال تاپتی

و همولکوندا والی بیک عرضه‌داشتین دوست محمد بهادرکیم مذکور بیک‌نینک خذمتکاریدور و سرپل حاکمی محمود خان و شاهمردان خانی شجاع الدین خان و بلخ حکمرانی ایشان اوراغ‌نینک عرضه‌داشت‌لارین محمد قربان بهادر و آنت‌خوی حکمرانی شاه ولی خان‌نینک عرضه‌داشتین محمد بیردی سردار ملازم‌لار دلالتی بیله نظر انورلاریغه منظور قیلدیلار والی بیک عرضه‌داشتی‌نینک سوادی بو تورور

تا جهان ایوانی‌نینک صفحاتی قویاش شعشعه‌سی لمعاتیدین یاروغلوق |65b| و درخشاندور همواره سعادت و اقبال کوکبی فتوت و اجلال

---

[1] بولوب above the line.

[2-2] Qur'ān IV: 59.

اختری حکومت‌مآب منزلت‌ایاب[1] عالیجاه رفیعجایکاه‌لیق حشمت و شوکت‌دستکاه‌لیق عظمت خاندانی نقاوه‌لاری‌نینک نوخروجی حشمت دودمانی عمده‌لاری‌نینک یانکی عروجی علوی‌مکان‌لیق اقبال‌نشان‌لیق عمر و دولت‌دین کامیاب و برخوردار اولغان عالیجاه امیدکاهیمیز جناب خان‌زاده‌میز شفقتلو شاهزادهٔ مهربانیمیز ادام الله تعالی ملکه و ابقی حشمته حضرت جلَّ شانه علی الاطلاق وجود شفقت‌آمودلارین بارچه زمان عوارضاتی و دوران حوادثاتیدین اوز حفظ و حمایتیدا محفوظ و مصون ایتیب دارین مطالبی‌غه کامیاب و نشاطین مقاصدیغه مقضی المرام دارین بولغایلار بحق محمد سید المختار |66a| اما انشراح اشواق ملاقات شفقت‌آیات‌لاریدین سونکرا رای مرحمت‌اقتضالاریغه معروض اولکیم الحمد لله تعالی بول نیازمندنینک طریق احوالاتی و کوایف اطواراتی حضرت واجب الوجودنینک فضل و عنایاتی بیرلان درجهٔ بهبودلیق و فیروزلیقدا عبور و مرور قیلیب جناب عالیجاه علوی‌مقامیمیز سلامتلیق و بلنداقبال‌لیق‌لارین حضرت تینکریتعالی‌دین خمس الاوقاتدا مطالب خلاصه‌سی و مآرب عمده‌سی بیلمیشدور و دیکر رای مرحمت‌اقتضالاریغه معروض توتارکیم بول آوان مسرت‌نشاندا استماع ایتدوک‌کیم ذو القعده آیی‌نینک یکرمه تورتونجی‌سی ایردی جناب همایون عالی خان حضرتیمیز شفقت و مرحمت‌لاری بیرلان اول علوی‌مکان بلنداقبال |66b| مهربانیمیز سانسیز قوشون آلیب مأمور چهار

[1] منزلت‌آیاب.

ولایت بولوب بو اخلاصمندنینک خاطری تسلی‌سی و استمدادی اوچون مرو اولکاسیکا دولت بیرلان شرف نزول باغیشلامیشدورلار فقیرکیم بول نوید فرحت‌جاویددین حددین آرتوق قوانیب سرافراز و ممنون بولدوق توقع و ترصد خذمت خورشیددرجه‌لاریدین آنداقدورکیم شفقت بیرلان اول شاهزادهٔ بلنداقبال مهربانیمیز حرکت ایتیب چهار ولایت ساری میمنه سرحداتیغه آیاق باسقودای بولسه‌لار انشاء الله بول فقیر و جمیع حکام بول ولالار توقف ایتمای شرف رکاب‌بوسلیق‌لاریغه فایز و بهره‌مند بولوب حضرت تینکریتعالی فضل و کرمی بیرلان اولوغ سودین بیری بالکلیه سبب دولت جاوید جناب همایون |67a| عالی و شفقت اول مهربان سعادتمندیمیز اوچون جماعهٔ منقیتیه شریدین و آفاتیدین امین و مطمئن[1] بولوب بول ولا فقراسی دعای دولت ظفرخاصیت‌لاریغه مشغول و موظف بولغومیزدور باقی لسانی مراتبین شجاعت‌نشان دوست محمد بهادر خذمت والامرتبت‌لاریغه کما ینبغی حالی و خاطرنشین ایتسه توقع اولکیم مقبول خاطر مرحمت‌مظاهر ایتیب قبول درجه‌سیغه بیتکوروب نوید مزاج وهاج سلامت‌لیغ‌لارین مرقوم ایتیب ارسال ایتسون‌لارکیم باعث سرافرازلیق و ممنون‌لیق بولغای باقی السلام علیکم

و چون قالغان تورت عرضه‌داشت داغی بو عریضه الفاظ و مضامینی‌غه مشتمل و محتوی ایردی اولجهت‌دین خامهٔ مشکین‌شمامه ادهمی |67b| بو تورتاو

[1] مطمئین.

نکارشی[1] میدانیغه قدم قویمادی و همولکون خذمت بابیدا راسخ‌دم و ثابت‌قدم قوتوش محرم بیله‌کیم آنی میمنه ولایتی ساری سفارت بیله سربلند قیلیب ییباریب ایردیلار حضرتقلی بیک‌کیم ولایت مذکوره حکمرانی مضراب خان‌نینک معتبر و معتمد کیشی‌سیدور مذکور خان عرضه‌داشتین درکاه فلک‌اشتباه‌لاری هواخواه‌لاری‌نینک واسطه‌سی بیله مطالعه‌لاری شرفیغه مشرف قیلیب عتبه‌بوسلیق رتبه‌سین تاپتی و اول عرضه‌داشت ترجمه‌سی بو تورور

> ایالت‌پناه شوکت و جلالت‌دستکاه حشمت و مناعت‌اکتناه عزت و اقبال‌همراه دولت و نصرت‌آکاه حکومت‌نشان رفیع‌مکان پادشاه‌زادۀ جهان زاد الله فتحه |68a| و نصرته‌نینک فلک‌بنیان بارکاه‌لاریغه بو نیازمندنینک عرضه‌داشتی اولکیم عالم‌پناها مرحمت و التفات یوزیدین عنایت‌نامۀکیم محرم بیله بو نیازمندنی نامزد ایتیب ییباریب ایردیلار اوقات اشرفی ساعات اسعدی‌دا وارد بولوب مطالعه‌سیدین ذات خجسته‌صفات‌لاری‌نینک صحت و عافیتمندلیک‌لارین خاطر اخلاص‌ذخایریمیزغه مفهوم و معلوم ایتیب جهان جهان خوشحالیق و عالم عالم سرافرازلیق واقع بولدی عالم‌پناها مطلب اعلی اولدورکیم چتر معلی سایه‌سیغه استظلال ایتیب دیدار فیض‌آثارلاریغه مشرف اولساق اما تزاحم امواج حادثه و تراکم افواج واقعۀ یومیه بو مطلب حصولی‌دین مانع‌دور و قالغان عرض بولسه مذکور محرم |68b| بیله حضرتقلی بیک حضورلاری شرفین تاپغان چاغدا عرض

[1] نکاریشی.

قیلسه‌لار مرحمت یوزیدین صدق بیلکایلار باقی عزت ایامی دوام بولغای

و اوشبو کوندین اوّل سه‌شنبه کونی کوشک قلعه‌سیدا اولتورملی طوایف مذکوره‌دین تورت مینک خانوارنی کوچوروب کیلتوروب معسکر معلی‌دین اوتکاریب توشوروب ایردیلار و ارسال تاپغان سرکرده‌لار داغی نهایت‌سیز نصرت و اقبال و غایت‌سیز شوکت و اجلال بیله کیلیب سُدّهٔ سنیه و عتبهٔ علیه‌لاری خاکبوسلیقی دولتین تاپیب شهزادهٔ نیکوصفات متعالی‌درجات ادام الله نصرته‌نینک ملاقات سراسرخاصیات‌لاری شرفیغه مشرف بولوب ایردیلار نظم

آبرو بیرله قایتیب اول لشکر	تاپیبان کوب فروحُ فتح و ظفر
کوچوروب ‎|69a|‎ مونچه‌ایلنی غایت‌سیز	شادُ مسرور اولوب نهایت‌سیز
مونچه نصرت تاپیب بی‌اندازه	سالیبان عالم ایچرا آوازه
دوست‌لار موندین اولدی کوب خرم	دشمن اهلی بولوب دوچار الم
مونچه یوز فتح و آبرو بیرله	مینک تومان خصلت نیکو بیرله
کیلیبان لشکر ظفرتزیین	قویدی‌لار خاک درکهْ اوزره جبین

و همولکون‌کیم چهارشنبه کونی ایردی نماز بامداد اداسیدین سونکرا اوشبو کوج بیله کیلکان کدخدا مردم‌لارنینک الله قلی بیک باشلیق‌کیم عبد الله بیک مذکورنینک اینی‌سیدور بارچه‌سین اطلس‌پوش قیلدیلار و همولکون اخال اولتورملی اوتامیش و توختامیش خلقی‌نینک اولوغ و کیچیک بارچه‌سیغه ضیافت کوناکون قیلیب ‎\|69b\|‎ التفات و احسان‌لاری جامه‌خانه‌سیدین حریر خلعت‌لار

و پاکیزه زربفت‌لار کیدوروب ولایت‌لاری ساری مراجعت و معاودت رخصتی بیله سرافرازلیق[1] بغیشلادیلار و ایرتاسی پنجشنبه کونی یوموت بابا سردار بیله‌کیم انت‌خوی و بلخ و شاهمردان و سرپل و تاش قورغان ساری سفارت‌نینک اعلی رتبه‌سی بیله سربلند قیلیب ییباریب ایردیلار منکلی بای بهادر و مُلک امان بیک [2]محمد والی آقسقال[2] والی بیک و بلخ حاکمی ایشان اوراغ‌نینک و حصار حاکمی صوفی دادخواه و سایر بلاد مذکوره حکمران‌لاری‌نینک عرضه‌داشت‌لارین آستانه معلّا مقیم‌لاری‌نینک واسطه‌سی بیله نظر کیمیااثرلاری منظوری قیلدیلار و تاش قورغان والی‌سی والی بیک عرضه‌داشتی‌نینک |70a| سوادی بو تورور

معروض رای مرحمت‌اقتضای سعادت و اقبال کوکبی فرخنده‌مآل و جهات ظفرخصال شهامت و نامدارلیق اورنکیکا زینت‌افزا عدالت و کامکارلیق مملکتیکا هدایت‌پیما سلطنت و جهانبانلیق ناصیه‌سیندا بهاسیز کوهر خلافت و کیتی‌ستانلیق باصره‌سیندا ضیابخش جوهر شفقت و مهربانلیق آسمانی‌نینک شرافت‌لیک محوری محبت و مرحمت‌اعیانلیق دیوانی‌نینک فتوت‌لیق نیکومنظری دانش محفلی‌نینک بلندمکانی بینش سریری‌نینک اقبال‌نشانی نصرت‌اعیان‌لیق مرحمت‌بنیان مروت‌نشانلیق علوی‌مکانلیق جناب شجاعت‌مآب کامکار عمر و دولت‌دین برخوردار |70b| شاهزادهٔ مهربان امیدکاهی‌میز ادام الله تعالی ملکه و ابقی

---

[1] لیق above the line.

[2-2] In margin. Hereafter read تاش قورغان والی‌سی.

سلطنته مکرمت یزدانی‌نینک سحاب رشحاتی و مرحمت سبحانی‌نینک امطار فیوضاتیدین حیات جاودانی کلشنیدا مخضر و ریان و شکفته و خندان بولوب حکومت مملکتی‌نینک اورنک‌نشینی ایکی جهان نشاءسی‌نینک مقضی المرام نشاطآیینی بولغایلار امّا اظهار دعاکوی‌لیک و رضاجوی‌لیق‌دین سونکرا رای مرحمت‌اقتضالاریغه معروض اولکیم الحمد لله تعالی بول نیازمندنینک طریق احوالاتی تینکریتعالی فضل و عنایاتی و یُمن دولت ظفرخاصیت‌لاریدین صحت و سلامت و فیروزلیق درجه‌سیندا عبور و مروردا بولوب ذرّه یانکلیغ ملالت و کلالت‌کیم خیال آیینه‌سین[1] مکدر قیلغای |71a| واقع ایرماس بول فقیر اول شفقت‌پناه مهربانیمیز وجود شریف میمنت‌مسعودلارین سلامتلیغ و اقبال‌بلندلیغ‌لارین تینکریتعالی درکاهی‌دین صبح شامدا خواهان و جویان‌دورمیزکیم جهان بارینچه سلطنت و کامکارلیق کشوریندا مقیم و مستقیم بولوب دهر و دوران دوست‌نوازی و عدوکدازی بولغایلار آندین سونکرا مستور بولماسون‌کیم شفقت و مهربانلیق قیلیب سرافرازنامه‌لاری‌کیم عالیشان‌لار شجاعت و مبارزت‌اعیان‌لار بابا بیک سردار و بیردی بیک صحابتی بیله پی‌درپی بول فقیر اوچون نامزد قیلیب ارسال ایتیب ایردیلار نکرانلیق و انتظارلیق زمانیندا شرف ورود ارزانلیق ایتی بول نیازمند اول مضمون مرحمت‌مشحون‌دین زیاده سرافراز |71b| و سعادتمند بولدوق بول آوان سعادت‌نشاندا عالیشان بیردی بیک‌نی حضوردا ساقلاب اتفاق رفاقت

---

[1] .ایینه‌سین

اوچون انشاء الله تعالی خذمت‌کذارلیق و فرمان‌بردارلیق‌دا عزیمت ایتیب سرپُل ولایتی‌غه داخل بولوب مستعد خذمتکارلیق بولوب امر و فرمان شریف‌لاریغه انتظارلیق و نکرانلیغدادور آنینک اوچون شجاعت و مبارزت‌اعیان بابا بیک مذکورنی موقوف ایتمای رخصت بیریب ییباردوک و مراتب تیل عرضین مومی الیه‌غه کما حقه تأکید ایتدوک‌کیم مبارزت‌پناه مذکور شرف دست‌بوسلیق‌لاریغه وصول پیدا ایتکان چاغدا تفصیل بیله عرض قیلغوسیدور امید اولکیم مقبول عتبۀ عالیه ایتیب کمال شفقت‌دین بهره‌مند ایتکایلار بول فقیر آنینک اوچون |72a| امر عالی‌لاریغه موقوف و فرمان همایون‌لاریغه منتظردورکیم شفقت بیرلان قایو خذمت و قایسی امرنی لایق کوروب کرم بیرلان بویورسه‌لار بول بندۀ درکاه سعی کورکوزکوسیدور بو فقیر اوّلدین تا آخرغه‌چه بارچه عرضه‌داشت‌نی بیر مضموندا عرض قیلیب امیدوار اول جواب‌دور و اخبارات دار السلطنۀ کابل آنداق صورت تاپیب‌دورکیم بول فقیر اخوان نور چشمی عالیجاه محمد رحیم بیک‌نی عساکر بیرلان معاونت اهل اسلام اوچون غزاغه بویوروب ییباریب ایردوک دوشنبه کیچه‌سی ذو الحجه آیی‌نینک اون ایکی‌لانجی‌سی ایردی اول نور چشمی‌نینک بیر ملازمی اخبارات کابل کتابتین کیلتوروب تسلیم ایتی و تیل‌دین داغی آنداق آیتیب‌دورکیم سردار محمد اکبر خان غازی امیر دوست محمد خان‌نینک اوغلی کفار فرنکی‌نی صلح بیرلان چاونی‌سیدین |72b| چیقاریب بُت خاک دیکان یردا قرار بیرکان ایرکان اسلام اهلی و سعادت‌فرجام غازی‌لار فرنکی‌لار بیله اوروشوب نیچه‌لارین قتل قیلیب سونکرا سردار غازی منع قیلیب

فرنکی‌نینک بارچه خزانه و اسلحه و توبخانه باری‌سین آلیب فرنکی جماعه‌سین نظربند قیلیب آلیب جلال آبادغه باریب‌دورکیم آندا چاونینی آلیب بارچه فرنکیکا رخصت بیرماکچی بولوب تورور لیکن بعضی‌لار آیتور ایرمیش‌لارکیم چاونی‌نی آلغاندین سونکرا فرنکی‌نی بارچه قتل ایتارلار الحمد لله کابل ولایاتی کفاردین پاک بولوب قرار سابق‌دا اهالی اسلام فارغبال ایرمیشلار باقی لسانی مراتبین اعتمادلیق منکلی بای بهادر شرف آستان‌بوسلیق‌غه مشرف بولوب عرض ایتکوسی‌دور آنداق امیدورکیم مقبول بارکاه فلک‌اشتباه ایتیب نوید |73a| سلامتلیق‌لاریدین و بارچه مرجوات‌دین قلسی قیلیب شفقت ایتکایلار و بول عرضه[1] دوشنبه کونی مذکور آی‌نینک اون ایکی‌سیدا بیتلدی باقی عمر و دولت مخلد و مستدام بولغای

و قالغان عرضه‌داشت‌لار داغی اوشبو مضمون‌دادور و ایرتاسی جمعه کونی اخلاص‌آثار میرداد سردار سمندوک طایفه‌سیدین یوز اویلیک‌نی کوچوروب لاله خان باشلیق کدخدا مردم‌لارین عتبه‌بوسلیق درجه‌سیغه ییتکوردی و سلطان صاحبقران داغی بارچه‌لارین[2] زرین لباس التفاتی بیله سرافرازلیق ییتکوردیلار و همولکون آقچه قایه‌دین کوچوب مذکور منزل محاذی‌سیداغی موری دریاسی‌نینک کذریدین اوتوب مرچاق طرفیکا عازم بولوب بیر نیچه مسافت یول

[1] عرضه above the line.

[2] Read بارچه‌لاریغه.

یوروب کیلیب پنجده قلعه‌سی‌نینک |73b| جنوبی طرفیکا عساکر ظفرمآثرلاری بیرله نزول بویوردیلار نظم

شاد اولوب اوشبو کون خدیو جهان — ایلاب اول ایلنی مرو ساری روان
کوچ‌لار آخرین تمام ایتی — اوزی هم آتلانیب خرام ایتی
حاصل ایلاب سرور ایله فرحت — لشکر اهلی هم ایتی‌لار نهضت
یولنی قطع ایتی‌لار بولوب مسرور — موری بحریدین ایلادیلار عبور
لشکری بیرله یوردی اول کامل — پنجده حدین ایلادی منزل

و اول کیچه مذکور موضع‌دا راحت‌کزین بولوب میمنه‌کا حضرتقلی بیک‌کا اخلاص‌آثار محمد نیاز خلیفه‌نی قوشوب عنایت‌نامه‌لارین تفویض ایتیب ییباردیلار و اول عنایت‌نامه سوادی بو تورور

عالیجاه رفیع‌جایکاه عزت‌همراه اخلاص‌نشان مضراب خانغه یارلیغ کورکاچ |74a| اولکیم حضرتقلی بیک بیله ییبارکان عرضه‌داشتینک آستانهٔ معلی ملازم‌لاری‌نینک واسطه‌سی بیله نظر امجد و اقدسیمیزغه منظور بولوب مضمونی کما ینبغی معلوم و مفهوم بولدی و بیز هم ظفرخروش لشکر بحرین جوش‌غه کیرکوزوب مرچاق جانبی عزیمت قیلیب پنجده سرحدیکا دولت و اقبال و اسرو شوکت و نصرت مالامال بیله نزول اجلال بویوردوق ایمدی کیراکدورکیم اوزینک یا اوغلینک درکاه

فلک‌اشتباهی‌میز ساری توجه کورکوزوب اطاعت طوقین کردنینک‌کا سالیب موندین بویان خذمت مراسمین تقدیمغه بیتکوروب بویروغ اداسیغه امتثال قیلسانک هرآینه التفات بیغایت و مرحمت بلانهایت کورکونک‌دور |74b| و اکر آنداق قیلماسانک هر امریکیم غیب مشیمه‌سیدین ظهور قیلسه کورولکوسیدور و قالغان تیل سوزی بولسه محمد نیاز خلیفه بیله مذکور بیک عند الحضور تقریر قیلغوسیدور دیب بو عنایت‌نامه ارسال تاپتی

و همولکیچه همول منزلدا خذمت بابیدا راسخ‌دم قلندر محرم‌نی تاش قورغان و حصار و سرپُل و شاهسردان و بلخ‌دین کیلکان کیشی‌لارکا کیم اسامی‌لاری یوقاریدا ذکر تاپیب ایردی قوشوب ییباردیلار و انت‌خویدین کیلکان‌لارکا اخلاص‌کیش خیریت‌اندیش درویش‌نی قوشوب هر بیرلارین سروپای شاهانه انعامی بیله سربلند و عنایت‌نامه‌لاری تفویضی بیله ارجمند قیلیب مُرخَّص قیلدیلار و اول |75a| عنایت‌نامه‌لار بارچه‌سی اوشبو مضموندا یازیلیب ارسال تاپتی

عزت‌آثارلار خیریت‌اطوارلار اخلاص‌کیش‌لار اعتقاداندیش‌لارغه یارلیغ کورکاچ اولکیم مذکور سفارت‌پیشه‌لار بیله ییبارکان عرضه‌داشت‌لاریکیم اول ارادت‌شعارلارنینک بو عتبهٔ علیه و سُدّهٔ سنیه خیریت‌خواه‌لیقی‌غه مشتمل ایردی،لار آستانهٔ معلی‌دا تورغان ملازم‌لار واسطه‌سی بیله بیتوشوب، مضمونی معلوم بولدی و همیشهٔ الاوقات عرضه‌داشت‌لار ارسالی بیله مونداق اظهار قیلور ایردینکیزلارکیم مرو ولایتی‌غه یا مرچاق طرفیکا تشریف بویورسه‌لار خذمت‌لاریغه اوزیمیز بارغومیز یا اوغلیمیزنی ییباریب

خذمت قواعدین اظهار قیلغومیزدور و بیز انشاء الله تعالی |75b| دییلکان موضعغه دولت بیله نزول اجلال بویورغومیزدور و سیزلار داغی قیلغان وعده‌لارینکیزکا موافق تیز دییلکان جایغه کیلیب خذمت قیلسانکیزلار و یا اوغلان‌لارینکیز کیلیب خذمت مراسمین تقدیمغه بیتکورسه انکا لایق التفات کورکونکیزدور و قالغان تیل سوزی بولسه مرسول توتولغان کیشی‌لار ملاقات هنکامیدا تقریر قیلغوسیدورلار دیب بو عنایت‌نامه بیتلدی

و ایرتاسی شنبه کونی دولت تمام و صولت مالاکلام بیله آتلانیب بیر نیچه مسافت یول یوروب بند نادر آتلیغ جاینی لشکرگاه قیلدیلار نظم

یوروب اول مصدر جلالُ جاه — بند نادرنی قیلدی لشکرگاه
مقدمیدین بولوب شرف ظاهر — بولدی مونداق شریف یر نادر

و ایرتاسی |76a| یکشنبه کونی فتح و نصرت‌لاری و کوچ اتمامی مژده‌سین عرضه‌داشت قیلیب حضرت پادشاه فلک‌بارگاه اوز قبله‌گاه‌لاری خوارزمشاه روحنا فداه‌نینک اکسیرخاصیت خذمت‌لاریغه اخلاص‌همدم‌لار اکرم و[1] بیرام یاغلی[2] بیله[3] ارسال قیلدیلار و اول عرضه‌داشت سوادی بو تورور

---

[1] و above the line instead of crossed-out بیله.

[2] یاغلی above the line.

[3] بیله altered from نی.

حضرت پادشاه معظم و شهنشاه مُکرَّم سلاطین زمان امیدکاهی و خواقین دوران تکیه‌کاهی آدمی‌لار مرحمت‌آکاهی عالمی‌لار پُشتُ پناهی آسمانجاه فلک‌بارکاه جناب مستطاب قبله‌کاهیمیز خوارزمشاه زاد الله ممالکه و مضافاته بنُصرت الآله‌نینک جهان‌مدار دربارلاریغه بو مخلص‌نینک عرضه‌داشتی اولکیم لله الشکر و المنه صحت و سلامت مع التوابع |76b| و اللواحق وَٱللَّهُ يُؤَيِّدُ بِنَصْرِهِۦ مَن يَشَآءُ[1] مؤداسینچه ارادت ازلیه و مشیت لم یزلیه تأییدی‌نینک اعانتی و دعوت اجابت‌آیت‌لاری خاصیتی‌دین فرحت اوزره فرحت و نصرت اوزره نصرت ظاهر بولوب قرا تیفه و قوش آسیا و سر چشمه و شهر خلیل و قاقچی و کوشک و کاریز و خواجه قلندر و بولارغه اوخشاش ینه نیچه قلعه‌لار فتحی میسَّر بولدیکیم بارچه‌سی جمشیدی طوایفی‌نینک سکون اختیار قیلغان بلادی تورور اول قلعجات اهلیدین اون آلتی مینک خانوارنی کوچوروب سونکین سونکلاب مرو ولایتی ساری یوللاب آقچه قایه‌دین کوچوب مرچاق جانبی عازم بولوب پنجده سرحدیدین اوتوب بند نادر آتلیغ جاینی منزلکاه قیلدوق و اوشبو بشارت عرضی‌نینک |77a| اظهاری اوچون خذمت بابیدا ثابت‌قدم‌لار اکرم بیله بیرام یاغلی‌نی اکسیرخاصیت خذمت‌لاریغه ییباردوک، قالغان لسانی عرایضین حضور باهر السرورلاری شرفین ادراک قیلغان چاغدا مشار الیهما عرض قیلغوسیدورلار دیب بو عرضه‌داشت بیتلدی باقی دولت ایامی مخلد بولغای

[1] Qur'ān III: 13.

و همولکون قلعهٔ نودا هزاره حاکمی کریمداد خان عرضه‌داشتین قاضی‌سی سید احمد خواجه ملازم‌لار واسطه‌سی بیله نظر فیض‌اثرلاری منظوری قیلدی و اول عرضه‌داشت تسویدی بو تورور

بختیارلیق عمانی‌نینک دُرِّ نابی شهریارلیق کانی‌نینک لعل سیرابی بسالت و بطالت‌پناه مبارزت و شجاعت‌اکتناه عظمت و رفعت‌آگاه حکومت و منزلت‌دستگاه |77b| ظفر و نصرت‌همراه سپهرمکان شهزادهٔ مهربان دام شوکته و نصرته‌نینک آستان فلک‌بنیان مقیم‌لاری‌نینک رای امجد و اقدس‌لاریغه تورلوک نیازمندلیک یوزیدین مونینکدیک معروض توتارکیم الحمد لله تعالی دولت ابدمدت‌لاری برکتی‌دین بو شوقمند باشلیق بو اطراف اولتورملی جمیع فقرا بارچه اموردین‌کیم[1] تشویش و تشتت باعثی بولغای فارغ و مطمئن بولوب حضرت ذی الجلال درکاهی‌دین فتح و نصرت‌لاری استدعاسیغه اشتغال‌لاری باردور دعا هدیه‌سی و ثنا وسیله‌سی اظهاریدین سونکرا عرض اولکیم بو اخلاصمند باشلیق جمیع فقرانینک جناب سپهرانتساب‌لاریدین توقع و چشم‌داشتی اولدورکیم مرچاق سرحدین بو فقرالارغه |78a| یارلیغ بیریب انعام قیلسه‌لار هرآینه هزاره فقرالاری کُلّاً کوچوب باریب اول سرحددا مکان توتوب عمر و دولت‌لاری ازدیادی‌نینک دعاسیغه اشتغال کورکوزسه‌لار و اوشبو عرض اظهاری اوچون قاضی سید احمد خواجه‌نی ییباردوک تا هر نیچوک

---

[1] کیم above the line.

مهربانچیلیق‌لاری بولسه کوروب و بیلیب مراجعت کورکوزکای دیب بو عریضة الاخلاص ارسال تاپتی باقی امرکم الاشرف مطاع

چون سلطان صاحبقران ادام الله سروره بو عرضه‌داشت مضمونیغه اطلاع پیدا قیلدیلار ایرتاسی دوشنبه کونی مذکور قاضی‌نی اجازت‌لاری بیله سربلند و سروپای شاهانه اعطاسی بیله ارجمند قیلیب ایراد ایتکان عرضه‌داشتی جوابین داغی بیتب آنکا تفویض قیلیب ییباردیلار و اول جواب تسویدی بو تورور

|78b| اخلاص میدانی‌نینک یکه‌تازی اعتقاد معرکه‌سی یکه‌تازلاری‌نینک سرافرازی عالیشان رفیع‌مکان کریمداد خان‌غه یارلیغ کورکاچ اولکیم فضیلت‌پناه فقاهت و سیادت‌دستکاه قاضی سید احمد خواجه بیله ارسال قیلغان عرضه‌داشتینک آستانهٔ دولت‌نشانه‌میز ساکن‌لاری‌نینک واسطه‌سی بیله ییتوشوب مضمونی ضمیر آیینه‌نظیریمیزغه وضوح طریقه‌سی بیله مفهوم بولدی و دیب‌دورسین‌کیم مرچاق سرحدین بیرسه‌لار بو فقرالار کوچوب باریب اول سرحددا متمکن بولغای ایردی بو طریقه عرضینک کوب خوب و خاطر فیض‌مآثریمیزغه اسرو مرغوب‌دور لیکن الآن‌کیم برودت عسکری‌نینک اردسامی چاغیدور تا ربیع هدکامی‌غه چه توقف لازم بیلیب اول ایش اداسیغه |79a| قدم قویمماق اولی و انسب‌دور نیدینکیم حالا مذکور امرنی ارتکاب قیلسه فقرا اَنْفُس و اموالی‌غه کوب ضرر

عاید و اول اخلاصمندکا اوز امثال و اقرانی اورتاسیدا نَقص[1] و ملامتی راجع بولغوسیدور نیدینکیم مونینکدیک امرنی بی‌جهت و بی‌سبب اختیار قیلماق خرد اهلی قاشیدا خوب و مرغوب ایرماستور و چون بیز مراجعت کورکوزوب ربیع فصلی هم وجود توتسه‌کیم تابستان ازمنه‌سی‌نینک مقدمه‌سی‌دور اولچاغ اختیاری اوز ایلیکیدادورکیم اولوقت مذکور امرکا اقدام کورکوزسه هیچ ضرری و ملامتی عاید و راجع بولماغوسی‌دور دیب لطف و مرحمت یوزیدین بو عنایت‌نامه ارسال تاپتی

و ایرتاسی سه‌شنبه کونی عاطفت خاقانیه و ملاطفت سلطانیه‌دین سربلند و ارجمند قیلیب |79b| بو فقیر الحقیر بیله مبارزت‌پناه جلادت‌دستکاه اخلاص‌توأم قارلی محرم‌نی پنجده قلعه‌سی توابعیدا اولتوروملی چارشنکی و ایرساری خلقی‌نینک‌کیم حمایت‌لاری تحتی‌کا داخل تورور اموال قایمه و مواشی سایمه‌سی زکوتین آلماق اوچون بویوروب ییباردیلار و ینه اول یردا اوچ کیچه توروب جمعه کونی لشکر اهلی کدخدا مردم‌لاری‌نینک خیریت‌خواه‌لیق یوسونیدا قیلغان عرض‌لارین قبول درجه‌سیکا ییتکوروب غایت‌سیز آبرو بیله اَلْعَوْدُ اَحْمَدُ حدیثی‌نینک مقتضاسینچه مراجعت و معاودت کورکوزوب لشکر اهلی داغی سرور علی سبیل الوفور اظهار ایتیب شکوه خسروانه بیله یول قطعی‌غه روانه بولوب بیراز یول یوروب موری دریاسی‌نینک کوپروکیدین اوتوب |80a| قریبی‌غه نزول بویوردیلار نظم

[1] نُقص.

تاپیب اول بختیار نام‌آور — ظفر و فتح و فرحت بیمر
آنچه فتح و ظفر تاپیب پیوست — ینه بیرکا جهاندا بیرمادی دست
تینکری لطف ایلابان بسی ارشاد — انکا مفتوح بولدی مونچه بلاد
نی تاپیب کیمسه زحمتی آندین — نی کیشیکا صعوبتی آندین
کامرانلارکیم ایردی جاهی رفیع — بولدیلار بویروغی‌غه باری مطیع
مونچه‌کیم نصرت ایلادی حاصل — آبرو تینکریدین تاپیب کامل
لشکر اهلی همه بولوب شادان — چمنستان ارا چو کل خندان
اوج توشتی بو کون صدای سرور — فلک اوزره چیقیب نوای سرور
عود ایتیب اول خدیو ایله لشکر — قطع ایتیب ره چو مه بیله اختر
موریدین چون کذر ایتیب سرکار — توشتی و اول یر اوزره |80b| توتتی قرار
ایلابان هم سپاه اهلی کذر — قیلدیلار اوشبو یرنی کیچه مقر
ای خدا بولسه مقصدی هر ایش — بیر ظفرنی همیشه بی‌تشویش

چون سلطان صاحبقران‌کیم کیچه مذکور یردا آرام آلدیلار ایرتاسی شنبه کونی یوز تومان دولت و اقبال و غایت‌سیز شوکت و اجلال بیله کیلیب اوروش توشکان آتلیغ مرحله‌کا قدوم شرافت‌لزوم‌لاری بیله طراوت تازه و نزول سعادت‌وصول‌لاری بیله نضارت بی‌اندازه بیتکوردیلار و بو منزلدا هسولکون بو فقیر بیله مذکور مبارزت‌پناه آستان‌بوسلیق شرفیغه مشرّف بولوب انعام‌لاری نقودیدین بهره‌یاب بولوب فقیرلیق فلاکتی‌دین استخلاص تاپیب غنی‌لیق‌نینک

اعلی مرتبه‌سیکا اختصاص تاپتی[1] و اولکون همولمنزلدا خفتن |81a| نمازی اداسیدین سونکرا مبارزت‌پناه شجاعت‌دستکاه اخلاص‌توأم ویس محرم حضرت پادشاه والاجاه انجم‌سپاه کیوان‌بارکاه جناب مستطاب خوارزمشاه روحنا فداه‌نینک سراسرخاصیت خذمت‌لاریدین کیلیب بلیغ یارلیغ‌لاری اصداری بیله‌کیم الفاظی لطافتدا نزاکت‌پیرا و عباراتی نزاهتدا مسرت‌افزادور وفور طریقی بیله سرور بیتکوردی نظم

قاصد بیتوشتی قیلدی کرم طرفه نامهٔ
پُرنور ایلاکیم ورق آفتاب و ماه
باشدین ایاغی لفظ دُرَرْ باری نامه‌نینک
توقیع مکرمت ایله طغرای عز و جاه

چون بو یارلیغ ورقیغه کوز سورتا آلمادیم اولوجه‌دین تحریر و ترقیمی‌غه خوفاً من الخطا جُرأت کورکوزا آلمادیم |81b| و ایرتاسی یکشنبه کونی همولمنزلدا علما و امرا بیرله جمیع سرکرده‌لار و سردارلارغه قویاش صفحه‌سیدیک زرین لباس‌لار و فلک‌رنک ماؤت[2] و شفقکون کلنار چاکمان‌لار انعامی بیله بارچه‌لاری تارکین سماوات طبقاتیدین آشوردی‌لار و توی شاهانه ترتیب بیریب سپهراشتباه بارکاه‌لاریغه تمامی‌سین اونداب رنکارنک اشربه و ملذّذ اطعمه‌لار تارتیب فرنکی قند و مصری نبات اولمجلس‌کا حاضر ایتی‌لارکیم موز شوشه‌سیدیک کثرتی

[1] Read تاپتی‌لار.
[2] Read ماهوت.

جهتیدین بیمقدار و توز قطعه‌سیدیک بی‌اعتبار ایردی و بو تکلفاتدین فی الجمله فراغت تاپغاندین سونکرا آت‌چاپارکاه جانبی‌غه دولت تمام و مسرت مالاکلام بیله آتلانیب باریب برق‌آثار و چرخ‌نمودار آتلارنی چاپتوروب شیرصورت |82a| فیل‌هیئت پهلوان‌لارنی کوراش توتتوروب هر بیری‌نینک جیب و ایتاکین زر و نقره‌دین تولدوردیلار و نهایت‌سیز تماشالار بیله خاطر عاطرلارین خوش قیلیب کیچ‌قورون مراجعت کورکوزوب ینه همولقوش‌غه نزول قیلدیلار نظم

مراجعت قیلیب اول بختیارُ کامروا
عنایت ایلاب همولقوشنی ایلادی مأوا
قویاش کیبی آچیب اولکوندا پنجهٔ احسان
جهانغه ایلادی زر ساچماق امرینی افشا
بو نوع جودُ کرم‌دین همه بولوب خرسند[1]
مدام ایلادیلار فتحین حق‌دین استدعا
خدای لطف ایتیبان بو دعالار عنقاسی
قبول قُلّه قافیدا ایلاکای پروا

|82b| چون خدیو جهان اعنی سلطان صاحبقران زاد الله تعالی[2] نصرته و فرحته اول کیجه مذکور منزلدا راحت کزین بولدی‌لار ایرتاسی دوشنبه کونی همول بردا پنجده قلعه‌سی‌نینک کدخدا مردم‌لاریغه سروپای شاهانه مرحمت و التفات

---

[1] خورسند.

[2] تعالی above the line.

ایتیب خذمت اموریدا راسخ‌دم و ثابت‌قدم قارلی محرم‌نی قلعهٔ مذکوره‌نینک حاکم‌لیغی توقیعی بیله باشین سپهر اوجیغه ییتکوروب اجازت‌لاری دولتی بیله سرافراز و ممتاز قیلیب ییباردیلار و همولکون همولمنزلدا عالیشان رفیع‌مکان عبد العزیز خاننی بُراق‌اطوار برق‌رفتار آت [1]سندس واستبرق[1] ماننّدی بولغان لباس انعامی بیله رتبه‌سین فلک‌دین آشوروب رفاقتی‌غه اخلاص‌همدم قوتوش محرم‌نی قوشوب لطف و مرحمت یوزیدین کریمداد خان اوچون بیر عنایت‌نامه تفویض قیلیب |83a| ییباردیلار و اول عنایت‌نامه سوادی بو تورور

> اخلاص‌کیش اعتقاداندیش عالیشان رفیع‌مکان کریمداد خان دام اخلاصه‌غه یارلیغ کورکاچ اولکیم اوتامیش و توختامیش تکه و سالور و ساریق و چارشنکی جماعه‌لاریغه بویوردوق و فرمان قیلدوق‌کیم چون اول اخلاص‌کیش‌کا حاجت و ضرورت یوزلانیب بیر واقعهٔ واقع و حادثهٔ شایع بولسه اعانت و امداد ییتکوروب اولواقعه دفعی‌غه کما ینبغی کوشش قیلینک‌لار و عبد العزیز خان‌نی مرخَّص قیلیب رفاقتی‌غه اعتقادتوأم قوتوش محرم‌نی قوشوب اول مخلص جانبی‌غه ییباردوک تاکیم اوشبو امر و فرمان صدورین اعلام ایتیب مراجعت کورکوزکای دیب بو عنایت‌نامه بیتلدی

|83b| چون سلطان صاحبقران اوشبو امرلار اهتمامی‌دین فراغ تمام حاصل ایتی‌لار اول منزلدین کوچوب روارو بابیدا دجلهٔ جیحون کیبی لشکر افواجی‌نینک

[1-1] Cf. Qur'ān XVIII: 31; XLIV: 53.

امواجی جوش قیلیب اسرو صولت بیله کیلیب صندوق قاچغان آتلیغ منزل دیده‌سیکا اشهب‌لاری توپناغی‌نینک توتیاآثار غباریدین ضیابخش بولدیلار و اولکیچه مذکور محل‌دا آرام آلیب دولت و نصرت بیله مراجعت ایتکان‌لارین عرضه‌داشت ایتیب حضرت ظل الله جناب مستطاب خوارزمشاه خدمت اکسیرخاصیت‌لاریغه ییباردی‌لار و اول عرضه‌داشت مُسوَّده‌سی بو تورور

حضرت کامکار عظیم و بختیار واجب التکریم ربع مسکون اهلی‌نینک فرمان‌فرماسی و دهر بوقلمون |84a| فرمان‌فرمالاری‌نینک[1] کامرواسی محب العلماء و الأُمَراء مربی الفقراء و الغرباء ملاذ الانام مرجع الخواص و العوام ذو المجد و العزت و الاحترام حافظ بلاد اهل الاسلام پادشاه باتخت و جاه داراشکوه اسکندردستگاه جناب مُطَهَّر و مقدس قبله‌کاهیمیز خوارزمشاه طول الله اغصان شفقته مُظَلَّلاً علی رؤس المهاجرین‌نینک عتبهٔ علیه و سُدَّهٔ سنیه‌لاریکا ادعیه و اثنیهٔ کثیره تحایفی ارسالیدین سونکرا بو شوقمندنینک عرضه‌داشتی اولکیم لله الشکر و المنه ایزد کامبخش فضلی فیضی‌نینک برکتی و مستجاب دعالاری خاصیتی‌دین صحت و سلامت مع التوابع و اللواحق آبروی تمام و فرحت و نصرت تام بیله کیلیب صندوق قاچغان آتلیغ جایغه نزول قیلدوق |84b| و انشاء الله تعالی مرو ولایتی‌غه دخول واقع بولغاندین سونک جمشیدی طایفه‌سیدین مینک خانوار آق اویلی‌سین کوچوروب خدمت‌لاری ساری

[1] فرمان above the line.

یوللاغومیزدور و کینی‌دین ایکی اوچ کون سونک بارچه‌لارین کوچوروب حضرت‌لاریکا ییبارکومیزدور و ینه امر عالی‌لاری نی نوع وجود توتمیش بولسه جهد موفور بیله اداسیغه امتثال کورکوزکومیزدور دیب اخلاص و اعتقاد فرطیدین بو عرضه‌داشت بیتلدی باقی دولت‌لاری ایامی مستدام بولغای

و ایرتاسی سه‌شنبه کونی دبدبهٔ سلطانیه بیله آتلانیب بیر نیچه مراحل‌نی قطع قیلیب عساکر ظفرمآثرلاری بیله چادر سپهراثرلاریغه چانکلی کذر آتلیغ[1] جاینی مقر قیلدیلار نظم

کوب شکوه ایله |85a| اول سپهرمدار	بادپاییغه چونکه بولدی سوار
تیبرادی صولت ایلابان پیوست	یتی آندین فلک کا اسرو شکست
هر قدم مینک تومان نشاط بیله	هر دمی اوزکا انبساط بیله
کیلیبان بیر یر اوزره قیلدی مقر	ایدی اول یرنینک آتی چانکلی کذر
مقدمیدین شرف تاپیب بو محل	بولدی آب و هواسی روضه مثل

و ایرتاسی چهارشنبه کونی اول جایدین کوچوب یول اثناسیدا قازوقلی بندین تماشا قیلیب بیر نیچه مسافت یول یوروب کیلیب جیکیرداکلی ساومه دیکان جایغه قدوم سعادت‌لزوم‌لاری بیله برکت و نزول دولت‌وصول‌لاری بیله

---

[1] اتلیغ.

شرافت ییتکوردی‌لار و ایرتاسی |85b| پنجشنبه کونی مذکور منزلدین رخش خوشخرام‌لاریغه راکب بولوب مرو دریاسی لبی‌دین شوکت تمام بیله یورروش کورکوزوب یول اثناسیدا زیبا تذرو بیرله خوش‌رفتار کاکلیک‌لارنی شکار قیلیب فیل‌صورت ببرهیئت خوک‌لارنی قتل‌غه ییتکوروب سلاطین ماضیه قبله‌سی خواقین سالفه قدوه‌سی ولایت‌مآب‌لار سرافرازی سلطان سنجر ماضی بندین تماشا ایتیب اول موضعدا دعا و فاتحه بیله روحین یاد و ذکر جمیل بیله شاد ایتیب صیاد قلعه‌سی پیشکاهیدین[1] اوتوب ریکزارلیق‌غه ییتوشکان چاغدا دار السلطنۀ خیوق صانها الله تعالی عن الحرق و الغرق‌دا قالغان بعضی شهزاده و بیک‌لارنینک سلطان عصر خذمت‌لاریغه |86a| ییبارکان خذمتکارلاری بیله تحایف و هدایالاری ییتوشوب مذکور شهزاده‌لار و بیک‌لارنینک صحت و عافیتمندلیک‌لارین خذمتکارلاری تقریریدین استماع ایتیب خاطر آیینه‌مآثرلاریغه جلای تازه و صفای بی‌اندازه حاصل بولدی و اول تحایف و هدایاکیم فلک جمازه‌سیدیک قوت‌لیغ و قدرتلیغ بُختی‌لارغه یوکلانکان ایردیکیم آلارغه نی غایت پیدا و نی نهایت هویدا ایردی و بو نوع فرحت فرخنده‌فر و شکوه قیامت‌اثر بیله کیلیب یول اوتان موضعی‌غه نزول و هبوط قیلیب تحایف مذکوره و هدایای مسطوره‌نی‌کیم بی‌غایت و نهایت ایردی سرکرده‌لار باشلیق سپاه اهلیغه تقسیم طریقه‌سی بیله مرحمت کورکوزوب |86b| التفات‌لاری بیله شادکام و شهدآشام ایتیب بارچه‌سین ممنون قیلدیلار نظم

[1] پیشکاه‌سیدین.

اول در بی‌بهای بحر کرم یعنی سلطان داور اعظم
یار اولوب مونچه نصرت ایله ظفر ممکن اولغانچه ایلابان کروفر
سالیب آوازه بو جهان ایچرا یوق جهان بلکه آسمان ایچرا
یول اوتان حدیکا یقین ییتکاچ آنداغی ریک‌دین عبور ایتکاچ
بیک‌لارکیم قیلیب ایدی ارسال تحفهٔ هدیهٔ همایون‌فال
خدماسی داغی یتیب اول آن خذمتی‌غه باریسی بولدی عیان
اولکروه سوزیدین بولوب عالِم بیلدیکیم بارچه‌سی ایرور سالم
ایشیتیب سمعی چون بو نوع نوید یتی کونکلیکا فرحت جاوید
بو صفت فرحت ایله اول کامل یول اوتان حدین ایلاکاچ منزل
تحفه‌لارکیم|87a|کیلیب ایدی فی الحال بیریب ایتی سپه ایلین خوشحال
خوش بولوب قیلدی‌لار سپاه دعا ایلادیلار دعانی بویله ادا
ربع مسکونغه حکمینی سورکای شوکتینی فلک‌دین آشورغای
یر اوزه صیت دولتین سالغای کوک اوزه کوس نوبتین چالغای

چون اولکیچه اول سرحدکا نزول بویوروب راحت ایتی‌لار ایرتاسی جمعه کونی دبدبهٔ سلطانیه و کوکبهٔ خاقانیه بیله آتلانیب یول اثناسیدا حضرت قبلة الاولیا قدوة الاتقیا طالقان بابا علیه الرحمه‌نی زیارت قیلیب خاطر عاطرلاریغه فیض وافر و فتوح متکاثر یوزلانیب غایت‌سیز صدقات و نذورات مجاورلاریغه ییتکوروب کونکول‌لاریغه نهایت‌سیز سرور بغیشلاب ینه آتلانیب کرنایلاتیب و توب آتدوروب |87b| کوه و کمر اعضاسیغه زلزله و بحر و بر اجزاسیغه ولوله سالیب مرو ولایتی اهلی‌نینک انتظارلیق دَردین چیککان دیدهٔ فراق‌دیده‌لاریکا تکاور

براق‌اثرلاری توپناغی‌نینک توتیاآثار غباریدین ضیا ییتکوردیلار نظم

داور کیتی‌پناه سلطان کردون‌اقتدار
صفدرُ لشکرشکن اسرو شجاع روزکار
حق تعالی التفاتیدین بسی نصرت تاپیب
بی‌نهایت آبرو بیرلان بو یان قیلدی کذار
ایل کوزی بی‌نور ایدی هجریدا یوز مینک شکر کیم
تاپتی خاک مقدمی‌دین توتیای افتخار
بولدی جان‌پرور هواسی ایلاکیم باغ جنان
مقدمی تشریفیدین تاپغاچ طراوت بو حصار
هر قایان عزم ایلاسه اول نامور کیتی‌ستان
فتح و نصرت یار و |88a| یاور ایلاکای پروردکار

چون سلطان صاحبقران قلعهٔ مذکوره‌غه دخول سعادت‌وصول‌لاری بیله طراوت تازه و نضارت بی‌اندازه ییتکوردیلار ایکی کون اوتوب یکشنبه کونی خدمتکارلیق بابیدا راسخ‌دم و ثابت‌قدم ویس محرم بیله مرو ولایتی‌غه یوز تورلوک فتح و نصرت بیله صحت و سلامت مراجعت کورکوزوب نزول قیلغانلارین ملاذ الخافقین قبله‌کاه‌لاری، خوارزمشاه حضرت‌لاریغه عرضه‌داشت ایتیب ییباردیلار و اول عرضه‌داشت الفاظی بو تورور

حضرت خاقان اعظم کردون‌حشم انجم‌خدم کامکار عالم فرمان‌فرمای امم چرخ‌درکاه سلیمانجاه دارادستکاه جناب مستطاب قبله‌کاهیمیز خوارزمشاه |88b| رقّاه الله تعالی رواج شوکته و اوصل الله صیت نصرته و دولته الی المشارق و المغارب بوفور عنایته‌نینک دربار کیتی‌مدار و آستانهٔ سپهرآثارلاریغه دعا تحایفی و ثنا هدایاسی ارسالیدین سونکرا بو شوقمندنینک عرضه‌داشتی اولکیم الحمد لله تعالی حضرت واهب النصرت عنایت بیغایتی و اولحضرت‌نینک دعوت اجازت‌آیت‌لاری[1] برکتی‌دین نصرت متکاثره و فرحت متوافره بیله صحت و سلامت مراجعت و معاودت کورکوزوب مرو ولایتی‌غه داخل بولوب[2] مرادات شاهدی وصالیغه[3] واصل‌دورمیز و انشاء الله تعالی جمشیدی طوایفی‌نینک مینک عدد آق اویلی‌سین کوچوروب سه‌شنبه کونی خذمت‌لاری ساری یوللاب کینینچه اوزکالارین داغی |89a| کوچوروب ییبارکومیزدور و قالغان لسانی عرایضین عریضة الاخلاص حاملی عتبه‌بوسلیق رتبه‌سین تاپغان چاغدا تفصیل طریقه‌سی بیله[4] عرض قیلغوسیدور دیب[5] اعتقاد و اخلاص نهایتی‌دین بو عرضه‌داشت ارسال تاپتی باقی امرکم الاعظم مطاع

---

1 .اجازت‌ایت‌لاری

2 بولوب above the line.

3 وصالیغه above the line.

4 بیله above the line.

5 دیب above the line.

و ایرتاسی دوشنبه کونی طوایف مذکوره‌نینک مینک عدد آق اویلی‌سین انتخاب بیله کوچوروب جلاویدا محمد امین بیک بیله سالور خلقی و کینی‌دا میرزا خان خلیفه نوکرلاری بیله یورسون دیب فرمان همایون عالی عز صدور تاپتی و عزیز قلی دیوان بیکی داغی آلار بیله همراه مأمور بولدی و بو طریقه بیله خوارزم جنت‌بزم تختکاهی ساری یوللادی‌لار و ایرتاسی سه‌شنبه کونی اوز کعبه‌لاری خوارزمشاه روحنا فداه‌نینک خلافت اورنکی |89b| اوزه صحت و عافیتمندلیک بیله مستقیم ایرکانلیک‌لاری خبری بیله مبارک یارلیغ‌لاری تبلیغی رسمین پهلوان کاکل‌لی آستان‌بوسلیق شرفین تاپغاندین سونکرا اظهار ایتیب غایت‌سیز سرور ییتکوردی و ایرتاسی چهارشنبه کونی جلالت‌پناه شجاعت‌دستکاه رفیع‌مکان کلات حکمرانی محمد علیخان بو نوع فتح و نصرت‌لاری آوازه‌سین استماع ایتیب خایف و هراسان بولوب اطاعت طوقین بوینیغه سالیب آستانهٔ دولت‌نشانه بنده‌لیکین اختیار قیلیب نهایت‌سیز پیشکش و تحایف بیله کیلیب عتبهٔ علیه‌لاری خاکبوسلیقی شرفیغه مشرف بولدی و ایرتاسی پنجشنبه کونی یوموت بیردی بیک بیله‌کیم آنت‌خوی و بلخ و شاه مردان و سرپل و تاش قورغان ساری سفارت طریقه‌سی بیله مرسول |90a| بولمیش ایردی بهبود بهادر آستانهٔ معلی خاکبوسلیقیغه مشرّف بولوب حصار حاکمی صوفی دادخواه باشلیق باقی بلاد مذکوره حاکم‌لاری‌نینک عرضه‌داشتین[1] ملازم‌لار واسطه‌سی بیله منظورلاری قیلدی و آنت‌خوی خانی شاه ولی خان عرضه‌داشتین حیدر قلی بیک کیلتوروب هواخواه‌لار دلالتی بیله نظر انورلاریغه فایز قیلدی و خدمتکار جان‌سپارلاری

---

[1] Read عرضه‌داشتلارین.

اخلاص‌کیش درویش داغی آلار رفاقتی بیله آستانهٔ معلی توفراغی‌غه جبهه‌سالیق درجه‌سین تاپتی و تاش قورغان حاکمی والی بیک عرضه‌داشتی‌نینک سوادی بو تورور

عرض بلاانتها و دعای لایعد و لایحصی‌کیم بول فقیر الحقیردین تحفه و هدایا اول سعادت‌مند اختر اقبال و کوکب فرخنده‌فال |90b| شهامت و نامدارلیق اورنکی‌نینک زیبنده‌سی عدالت و کامکارلیق سریری‌نینک طرازنده‌سی شفقت و مهربانلیق آسمانیدا محور مرحمت و محبت عمانیدا درخشنده کوهر سلطنت و جهانبانلیق ناصیه‌سی‌نینک غرۀ بیضاسی جلالت و کیتی‌ستانلیق باصره‌سی‌نینک قُرَّۀ نورافزاسی سخاوت و کرم محفلی‌نینک بلندمکانی دانش و بینش مجالسی‌نینک اقبال‌نشانی شفقت‌اعیانلیق مرحمت‌بنیانلیق علوی‌مکانلیق امیدکاهی‌میز شاهزادۀ سعادتمند مهربانیمیز ادام الله تعالی ملکه کامروالیق افقیدین طالع و لامع بولوب مکرمت یزدانی‌نینک سحابی رشحاتیدین و مرحمت سبحانی‌نینک فیوضاتی قطراتیدین حیات جاودانی کلشنیدا سبز و ریان شکفته و خندان بولوب سلطنت |91a| مملکتی‌نینک اورنک‌نشینی و ایکی جهان‌نینک نشاطی‌دین سرافراز و برخوردار بولغایلار بحرمت سید المختار آندین سونکرا رای شفقت‌اقتضالاریغه معروض توتارکیم الحمد لله تعالی و تقدس بول نیازمند درکاه آله‌نینک طریق احوالاتی و کیفیت اطواراتی حضرت تینکریتعالی‌نینک فضل و عنایاتی و ظل السبحان خان حضرتیمیز خلد الله ملکه و اوضح برهانه و اول مرحمت‌پناه

مهربانیمیز توجهات خاطر شریف‌لاری برکتی‌دین بول فقیر سلامتلیق و فیروزلیق درجه‌سیدا ذو الحجه آیی‌نینک یکرمه ایکینجی تاریخیدا عبور و مروردا بولوب ذرّه یانکلیغ ملالت و کلالت‌کیم خیال آیینه‌سین مکدّر قیلغای واقع ایرماستور بول فقیر اول شفقت‌اعیان مهربانیمیز وجود شریف‌لاری سلامت‌لیغین |91b| تینکریتعالی درکاهی‌دین صبح و شام مستدعی‌دورمیزکیم جهان باریچه سلطنت و کامکارلیقدا مقیم حکومت و نامدارلیق مملکتیندا مستقیم بولوب دهر و دوران دوست‌نوازی عصر و آوان عدوکدازی بولغایلار آمین یا رب العالمین آندین سونکرا مستور و محجوب بولماسون‌کیم چنانچه ذرّه‌نوازلیق مرحمتی بیرلان سابق الیومدا شجاعت‌نشان بابا بیک محرم صحابتی بیله تشریف ایتماک‌لارین بول فقیرغه سرافرازنامه‌لارین نامزد ایتیب ییباریب آندین سونک عالیشان شجاعت‌بنیان ملازم دربار عالی بیردی بیک‌نی بول کمترین بندۀ درکاه آله اوچون مرحمت‌نامه‌لارین بیریب ارسال ایتیب ایردی‌لار بول فقیر نوید سعادت‌جاویددین حددین زیاده سرافراز بولوب شرف ورود |92a| کیلتورماک‌لاری اوچون عالیشان بابا بیک محرم مذکورنینک رفاقتی‌غه معتمدی‌آکاه منکلی بای بهادرنی قوشوب ورود ایتماک‌لاری اخبارین معین بیلماک اوچون آستان‌بوسلیق‌غه ییباریب عالیشان بیردی بیک مذکورنی حضوردا ساقلاب بیغین‌غه سررشته و انجام بویوروب آماده و طیار بولوب انتظارلیقدا و نکرانلیقدا حددین آشه معطل بولدوق بل‌کیم انتظارلیق حددین آشیب شرف ورود ایتماک‌لاریدین نوید جدید مسموع بولمای بول آوانده آنینک اوچون اخوان نور چشمی‌میز عالیجاه محمد نظر

بیک‌نی عساکری بیرلان ذو الحجه مذکوره‌نینک یکرمه اوچونجی‌سیغه سرپل ولایتی‌غه استقبال اوچون بویوردوق‌کیم مذکور الالقاب ایلکاریراق باریب خذمت‌لاریغه یقین بولوب |92b| آماده و مستعد خذمتکارلیق بولوب کیلماک‌لاریکا انتظار و نکرانلیقدا بولسون‌لار و بول فقیر کما حقه منتظرلیق بیرلان کیچه و کوندوز نکران بولوب اخبارات جدید اول شفقت‌پناهیمیزدین بیتماسلیک اوچون متحیردورمیز بول سبب‌دین عالیشان عزت‌نشان بیردی بیک موصوف‌نی رخصت قیلیب اعتمادلیق مبارزت‌اعیان بهبود بهادرنی مذکور الالقاب‌نینک رفاقتیغه قوشوب تیل سوزین کما حقه مشار الیهمالارغه تعیین و تأکید ایتیب آستان‌بوسلیقغه ییباردوک مذکور الالقاب‌لار اول بارکاه فلک‌اشتباه‌غه فایز و بهره‌مند بولوب کما حقه عرض درجه‌سیکا بیتکورکوسیدورلار امید اول جناب مهربانیمیزدین آنداقدورکیم قبول عتبه‌لاری ایتیب نوید مزاج وهاج سلامت‌لیک |93a| و تشریف کیلتورماک‌لارین تفصیل ایتیب ارسال ایتسون‌لار تاکیم سبب تسکین انتظارلیق بولوب موجب ممنونلیق و سرافرازلیق بولغای و بول فقیر منتظرلیق‌دا آماده و طیار بولوب موقوف‌دور باقی التقصیر التقصیر التقصیر

و شاه ولی خان عرضه‌داشتی‌نینک الفاظی بو تورور

عالیحضرت رفیع المنزلت بهرام‌سطوت کیوان‌رفعت کسری‌صلابت سکندرصولت مؤسس قواعد عدل و احسان هادم مبانی ظلم و

طغیان ادام الله ظلال لطفه علی مفارق الانام‌نینک آستان عرش‌بنیان ملازم‌لاری‌نینک ذروه‌سیغه بو عبودیت‌فرجام غلام‌نینک عرضه‌داشتی بیتوشیب مفتوح بولسونکیم الحمد لله تعالی بو ولا احوالاتی دولت بیله سلامت‌لیق |93b| درجه‌سیدا مرور و عبور قیلیب ذات ملکی‌صفات عمری استدامتین و اول عالیجاه‌نینک دولت و اقبال مدارجی‌غه ارتقاسین مطالب اعلی‌سیدین بیلور ثانیاً عرض موقفی‌غه بیتوشسونکیم بو کمترین بو چاغغه تیکرو خذمتکارلیق شرایط و لوازماتین مهیا ایتیب و همسایه‌لاریمیزنی داغی اوشبو بابدا ترغیب قیلیب برادرلاریمیزدین بیراونی دربار معلی آستان‌بوسلیقی اوچون ارسال قیلماقچی ایردوک و خذمتکارلاری بیردی بیک مراجعتی اوچون منتظر ایردوک‌کیم بو حین‌دا بارکاه عالمپناه استرجاعی‌نینک خبری ایشیتلدی اولجهت‌دین خذمت‌آثار[1] حیدر قلی بیک‌نی[2] خذمتکارلاری بیردی بیک و درویش بیک مصحوبی قیلیب خذمت‌لاریغه روانه ایتدوک‌کیم عرایضات |94a| بنده‌لیک و هواخواهلیق مراسمین بو کمترین جانبی‌دین معروض توتوب اول ولا اخباراتین معین بیلیب مراجعت کورکوزکای باقی زبانی مراتبین اوز آدم‌لاری بیردی بیک و درویش بیک کوروب ایشیتکان‌لاریدیک معروض قیلسه‌لار باور توتغایلارکیم بو جانب‌لینک عتبهٔ علیالاریدین اوزکا هیچ متکا و امیدکاهی یوقتور آلهی سلطنت شجره‌سی وجود شریف و عنصر لطیف‌لاری بیله بارور و سایه‌کستر بولغای

---

1 خذمت اثار.

2 Hereafter crossed-out مصحوب.

و اوزکا عرضه‌داشت‌لار داغی بو ایکی عرضه‌داشت مضامین و عباراتیغه مشتمل ایردی اولوجه‌دین قلم یوکروک‌رقم آلار تحریری میدانیدا جولان قیلمادی و یکشنبه کونی علما و اُمرا مذکور خان و ایلچی‌لارکا و جمیع سالور و ساریق و یموت و چادور[1] |94b| و جمیع تورکمان اهلیکا ضیافت قیلیب کوناکون طعام‌لار و رنکارنک فواکه‌لار تارتیب کردون بوشقابیدیک لعلی‌لار ایچرا قندلار حاضر قیلدیلارکیم هر بیری بیر فلک کنکریدیک بزرکوار و شیرین‌لیک‌دا بهشت ثماریدیک خوشکوار ایردی و نبات‌لار کیتوردیلارکیم هر بیر بولاکی جان شیره‌سی و حیات سرمایه‌سی ایردی اولمجلس‌داکی حاضرلار بارچه‌سی اشیای مذکوره‌دین بهره‌مندلیک تاپتی‌لار و حاضرلار بارچه‌سین محمد علیخان باشلیق زرین لباس‌لار ایصالی بیله خوشحال قیلدی‌لار نظم

ضیافت ایتیب نعمت بیقیاس   باریغه بیریب آت و زرین لباس
خدیو فلک‌جاهُ دریانوال   کرم بیرله باریغه بیردی جمال
اولوس جمله تاپتی بغایت فرح   آینکدیک که|95a|مخمورایچکای‌قدح

چون سلطان صاحبقران دام فرحته مذکور اولوس‌کا کرم‌لاری جویباری‌دین سرشارلیق بیتکوردیلار دبدبهٔ سلطانیه بیله آتلانیب آت‌چاپارکاه‌غه باریب سرعت بابیدا چون طیر و فلک یانکلیغ سریع السیر آت‌لارنی چاپتوروب تماشاسی کل‌لاری بیله خاطرلاری کلشنی‌کا زیب و آرا بیتکوردیلار نظم

[1] Read چاودر.

شتاب ایچرا بعضی کیلیب مثل باد فلک رخشیغه بیردی چاپماقنی یاد
کیلیب بعضی چاپماق ارا مثل برق عرق بحری ایچرا بولوب جسمی غرق
کونکول‌لار تاپیب موندین اسرو حضور باری ایلکا بتی بغایت سرور

چون رخش فرحت‌بخش‌لارنینک[1] چاپماق طریقیدا رفتار مسرّت‌آثارلارین تماشا قیلیب تمام ایتی‌لار پهلوان‌لاریکیم |95b| پیکرلاری چون کوه و غضنفرشکوه ایردیلار آلارنی کوراش توتتوروب هر بیریکا خاطرلاریغه خطور قیلماغان بایراق بیریب بارچه‌سین سربلند و ارجمند قیلدیلار و بو یانکلیغ تماشالار صیقلی بیله کونکول‌لاری مرآتیغه صفا بیتکوروب کیچ‌قورون ینه مراجعت کورکوزوب قلعهٔ مذکوره‌نی آرامکاه قیلدیلار و ایرتاسی دوشنبه کونی حضرت پادشاه عالم و خاقان اعظم کیوان‌بارکاه اوز قبله‌کاه‌لاری خوارزمشاه روحنا فداه خدمت سراسرخاصیت‌لاریدین اکرم بیله بیرام یاغلی کیلیب صحت و سلامت کامرانلیغ اریکه‌سیدا مقیم ایرکانلارین و باقی شهزاده‌لار و بیک‌لارنینک عافیت مسندیدا مستقیم‌لیق‌لارین بیتکوروب غایت‌سیز فرحت و نهایت‌سیز مَسرَّت حاصل بولدی |96a| و بلیغ یارلیغ‌لارین داغی سلطان صاحبقران ایلیک‌لاریکا تسلیم قیلدی‌لار و اوشبو یارلیغ صفحه‌سیکا داغی نظر قیلماق بیله کوز یاروتا آلادیم و هسولکون اعتقادهسدم قوتوش محرم قلعهٔ نودین کیلیب عتبه‌بوسلیق رتبه‌سین تاپیب کریمداد خان‌نینک عرضه‌داشتین منظورلاری قیلدی و اول عرضه‌داشت سوادی بو تورور

[1] نینک above the line.

نواب مستطاب فلکجناب قمررکاب خورشیدانتساب جلالت و خان‌لیق نکینی‌نینک کوهر قیمت‌بهاسی ملکت و قاآن‌لیق انکشتی‌نینک خاتم جهان‌آراسی نصفت و حکمرانلیق شمشیری‌نینک جوهر زینت‌فرجامی عظمت و خاقان‌لیق نیامی‌نینک حدت‌آثار حسامی اشرف ارفع امجد اعظم |96b| افخم والاحضرت توره خان شید ارکان دولته‌نینک مقدس عرضی ذروه‌سیغه موندا غ بیتکوروركیم عنایت و چاکرنوازلیق یولیدین مبارک یارلیغ بلیغ‌کیم عالیشان عزّت‌بنیان قوتوش محرم صحابتی بیله عز اصدار تاپیب ایردی زیارتیغه مشرف بولوب مفاخرت و استظهار مراسمی‌نینک ازدیادیغه باعث بولوب فرمایشات علیه و احکام سنیه‌کیم[1] مرحمت و التفات یوزیدین بویوروب ایردیلار حالی و خاطرنشان ایتیب سرافرازلیق مزیدیکا سبب بولدی و بو عنایت خاص‌دین‌کیم غلام‌نی آنکا اختصاص بیرمیش‌دورلارکیم تورکمان سالور و ساریق و تکه و چهارشنکغی آتلی‌سی هرکاه بو چاکرکا مقدمهٔ و حادثهٔ[2] یوزلانسه هر بیری کیلیب مقدمه و احوال مدافعه‌سیغه سعی کورکوزسون‌لار |97a| و اول التفاتی‌کیم اخوی عبد العزیز حقیدا معمول بویورمیشدورلار بین الانام قرین مباهات و افتخار بولدی و ایل و جمیع طایفه‌غه امیدوارلیق مزیدی‌نینک باعثی بولدی و عقیدت‌اثر چاکرنینک آمالی تارکین فلککا بیتکوردی و انشاء الله تعالی تا حیات بارینچه ارادت و خذمتکارلیق کمرین بیل‌کا باغلاب دربارلاریدین اوزکا جانب‌دین امیدنی اوزوب خاطرنی یکجهت قیلیب بو

---

[1] سنیهٔ‌کیم.

[2] جادثهٔ.

آستان دولت‌بنیان خذمتکارلیقی قواعدی‌نینک[1] اظهاریدا تهاون و تقصیر قیلماغوسی باقی بو چاکر عقیدت‌سیرنینک ارادت و اخلاصی مراتبین رکاب‌بوسلیق شرفی‌نینک ادراکی حینی‌دا محرم‌باشی زبانی عرضه‌داشت قیلغوسیدور صدق مقرونی بیلکایلار امره الاشرف الولا مطاع

|97b| و همولکون والی بیک و شاه ولی خان باشلیق باقی حاکم‌لار طرفیدین کیلکان کیشی‌لارکا بیردی بیک‌نی قوشوب سروپای شاهانه انعامی بیله هر بیرین سربلند و عنایت‌نامه‌لاری تفویضی و اجازت ذی‌سعادت‌لاری بیله ارجمند قیلیب ییباردیلار انت‌خوی حکمرانی شاه ولی خانغه ارسال تاپغان عنایت‌نامه سوادی بو تورور

ارادت‌آثار عقیدت‌اطوار اخلاص‌نشان شاه ولی خانغه یارلیغ کورکاچ اولکیم حیدر قلی بیک بیله ارسال قیلغان عرضه‌داشتینک دربار کیتی‌مداریمیز هواخواه‌لاری‌نینک وساطتی بیله ییتوشیب مضمونی کما ینبغی مفهوم بولدی و سین خود بو جانب کیشی و عرضه‌داشت ییبارماک خذمتین برجا ایتیب دقیقهٔ نامرعی قویمادینک و موندین سونک نی نوع خذمت قیلسانک |98a| آنکا یاراشه پاداش کورکونک‌دور دیب، بو عنایت‌نامه بیتلدی

[1] نینک above the line.

والی بیک اوچون مفوَّض بولغان عنایت‌نامه تسویدی بو تورور

عالیجاه رفیع‌جایگاه اخلاص سپهری‌نینک مهر درخشنده‌سی اعتقاد بحری‌نینک گوهر تابنده‌سی خیریت‌خواه‌لیق یوسونیدا اطواراتی خوب و نیک والی بیک‌کا یارلیغ کورکاچ اولکیم بهبود بهادر بیله مرسول توتولغان عرضه‌داشتینک آستانهٔ دولت‌نشانه‌دا تورغان ملازم‌لار واسطه‌سی بیله بیتوشیب خاطر رافت‌ذخایریمیزغه اخلاص و اعتقادینک کثرتی کما ینبغی معلوم و مفهوم بولدی ایمدی کراکدورکیم اعتقادینک وفوریغه لایق قراوُل خانه یا چهارشنبه‌دا اوغلینک یا اوزینک کیلیب خدمت مراسمین تقدیمغه بیتکورسه بیز داغی انشاء الله تعالی |98b| مواضع مذکوره ساری دولت بیله متوجه بولوب رایت ظفرآیتیمیزنی اول اطراف‌دا جلوه‌نما قیلیب غایت‌سیز التفات و نهایت‌سیز عنایات اول اخلاصمند حقیدا ظهورغه کیلتورکومیزدور دیب لطف و مرحمت یوزیدین بو عنایت‌نامهٔ عالیه ارسال تاپتی

[1]و اوزکالاری هم بو عنایت‌نامه مضمونیدا بیتیلیب ارسال تاپتی[1] و همول کوندا محمد علیخانغه داغی اسرو مرحمت کورکوزوب آت و سروپای خسروانه و اجازت دولت‌علامت‌لاری بیله سربلند و تکه طایفه‌سی‌نینک آنکا حاجت وقتی‌دا خدمت قیلماقی اوچون عنایت‌نامهٔ عالی اعطاسی بیله ارجمند قیلیب

[1-1] In margin.

ولایتی ساری مرخّص قیلدیلار و اول عنایت‌نامه سوادی بو تورور

دربار فلک‌اقتدارپمیز خذمتکارلاری و اول دربار خذمتی اداسیدا فدوی‌آثارلاری |99a| ارادت‌کیش‌لار اعتقاداندیش‌لار اوراض خان و خواجمشکر آقسقال باشلیق اوتامیش و توختامیش تکه خلقی‌نینک ییکیت و یالانک بارچه‌سیغه یارلیغ کورکاچ اولکیم چون عالیجاه عزت‌پناه عقیدت‌نشان محمد علی خان‌غه بیر حادثه و واقعهٔ واقع بولوب حاجت و ضرورت یوزلانسه کما ینبغی اعانت و امداد ییتکوروب بویروغی اداسیغه ساعی بولوب کهالت یوزیدین تهاون و تقصیر قیلمانک‌لار و هر کیمسه‌کیم یارلیغ مضمونیغه خلاف قیلسه سیاست سلطانیه‌غه سزاوار بولغوسیدور دیب اوشبو یارلیغ عالی مرقوم بولدی

و همولکون خذمتکار فدوی‌لاری اخلاص‌نمای اسماعیل بای بیله جمشیدی طایفه‌سیدین کولوک و اولاغ‌غه |99b| قدرت پیدا قیلغانیدین تورت مینک خانوارنی کوچوروب خوارزم تختکاهی ساری یوللادی‌لار و ایرتاسی سه‌شنبه کونی محمد نیاز خلیفه‌کیم میمنه جانبی‌غه سفیر قیلیب ییباریب ایردیلار عتبهٔ علیه توفراغی‌غه جبهه‌سالیق درجه‌سین تاپیب مضراب خان عرضه‌داشتین نظر انورلاریغه فایز قیلدی، و اول عرضه‌داشت الفاظی بو تورور

عرضه‌داشت بندهٔ کمترین اخلاص‌کیش عقیدت‌اندیش اول جناب مستطاب معلی‌القاب قمررکاب پادشاه کردون‌اشتباه انجم‌حشم

ملایک‌خدم قطب فلک ابهت و دولت و اجلال مرکز محیط سطوت و عزّت و اقبال قدوة السلاطین الایام ملاذ الکافة الانام ملجاء الامراء العظام سلطنت و کامکارلیق مسندی‌نینک وارثی |100a| امن و امان بساطی‌نینک باعثی تاج‌بخش کشورستان و کامکار عظیم الشأن دارین مراداتی اعلی‌سی‌نینک کامیابی بولوب عاطفت و مرحمت‌لاری سایه‌سی اخلاص‌کیش خذمتکارلار مفارقیغه دایم و پایدار بولغای اخلاص و اعتقاد مراسمی اداسیدین سونک رای عالم‌آرای و ضمیر منیر کیمیاتأثیر عقده‌کشای‌لاریغه روشن و مشهود اولسونکیم مرحمت‌نامهٔ عنبرین‌شمامهٔ لازم التکریم و مفاوضهٔ واجب التعظیم الطاف و اعطافدین بو اخلاصمند دعاکوی‌لاریغه عزت‌مکان حضرتقلی بیک بیله مصدر جاه و جلالدین ارسال قیلیب ایردیلار ایمن ساعات و اشرف اوقاتدا یتیب مطالعه‌سیدین ذات عالیصفات‌لاری‌نینک خاطر اخلاص‌ذخایریمیزغه |100b| صحت و عافیت‌مندلیکی مفهوم و معلوم بولوب[1] جهان جهان خوشحال‌لیق و عالم عالم سرافرازلیق واقع بولدی اخلاص و اعتقادغه ازدیاد باعثی عالم‌پناها بیر نیچه زماندین بیری آباء بزرکوار و اجداد عالی‌تباریمیز عصریدین بو فرخنده‌نشان زمانغه‌چه بیراز طایفه مسلمان‌میزکیم پادشاه عالم‌پناه‌لارنینک ازدیاد دولت و حشمت و اقبال و ترقی عزّت و شوکت و اجلال‌لارین الله تعالی‌نینک درکاهی‌دین استدعا ایلاب جبههٔ نیاز درکاه بی‌نیازه قویوب التجا ایلارمیزکیم پادشاه عالمپناه کفار فجار ضلالت‌شعارلار دفعی‌غه

---

[1] Altered from بولدی.

عازم بولسه‌لار خذمتکارلیق و جان‌نثارلیق رسمیغه ایلکیمیزدین کیلکان خذمت‌لارغه سعی قیلساق آندین سونک عالم‌پناها |101a| مطلب اعلی اولدورکیم چتر معلی سایه‌سیغه استظلال ایتیب دیدار فیض‌مدارلاریغه مشرف اولماقغه تزاحم امواج حادثه و تراکم افواج واقعهٔ یومیه بو مقصد اعلی‌غه مانع و مهجور اولماقغه باعث‌دور قالغان عرض اولسه مشار الیه بیله عزت و رفعت‌مکان خلیفه محمد نیاز وقت شرفیاب حضور معدلت‌دستور سمع همایون اشرف اعلی‌غه عرض ایلاسه‌لار مرحمت و شفقت‌دین صدق بیلسون‌لار باقی ایام عزت و دولت دوام بولغای

و موندین ایکی کون سونک[1] پنجشنبه کونی عالیجاه فضیلت‌پناه ملا دولتنظر بی‌کیم هرات جانبی مرسول بولوب ایردی وزیر بیله شاه کامران اورتاسیدا عهد و پیمان باغلاتیب صلح بنیادی طرحین استحکام بیله سالیب |101b| مراجعت قیلیب عتبه‌بوسلیق رتبه‌سین تاپیب وزیر عرضه‌داشتین منظورلاری قیلدی و اول عرضه‌داشت ترجمه‌سی بو تورور

فلک‌جناب قمررکاب خورشیدانتساب سلطنت و حکمرانلیق خاندانی‌نینک سلاله‌سی حکومت و کامرانلیق دودمانی‌نینک خلاصه‌سی عارج معارج شوکت و اجلال مرتقی مدارج دولت و اقبال شید الله ارکان دولته‌نینک جناب مستطاب‌لاری ملازم‌لاری‌نینک رای امجد و اقدس‌لاریغه بو نوع

[1] Hereafter crossed-out عالیجاه.

عرض قیلورکیم نامهٔ مرحمت‌ختامه‌کیم فضیلت‌پناه ملا دولت نظر بی بیله شفقت و التفات یوزیدین بو مخلص‌نی نامزد ایتیب ییباریب ایردیلار بیتوشیب افتخار فرقین سماوات طبقاتیدین آشوردی ابتدادین تا بو چاغغه‌چه سلطان طوران حضرت‌لاری |102a| اعانتی‌دین امیدوار ایردوک الحمد لله جناب عالی‌لاری بو یان تشریف کیلتوروب‌دورلار و بعضی امورلارکیم اول معلی‌اَلقاب‌دین بو اخلاصمند حقیدا عز صدور تاپیب ایردی امیدوارلیق سلسله‌سی‌نینک انقطاعی‌غه داعی بولوب ایردی چون میرزا ابو القاسم جناب‌لاری‌دین مرخص بولوب دولت نظر بی بیله کیلیب مراحم و مکارم‌لارین بو اخلاصمند حقیدا تقریر قیلدیلار آنداق معلوم بولدی‌کیم شفقت و مرحمت‌لاری سابق‌داغی قراردا کمال سرحدیدا ایرکان بو زمانداکیم تورت طرفدین حضرت رسالت‌آیین دینی‌نینک مخالف‌لاری تسلُّط و قدرت رایت‌افرازی‌دورلار و حضرت پیغمبر علیه السلام دینی‌نینک حمایتی ذات شریف‌لاریغه منحصردور بو مخلِص‌نینک آرزوسی |102b| بودورکیم رکاب والالاریغه مشرف بولوب جان‌فشان‌لیق و خذمت‌کذارلیق مراسمین تقدیمغه بیتکورسه و ینه آرزوسی اولدورکیم شرف حضور والالاریغه مشرف بولسه ایمدی‌کیم دلالت و التماس‌لاری برکتی‌دین منازعت و مخالفت برطرف بولوب فراغت حاصل بولدی بیغین و لشکر اسبابی اوچون کوب سعی کورکوزوب بو صدددادورکیم سپاه رزمخواه ظفرهمراه و توبخانه و قورخانه بیله خذمت عالی‌لاریغه بیتوشسه و مارچاقدا حضورلاری شرفیغه مشرف بولسه خواه خراسان طرفیغه خواه بخارا طرفیغه صلاح بیلیب خذمت بویورسه‌لار جان بیله

خذمت قیلسه لیکن سفر اسبابی اوچون مبلغ خطیر و کوب نمرسه خرج و صرف قیلغاندورلار بیر ایشی قیلسه‌لارکیم مبلغ مذکور بیهوده صرف بولماغای امید بودورکیم |103a| مارچاقدا یکرمه کون توقف قیلسه‌لار تا همه اسباب مهیّا بولوب خذمت‌لاریغه مشرف[1] بولسام فرمایش عالی‌لاریغه منتظردورمن‌کیم بیر آدم و مرحمت‌نامهٔ ییتوشسه بی‌توقف خذمت عالی‌لاریغه ییتوشکوم‌دور دیب عرضه‌داشت[2] بیتلدی

و شنبه کونی قاصد بادیه‌پیمای نظر بای حضرت پادشاه عالم و شهنشاه مکرم سلیمانجاه دارادستگاه قبله‌گاه‌لاری خوارزمشاه روحنا و روح العالمین فداه‌نینک جانب دولت‌جوانب‌لاریدین مبارک یارلیغ‌لاری ایصالی بیله‌کیم مضمونی روضه‌سی‌نینک فرحت‌شمیم نسیمی جان مشامین معطر و عطرپرور قیلیب بهجت و مسرت ریاحینی انواعین کونکول‌لار گلستانیدا آچتی و اوشبو یارلیغ سطوریغه نظر سالماق بیله داعی کوزیمنی |103b| پرنور قیلا آلمادیم و یکشنبه کونی مبارک وجود مسعودلاری‌نینک مع التوابع و اللواحق صحت و عافیت‌غه مقرون ایرکانین اخلاص و اعتقادلی بیرام یاغلی بیله پادشاه باتخت و جاه قبله‌گاه‌لاری خوارزمشاه دام دولته حضرت‌لاریغه عرضه‌داشت قیلیب ییباردیلار و سه‌شنبه کونی قاصد سریع السیر و سرعت بابیدا چون طیر اخلاص‌همدم ویس محرم حضرت بادشاه والاجاه فلک‌بارگاه جناب مستطاب خوارزمشاه سلمه الله تعالی‌نینک میمون و مبارک یارلیغ‌لاری اصداری بیله‌کیم الفاظی نزاهت‌دا

---

1 مشرف above the line.

2 عریضه‌داشت.

فرحت‌بخشا و عباراتی نزاکتدا مسرّت‌افزادور شهزادهٔ سپهرمرتبت بهرام‌صولت دام نصرته باشلیق مهاجرلار فرقین فرقدان |104a| فرقیدین اوتکاردی و اول یارلیغ الفاظی جواهری تحریر سلکیکا بو نوع[1] انتظام تاپمیش‌دور

کرم محیطی‌نینک درخشان کوهری حکومت بُرجی‌نینک تابان اختری عزت‌پناه شوکت و عظمت‌دستکاه رفیع‌مکان قرة العینی‌میز شهزاده رحیم قلی سلطان زاد الله فتحه و نصرته‌غه یارلیغ کورکاچ اولکیم الحمد لله تعالی فقرا و رعایا حمایتی‌میز چتری‌نینک سایه‌سیدا فارغ البال‌لیق بیله دولت ابدمدتیمیز استدامتی‌غه تینکریتعالی درکاهی‌دین مستدعی بولوب بارچه متعلقاتیمیز صغاراً و کباراً ذات والاسماتیمیز باشلیق صحت و عافیت مسندی اوزه مقیم فرحت و مسرت اورنکی‌دا مستقیم بولوب اول نور چشمی‌نینک فتح |104b| و نصرتی دعاسیغه صلوات خمسه اداسیدین سونک[2] اشتغال کورکوزورمیز دعادین سونک اول نور چشمی‌نینک خاطر اخلاص‌ذخایریغه واضح بولسونکیم بو عنایت‌نامهٔ عالیه بیتوشکاچ زیارت سراسرخاصیتیمیز ساری مراجعت کورکوزوب متوجه بولسون دیب اشتیاق نهایتی‌دین بو عنایت‌نامه بیتلدی

و جمعه کونی مشهد حاکمی آصف الدوله‌نینک ایلچی‌لاریکیم محمد حکیم خان بیله محمد حسن بیک تبریزی‌دور مذکور حاکم عرضه‌داشتین آستانهٔ معلی

---

1 بو نوع above the line.

2 سونک above the line.

ملازم‌لاری‌نینک واسطه‌سی بیله نظر اقدس‌لاری‌غه منظور قیلیب اوزلاری هم بارکاه سپهراشتباه‌لاری عتبه‌بوسلیقی شرفیغه اول کون[1] مشرف بولدی‌لار |105a| و آلارنینک کیلمیش‌لاری بیر آز کفتکُوی اِداره‌سیدین سونک خفا پرده‌سیدین چهره‌نما بولدیکیم اولوجه‌دین ایرکانکیم خان‌نایب‌کیم محمد شاه قاچارنینک اقرباسیدین آصف الدولهٔ مذکوره‌غه مصاهرت[2] نسبتی باردور و تبریز شهری‌نینک حاکمی‌دور سالور خلقی‌نینک مبارزت‌پناه غازی‌لاری مشهد اطراف و جوانبی‌دا اولتورملی شیعهٔ شنیعه‌نی بو سنه‌دین بورونغی سنه‌دا تاخت و تاز قیلیب مذکور نایب‌نی اسارت قیدیغه چیکیب یانیداغی بیحد لشکریکا هزیمت بیریب آندین کوب کیشی‌نی قتل‌غه بیتکوروب اوزین حضرت خوارزمشاه روحنا فداه دربارلاریغه آلیب باریب خوارزم دار السلطنه‌سی زندانیدا محبوس قیلیب |105b| ایردی‌لار آنی اسارت قیدیدین خلاص قیلیب مرخَّص قیلسه‌لار و تازه‌دین عهد و پیمان باغلاب موندین بویان تاخت و تاراج مراسمین[3] برهم اورولوب ایکی دولت اورتاسیدا مزاحمت و مداخلت قواعدی‌نینک بناسی انهدام تاپسه چون سلطان صاحبقران زاد الله رواج شوکته مذکور ایلچی‌لار کیلمیش‌لاریدین اغراضی‌غه وقوف پیدا قیلدیلار حضرت پادشاه کیوان‌بارکاه قبله‌کاه‌لاری خوارزمشاه دام دولته خذمت‌لاریغه یوللاماقچی بولوب موقوف بیر نیچه کون قویدی‌لار و صفر[4] آیی‌نینک ایکینجی دوشنبه کونی غلام اخلاص‌توأم‌لاری عابدین محرم

---

[1] Altered from سرکشته‌لار (?).

[2] مصاهرة.

[3] Read مراسمی.

[4] سفر.

حضرت پادشاه انجم‌سپاه جناب مستطاب خوارزمشاه روحنا فداه |106a| طرف‌لاریدین مبارک یارلیغ تبلیغی بیله سلطان سپهرمکان باشلیق درکاه عالی دولتخواه‌لاری‌نینک باشین سماوات طبقاتیدین اوتکاردی نظم

قاصد بو کون بیتوردی عجب یارلیغ بلیغ
کیم ایردی سر بسر فرح و جانفزا نوید
فرحت‌فزا عبارتی انفاسی عیسوی یانکلیغ
فسرده جسمیمه جان ایلادی کرم جاوید

و مذکور آی‌نینک تورتونجی چهارشنبه کونی مذکور ایلچی‌لارنینک نی یوسوندا کیلمیش‌لارین عرضه‌داشت قیلیب پادشاه والاجاه کردون‌دستکاه خوارزمشاه سلمه الله تعالی حضرت‌لاریغه یوموت نظر بای سابق الذکر بیله ارسال قیلدی‌لار و همولکون محمد نیاز خلیفه‌غه عنایت‌نامه‌لارین تفویض قیلیب دری جز حاکمی سلیمان خان ساری یوللادی‌لار و همولکون |106b| شجاعت‌پناه‌لار جلادت‌دستکاه‌لار آدینه بای اتالیق و شاهمراد ایناق بیله ینه نیچه سرکرده‌لارکیم حضرت خوارزمشاه مد ظله العالی سلطان صاحبقران خدمت‌لاریغه بویوروب ییباریب ایردیلار آستانهٔ دولت‌نشانه‌لاری خاکبوسلیقی شرفیغه مشرف بولدیلار و بو ایکی سپهبد ذکریکا اکتفا ایتیب اوزکا سرکرده‌لار اسامی‌سی ذکریدین کلک عاجزی‌سلک خوفاً للاطناب اوزنی معاف توتتی و ایرتاسی پنجشنبه کونی مذکور ایلچی‌لارنی اخلاص‌کیش اعتقاداندیش خلیفه بیکیش بیله قوشوب قبله‌کاه‌لاری روحنا فداه خدمت‌لاریغه یوللادیلار و موندین ایکی کون

سونک کیم شنبه کونی ایردی امیر الامرا خلاصة الوزرا دستور آصف‌نهاد اتا مراد قوشبیکی‌نی بویوردیلارکیم جمشیدی طوایفی‌نینک |107a| قالغان بارچه‌سیغه تیوه بیریب کوچوروب ییبارکای[1] چون وزیر صایب‌تدبیرکیم مأمور بولدی فرمان واجب الاذعان مؤدّاسینچه طوایف مذکوره ایچیکا هر کون باریب طایفه طایفه تیوه بیریب کوچوروب دوشنبه کونی نماز شام وقتی تمام قیلیب درکاه کیهان‌پناه ساری مراجعت کورکوزوب کوچ اخیری‌نینک اتمامین عرض طریقیدا اعلام قیلغان‌دین سونک نیاز محمد بای مذکورنینک اوغلی خدای بیرکان بای بیله عبد الله یساولباشیغه طوایف مذکوره‌نینک آب و آزوقه‌سی اوچون نیچه تیوه‌نی سو و آزوقه یوکلاتیب تفویض قیلیب کوچ‌نینک ایلکاری و کینی‌دین و میمنه و میسره‌سیدین |107b| خبردارلیق قیلینک دیب بویوروب ییباردیلار و موندین سونک[2] ایکینجی چهارشنبه کونی علما و اُمرا اهلیغه ضیافت کوناکون قیلیب سالور و ساریق‌نینک حاکم‌لاری باشلیق بیک و کدخدا مردم‌لارین[3] سروپای شاهانه اعطاسی بیله سربلند و ارجمند قیلدیلار و ایرتاسی پنجشنبه کونی حضرت خدیو کامکار و خسرو بختیار پادشاه سپهردرکاه قبله‌کاه‌لاری خوارزمشاه روحنا فداه خذمت‌لاریغه آبروی تمام بیله مراجعت کورکوزوب متوجه بولغان‌لارین عرضه‌داشت ایتیب خذمت بابیدا ثابت‌قدم ویس محرم بیله ارسال قیلیب اوزلاری هم صولت تمام و هیبت مالاکلام بیله[4] کرنایلاتیب و توب

---

[1] ییبارکای altered from ییبارماک. Hereafter crossed-out اوچون بویوردیلار.

[2] سونک above the line.

[3] مردم added later.

[4] بیله above the line.

آتدوروب بنی آدم اورتاسیغه غلغل و یر و کوک اجزاسیغه تزلزل سالیب |108a| زرین‌لجام اشهب‌لاریکا راکب بولوب آفتاب عالمتاب فلک قورغانیدین اشراق قیلغاندیک بای مذکورنینک بنا قیلغان حصاریدین چیقیب اساسه و دبدبه بیله یوروش کورکوزوب قبله‌گاه‌لاری خوارزمشاه طول الله ایام عمره و دولته‌نینک سراسرخاصیت خذمت‌لاریغه متوجه بولدیلار نظم

چیقتی اولکون خدیو فرخ‌فال　　بولوبان طرفه خوشدل و خوشحال
آنچه‌کیم شوکت ایلادی صادر　　تاغ‌دین بولدی رعشه‌لار ظاهر
زلزله توشتی بحر و بر ایچرا　　ولوله کوه ایله کمر ایچرا
صولتی‌دین سپهر بولدی پست　　قلّه‌لارغه شکوهی بیردی شکست
کرنای آوازی هم فلک‌دین آشیب　　توب صداسی داغی آنکا یاناشیب
تاپیبان نصرت اوستیکا |108b| نصرت　　ینه فرحت اوزه تاپیب فرحت
بیعدد شوقُ آرزو بیرلان　　مینک تومان فتح و آبرو بیرلان
داور دادکر خدیو جهان　　بولدی خوارزم جانبی‌غه روان
تینکری لطف ایلابان آنکا موفور　　حاصل ایتکای باری ایشیدا سرور

چون سلطان صاحبقران بو نوع شوکت و صولت بیله روان بولدی‌لار یول اثناسیدا بیرام علی خان‌نینک خراب بولغان قلعه‌سین تماشا قیلیب سلطان قلعه‌سی محاذی‌سیدین عبور ایتیب قوی قلعه‌سی آتلیغ جایغه‌کیم قلعهٔ مذکوره‌نینک جنوبی طرفیدا واقع‌دور نزول قیلدی‌لار بیت

قدومـی بیلـه داور جم‌شـیم بـو منزلنـی قیلدی چو بـاغ ارم

و اول اقشام مذکور جایدا آرام آلیب ایرتاسی جمعه کونی غایت‌سیز آبرو و نصرت |109a| و نهایت‌سیز فرح و بهجت بیرله مراجعت‌لاری خبرین عنایت‌نامه‌لاری ایچیدا دَرج ایتیب تاش قورغان حاکمی والی بیککا و سرپُل خانی محمود خانغه و شاهمردان خانی شجاع الدین خانغه و بلخ حکمرانی ایشان اوراغغه و آنت‌خوی خانی شاه ولی خانغه یوموت بابا سردار بیله ارسال قیلدی‌لار و محمود خانغه ارسال تاپغان عنایت‌نامه سوادی بو تورور

ارادت‌اطوار عقیدت‌کردار رفیع‌مکان محمود خانغه یارلیغ کورکاچ اولکیم حضرت پادشاه انجم‌سپاه جناب مستطاب قبله‌کاهیمیز خوارزمشاه سلمه الله تعالی جانب شرافت‌جوانب‌لاریدین بیزکا موندینکدیک یارلیغ کیلدیکیم درکاه جهان‌پناهی‌میز ساری توجه کورکوزوب ملاقاتیمیز دولتی‌غه فایز بولسون لهٰذا |109b| بو امر دولت‌اثر امتثالین لازم بیلیب دولت بیله مراجعت کورکوزوب اوز حضرتیمیز خدمت‌لاری ساری عازم بولدوق انشاء الله تعالی ینه بوغدای پیشکان وقتدا رایت ظفرآیتیمیز بو اطرافدا شقه‌کشا بولوب بعضی معاند و سرکش‌لارنینک تنبیه و کوشمالین کما ینبغی بیتکورکومیزدور دیب صفر[1] آیی‌نیدک اون اوچونجی جمعه کونی بو عنابت‌نامهٔ عالی بیتلدی

---

[1] سفر.

و اوزکا عنایت‌نامه‌لار داغی اوشبو مضموندا بیتیلیب مرسول توتولدی چون سلطان صاحبقران مذکور امور اهتمامی‌دین فارغ بولدی‌لار دبدبۂ سلطانیه بیله آتلانیب بیر نیچه مرحله‌نی قطع قیلیب مجاور کولی‌نینک لبیکاکیم سلطان قلعه‌سی‌نینک غربی طرفیداکیم اول قلعه‌غه بیر فرسخ مسافتینچه یول باردور |110a| نزول و هبوط بویوردیلار نظم

ایلابـان کـوب شـکوهٔ کیـرُدار　　کامـکار جهـانُ دهرمـدار
قیلـدی اول داور فریدون‌فـر　　دولـت ایله کیلیب بـو یرنی مقر

چون خدیو کامکار و کامل بختیار اول یرنی آرامکاه قیلدی‌لار اولکیچه اولجایدا آرام آلیب ایرتاسی شنبه کونی دولت بیله آتلانیب لشکر اهلی اوچون بی‌نهایت تیوه‌لارکا سو یوکلاتیب بیر نیچه منزلنی طی قیلیب کشمان میدانین نزول شرافت‌وصول‌لاری بیله چون روضۂ رضوان قیلدیلار بیت

توشـوب اول یرکا صفـدر دوران　　قیلـدی آنی چو روضـۂ رضوان

چون حضرت سلطانکیم اول میداندا سرادق چرخ‌فایق‌لارین برپا قیلدوردیلار تا کیچه یاریمی‌غه‌چه راحت ایتی‌لار آندین سونکرا صباسیرلاریکا |110b| سوار بولوب بامداد نمازین یولدا ادا قیلیب یکشنبه کونی چاشت وقتی کیلیب ترخان قودوقیدین اوتوب نزول و هبوط قیلدی‌لار و اول منزلدا پیشین‌کا تیکرو استراحت قیلیب پیشین نمازی اداسیدین سونکرا حرکت کورکوزوب عصر چاغی یانتاقلی

سرحدیکا قدوم‌لاری شرفی بیله شرافت ییتکوردیلار نظم

سپاهی بیرلـه اول دارای دوران	طی ایلاب بیر نیچه دشتُ بیابان
مسـرَّت بیرلـه اول دوران همامی	کیلیب یانتاقلی‌نی قیلدی مقامی
قدومـی بیرله اول کان سـعادت	بو سرحد ایچرا ییتکوردی طراوت

چون اول بهرام‌صولت فریدون‌مکنت عطاردفطرت مشتری‌خاصیت اعنی سلطان صاحبقران |111a| زاد الله[1] فرحته و نصرته‌کیم مذکور یرنی[2] قدوم شرافت‌لزوم‌لاری بیله بهشت‌آیین و نزول سعادت‌وصول‌لاری بیله ارم‌تزیین قیلدیلار اول کیچه مذکور سرحددا آرام آلیب ایرتاسی دوشنبه کونی ایرتانک نمازی اداسیدین سونکرا رخش راحت‌بخش‌لاریغه رکوب قیلیب سپاه نصرت‌پناه‌لاری بیله بیر نیچه مسافت راه قطعین تقدیمغه ییتکوروب سِرطلانلی بیله یانتاقلی اورتاسیدا واقع بولغان بیر ریکزار اوستیکا دولت تمام بیله کیلیب توشتی‌لار و اول ریکزار اوستیدا تا کیچه نصفیکاچه توقف کورکوزوب کیچه نصفی‌دین سونک دولت بیله آتلانیب شبکیر قیلیب تانک نمازین یولدا ادا قیلیب سه‌شنبه کونی چاشت وقتی سرطلانلی قودوقیدین اوتوب نزول بویوردیلار |111b| نظم

توتتی سـلطان بو یـردا جون آرام	قیلدی پیشین‌کا تیکرو آنی مقام
سونکرا آتلاندی اول خدیو جهان	کوب شکوه ایله یولغه بولدی روان

---

[1] لله.

[2] Altered from یرکا.

قطع ایتیب نیچه یولنی اول کامل　　　کیلیب ایتــی اوجارلی‌نــی منزل

چون سلطان صاحبقران نزول سعادت‌وصول‌لاری بیله اوجارلی سرحدین فردوس‌آیین قیلدیلار دستور آصف‌نهاد اتا مراد قوشبیکی سلمه الله تعالی‌غه بویوردیلارکیم یوزباشی‌لارغه بیر بلند قوم اوستیکا اوتون جمع ایتدورکای و بو امردین غرض‌لاری اولکیم بیر بیچاره و غریبی یولدین آزمیش بولسه بو علامت و نشانه‌نی کوروب یولین توز و راست قیلا آلغای و چون بو فرمان واجب الاذعان صدورین استماع قیلدی‌لار یوزباشی‌لار توش توش‌دین |112a| اولمقدار اوتون جمع ایتی‌لارکیم کوییا اوتوندین بیر کوهی نمودار بولدیکیم اولمنزل سلطان اویوقی دیب لقب کوتاردی نظم

وزیــر صــاف‌رایُ پاک‌تخمیــر　　　ســپهبدلارکا اعلام ایتــی بیر بیر
باری یوزباشی‌لار بی‌قال ایله قیل　　　اوتون جمع ایلاماککا قیلدی تعجیل
نفس آلغونچه اول خیل ایله سرکار　　　اوتوندیــن قیلدیلار کوهی نمودار
نی یانکلیغ کوه عظیم الشأن کوهی　　　یر و کوک صورتین بوزدی شکوهی
باشی ایلاب فلک سطحینی سوده　　　اشــاغی یرنی ایــلاب ریک‌توده
بو یانکلیغ امرنی کیم کوردیلار ایب　　　ملقّب بولدی سلطان اویوقی دیب

چون خدیو فرخ‌سیر و بختیار فریدون‌فرکیم اوشبو منزلنی آرامکاه قیلدیلار کیچه یاریمی‌غه‌چه توقف کورکوزوب آندین سونک اسرو کروفر |112b| بیله آتلانیب لشکر ظفراثرلاری بیله حرکت قیلیب شبکیر اوروب تانک نمازین

یول قطعی اثناسیدا ادا قیلیب چهارشنبه کونی چاشت وقتی بیر قوم اوستیکا کیلیب توشتی‌لار و اول یردا تا پیشین‌کا تیکرو مکث کورکوزوب پیشین نمازی اداسیدین سونکرا رخش خوشخرام‌لاریغه رکوب تمام کورکوزوب مذکور یردین جنود نصرت‌نمودلاری بیله حرکت قیلیب شوکت مالاکلام بیله بیر نیچه منازل قطعین تقدیمغه بیتکوروب تخت‌نی مقام قیلدی‌لار نظم

داور عادل جهان‌آرا تخت‌نی چونکه ایلادی مأوا
مقدمیدین بیتوردی پیرایه تخت‌نی ایلادی بلندپایه

چون سلطان عادل و شجاع کامل‌کیم تخت‌نی آرامکاه قیلدی‌لار تا یاریم کیچه‌کا تیکرو توقف قیلیب آندین سونکرا بُراق‌نمودار |113a| برق‌رفتار آت‌لاریغه راکب بولوب شبکیر ایتیب بامداد نمازین اعتقاد بیله یولدا ادا قیلیب بیر نیچه بلند و پست ریکزاردین اسرو کیرُدار بیله کذار قیلیب اول جمشیداطوار پنجشنبه کونی چاشت وقتی حوض خانغه توشوب آنی بهشت‌آثار قیلدیلار و اول منزلدا خادم معظم ناظم مصالح بنی آدم خذمتکارلار خوب و نیکی بکنیاز دیوان بیکی‌کیم آنی[1] حضرت پادشاه کیوان‌بارکاه دارادستکاه ابو المظفر و المنصور خوارزمشاه مد ظله العالی جمشیدی‌لار کوچی اهتمامی اوچون بویوروب قاباقلی سرحدیکا ییباریب ایردیلار غایت‌سیز خوشحال‌ایق بیله استقبال یوسونیدا اول سلطان بلنداقبال عتبهٔ علیه‌سی‌نینک توتیا |113b| مثال خاکی

[1] آنی above the line.

بیله کوزین روشن و دیدار فیض‌آثارلاری کلی‌نینک بهجت‌شمیم نسیمی بیله خاطرین کلشن قیلدی و مذکور جایدا آفتاب‌نینک نصف النهار خطی‌دین نزولیغه‌چه توقف قیلیب صلوة ظهر اداسین داغی اول یردا تقدیمغه بیتکوروب کوب شوکت بیله آتلانیب دبدبۀ خسروانه بیله یول قطعی‌غه روانه بولوب عصردین بورونراق کیلیب قاباقلی سرمنزلین آرام اوچون مقام قیلدی‌لار نظم

داور جم‌شیم سیامک‌رزم — قطع ایلاب چو هفت ریک خوارزم
چیقتی صحت سلامت اول قوم‌دین — تشنه‌لیک خوفیدین بولوب ایمن
تاپیبان فتح حد و غایت‌سیز — فرح و شادلیق نهایت‌سیز
آبروی تمام ایله سلطان — توتتی دریا کناری|114a|ایچرا مکان
لشکر اهلی داغی بولوب مسرور — تاپتی‌لار بحر ساحلیدا حضور
قایسی دریاکیم آتیدور جیحون — سویی آب حیات‌دین افزون
یعنی خاصیتی حیات‌افزا — یوق مونینکدیک جهان ارا دریا
سویین ایچکان کیشیکا بو که اُمید — کورماکای دوزخ اوتینی جاوید
بویله دریا لبی‌نی لشکرکاه — ایلادی آندا توتدوروب خرکاه

چون سلطان صاحبقران دام فرحته اولکیچه‌کیم جمعه کیچه‌سی ایردی مذکور سرمنزلدا آرام آلدیلار ایرتاسی جمعه کونی امارت‌پناه وزارت‌دستکاه دستور آصف‌نهاد اتا مراد قوشبیکی‌نی سابق الذکر سرکرده‌لارکا باش قیلیب طوغ ظفرفروغ‌لار یانیدا دریا کناریدین بویوروب ییباردی‌لار |114b| و اوزلاری بیر نیچه مخصوص محرم و چاکرلاری بیله هلال‌مثال زورقچه‌لارغه مینیب دریای آمویه

ایچی بیله سیر قیلیب ماه‌مانند سیمکون ماهی‌لارنی سانچتوروب کیچ‌قورون بولغاندا کیلیب دریا کناریغه دایه خاتون سرمنزلیغه چیقیب آرام آلدیلار نظم

اول سحاب کرم محیط اعطا — اوشبو کون سیر و کشت ایتیب دریا
زورق ایچرا خدیو دریادل — کوب تماشالار ایلابان حاصل
کیچ چیقیب اول غضنفرصفدر — دایه خاتون محلین ایتی مقر

چون سلطان سپهرمکان کیم مذکور منزلنی آرامگاه قیلدی‌لار خفتن نمازی اداسیدین سونکرا تینکریتعالی هدایتی بیله صحت و سلامت مع التوابع و اللواحق چولدین چیقیب بو منزلکا کیلیب نزول قیلغان‌لارین |115a| عرضه‌داشت ایتیب حضرت پادشاه اعظم و شهنشاه مکرم کیوان‌بارگاه قبله‌گاه‌لاری خوارزمشاه روحنا فداه‌نینک سراسرخاصیت خذمت‌لاریغه بیرام یاغلی بیله ارسال قیلدی‌لار ایرتاسی شنبه کونی ینه بورونغی دستور بیله وزیر مذکورنی سرکرده‌لار بیله دریا ساحلیدین طوغ‌لار بیرله ییباریب اوزلاری بیر نیچه محرم‌لار بیله مقوّس کیمه‌لارکا سوار بولوب دریا عجایب و غرایبین تماشا قیلیب کیچ بولغان چاغدا آت‌خور سرحدیکا چیقیب دریا کناریدا قرار توتتی‌لار نظم

ینه اول اختر برج جلالت — درخشان گوهر بحر عدالت
بولوب دریا ایچی بیرله روانه — ایتیب کوب کیرودار خسروانه
|115b| بو کون زورق ارا اول عالم‌آرا — ایتیب کیچکا دیکین سیر و تماشا
چیقیب کیچه مقامی بولدی آت‌خور — سراسر مقدمی‌دین بولدی پرنور

چون ایرتاسی یکشنبه صبحی خورشید سلطانی سپهر عمّانی ایچرا روان بولوب شعاع چاووش و چاکرلاریکا امر قیلیب الویۀ لمعات بیله اول بحر کناریدین ارسال قیلدی سلطان صاحبقران عظّم الله شانه ینه اولغی کونداکی یوسوندا وزیر مذکورنی مزبور آدم‌لار بیله رأیت نصرت‌آیت‌لار یانیدا قیراغ بیله ییباریب اوزلاری بیر نیچه مخصوص‌لار بیله کیمه‌کا مینیب دریا غرایبی تماشاسی بیله روان بولوب کیچ بولغاندا دریادین چیقیب قرا آیغیر بیشه‌سین |116a| خیمه و خرکاه‌لاری بیله عسکرلاریکا قرارکاه قیلدیلار چون ایرتاسی دوشنبه صبحی غایت‌سیز طُمطراق بیله سلطان بیضا کیچه‌دا فراقی وادیسی‌نینک لب‌تشنه‌لاریکا وصالی ضیاسی‌نینک زلالی بیله سیراب‌لیق و شاداب‌لیق ییتکوردی سلطان بختیار و کامران نامدار ینه سابقداغی دستوردا وزیر صایب‌تدبیر بیله مزبور سپهبدلارنی لوای ظفرانتمالار یانیدا ییباریب اوزلاری بیر نیچه مخصوص‌لار بیله بادرفتار کیمه‌لارکا سوار بولوب بحر امواجی تلاطمی‌نینک[1] تماشاسین قیلیب مقصد ساری روان بولدیلار[2] و همولکون حکومت دودمانی‌نینک سلاله‌سی منزلت و خلافت خاندانی‌نینک خلاصه‌سی کامکارلیق بحری‌نینک |116b| در یکدانه‌سی بختیارلیق تاجی‌نینک لعل شاهانه‌سی نظم

خلافت برجیدا رخشنده اختر	حکومت درجیدا تابنده کوهر
ایالت بوستانی نونهالی	سماء منزلت فرخ هلالی
یوزیدین مکرمت آثاری پیدا	سوزیدین معدلت امری هویدا

[1] طلاطمی‌نینک.

[2] بولدیلار above the line.

الٓهــی تــوت وجودین تــا قیامت حکومت مسندی اوزره سلامت

اعنی رفیع‌مکان بابا جان توره طول الله عمره و شوکته غایت‌سیز خوشحاللیق‌لار بیله اقالاری استقبالی اوچون سودوک سرحدیکا تشریف بویوروب ایرکانلار چون وزیر صایب‌تدبیر مذکور سرکرده‌لار بیله مزبور موضع‌غه کیلیب شهزادهٔ مذکورنینک دیدار فیض‌آثارلاریدین بهره‌مندلیک درجه‌سین تاپتی‌لار و آلار تقریریدین سلطان |117a| صاحبقران اعلی الله قدره‌نینک بحر ایچی بیله کیلمیش‌لارین استماع ایتی شهزادهٔ عالیجناب‌نینک شوقی غالب بولوب اول یردا استقرار قیلا آلمای قاییق‌غه مینیب دریا ایچی بیله آلدلاریکا روان بولوب بیراز مسافت‌نی قطع قیلغاندین سونک دریا ایچیدا ملاقات مسرت‌علامات واقع بولوب بیراو بیراولاری‌نینک دیدار فیض‌آثارلاریدین فرحت اوزره فرحت تاپیب وصال زلالی بیله بیراو بیراونینک فراقی تشنه‌لیکی‌نینک اوتیغه تسکین بیردیلار و مونینکدیک نهایت‌سیز مسرت بیله ایکی شهزادهٔ آزاده[1] قوشولوب کیلیب ایکی اختر سعد بیر برجدا قران قیلغاندیک مذکور منزلنی مکان قیلدیلار و اوزکا کیچیک شهزاده و بیک‌لار داغی |117b| همول منزلدا دیدار مسرت‌آثارلاریدین بهره‌مند بولدیلار و هزاراسب علمالاری داغی فرحت مالامال بیله استقبال قیلیب تومان مینک امانی[2] و آمال[3] بیله عتبه‌بوسلیق شرفیغه مشرف بولوب ملاقات‌لاری دولتین تاپیب دعا مراسمین تقدیمغه بیتکوردیلار و ایرتاسی

---

1 .ازاده

2 .آمابی

3 .امال

سه‌شنبه کونی مذکور منزلدا علما و امرا اهلیکا ضیافت شاهانه بیریب بارچه‌سین قویاش صفحه‌سیدیک زرین لباس‌لار انعام و ایصالی بیله خوشحال قیلدیلار آندین سونکرا اسرو کروفر و شکوه قیامت‌اثر بیله آتلانیب آت‌چاپارکاه‌غه باریب بادرفتار براق‌نمودار آت‌لارنی چاپتوروب شجاعت‌اطوار رستم‌وار پهلوان‌لارنی کوراش توتتوروب هر بیرین انعام‌لاری نقودی بیله غنا مقامی‌غه ییتکوردیلار و آفتاب‌نینک نصف النهار |118a| خطیدین توشوب مغرب ساری میلانیغه‌چه بو نوع تماشالار صیقلی بیله کونکول‌لاری مرآتیغه صفا ییتکوروب آندین سونک ینه اسرو کیرودار بیله کیلیب بادرفتار کیمه‌لارکا سوار بولوب وزیر صایب‌تدبیرنی مذکور سپهبدلار بیله کناردین ییباریب دریا تماشاسی بیله روان بولوب کیچ بولغاندا چیقیب تیوه بویون سرمنزلین قدوم شرافت‌لزوم‌لاری بیله ارم‌نمون قیلدیلار چون ایرتاسی چهارشنبه کونی‌نینک صبحی مهر سلطانی نور عسکری بیله مشرق سرمنزلیدین طلوع ایتیب[1] افلاک قلعه‌سی ساری توجُّه کورکوزدی سلطان صاحبقران عظَّم الله قدره غایت‌سیز شوکت و نهایت‌سیز صولت بیله رخش خوشخرام‌لاریغه راکب بولوب اول یردین حرکت |118b| کورکوزوب یول قطعی اثناسیدا بیر نیچه جلد و چالاک بهادرلار شمشیربازلیق و تفنک‌اندازلیق[2] بیله طَرید[3] آغاز قیلیب اولمقدار ایش‌لار اظهار قیلدیلارکیم فلک دوار شعبده‌بازی حیرت کوزی بیله نظاره‌کر بولوب حسرت انکشتین تیشلادی و بو نوع اساسه و دبدبه بیله فتناک قلعه‌سیدین عبور ایتیب بیر میدانغه‌کیم قلعه مذکوره

---

1 آیتیب.

2 توفنک‌اندازلیق.

3 طُرید.

بیله هزاراسب توابعاتی اورتاسیدا واقع‌دور دولت تمام بیله[1] بیتکان وقتلاریدا حقایق‌پناه‌لار معارف‌دستکاه‌لار هدایت اهلی مقتدالاری ولایت زمره‌سی‌نینک مرشد و پیشوالاری معرفت‌نشان‌لار الله قلی ایشان بیله[1] قاضی محمد صادق خواجه ایشان ایکاولاری استقبال طریقه‌سی بیله چیقیب مصافحه‌لاری دولتی بیله خوشحال |119a| بولوب دعای خیر قیلغان‌لاریدین سونکرا بویوردیلارکیم اول ایکی عزیز رایت نصرت‌آیت‌لار یانیدا پیشکاه‌دا یورسون‌لار و بو امر دولت‌اثر موجبینچه اول ولایت‌پناه‌لار داغی لشکر ظفراثر آلدیدا خضر بیله الیاس رهبر بولغاندیک روان بولدیلار و چون سلطان صاحبقران اول ایکی عزیزنی زیارت ایتیب شوکت خسروانه بیله یول قطعی‌غه روانه بولدیلار مذکور بهادرلار ینه بیر بیرلاریکا حملات متعاقبه و ضربات متوالیه بیله اویون‌لار آشکار ایتی‌لارکیم خلایق حیرت غلبه‌سیدین سکوت اختیار قیلیب سپهر بوقلمون طریدپردازلاری بو امور ظهوریدین دنک و مبهوت بولدیلار نظم

بولوب نیزه‌ورلار باری بیر طرف تفنکچی[2] داغی بیرطرف |119b| نیچه‌صف
نیچه مینک او یان و نیچه مینک بو یان بولوب بویله پرخاش رسمی عیان
ایرور کوییا بارچه رخشنده برق بولوب پیکری کوک تیمور ایچرا غرق
بهادرلار اولنوع جولان قیلیب فلک چهره‌سین کرد پنهان قیلیب
هوا اوزره کرد ایلا ساکن بولوب که آت یورسه کرد اوزره ممکن بولوب
ایتیب بیر بیریکا عیان حمله‌لار یتیب بیر بیریدین بسی ضربه‌لار

---

[1] بیله above the line.

[2] توفنکچی.

تفنک[1] اژدری آغزیدین اوت ساچیب   فلک خصمی نینک هوشی آندین قاچیب
شهاب سنان هر قایان کیم سونوب   آنینک بیمی‌دین چرخ رنکی دونوب
مونینکدیک نیچه صف مهیا قیلیب   آتیب چاقماقی چاقماقی چاقیلیب
ایتیب کرنای آوازی آنداق اثر   فلک سمعینی بو زمان ایتی کر
توب آوازی |120a| داغی فلک‌دین عبور   ایتیب بولدی کویا که یوم النشور

بو نوع اساسه و دبدبه بیله کیلیب هزاراسب قلعه‌سیغه دخول شرافت‌وصول‌لاری بیله شرافت بیتکوروب قلعهٔ مذکوره اهلی‌نینک دیدهٔ فراق‌دیده‌لارین تکاورلاری توپناغی‌نینک غبار توتیاآثارلاری بیله روشن و خاطرلارین دیدار مسرت‌نمودارلاری کلی بیله کلشن قیلدیلار نظم

دولت ایله بو قلعه‌غه سلطان   کیریب ایتی آنی چو باغ جنان
آتی توزیدین ایل کوزی روشن   بولدی قلعه قدومیدین کلشن
تاپتی اهلی بسی سرورُ فرح   کیشی ایچکان کیبی مدام قدح

چون سلطان صاحبقران کیم قدوم ظفرلزوم‌لاری بیله[2] قلعهٔ مذکوره‌غه طراوت تازه و نضارت بی‌اندازه بغیشلاب کیچه آندا استراحت ایتی‌لار |120b| ایرتاسی پنجشنبه کونی مذکور حصاردا علما و اُمَرا اهلیکا کوناکون ضیافت قیلیب دعای خیرلارین آلیب آفتاب عالمتاب مشرق حصاریدین طلوع ایتکاندیک

---

1 توفنک.

2 بیله above the line.

قلعهٔ مذکوره‌دین اساسهٔ تمام و دبدبهٔ مالاکلام بیله چیقیب خیوق صانها الله تعالی عن الحرق و الغرق دار السلطنه‌سی ساری نهضت ایتیب متوجه بولدیلار و بو کون داغی مذکور مبارز و بهادرلار یول قطعی اثناسیدا اوتکان کونداکی یانکلیغ اولمقدار اویون‌لار آشکار ایتی‌لارکیم سپهر مبارزی حیرت استیلاسیدین تحسُّر ابهامین تیشلادی و بو طریقه کیردار قیامت‌آثار بیله بیر نیچه میدان قطعین تقدیمغه بیتکوروب صولت و شوکت مالامال بیله کیلیب یانکی آریق حولی‌لاریکاکیم موروثی هامن‌لاریدور |121a| نزول اجلال بویوردیلار نظم

اول کوکب سعد برج اقبال | بو کون بویوروب نزول اجلال
بو حولیکا بیتکوروب طراوت | آندا کیچه ایلادی حلاوت

چون سلطان صاحبقران اعلی الله قدره مذکور حولیکا نزول سعادت‌وصول‌لاری بیله طراوت بی‌نهایت و نضارت بیغایت بیتکوروب کیچه آندا استراحت ایتی‌لار ایرتاسی جمعه کونی غایت‌سیز دولت و اقبال و نهایت‌سیز شوکت و اجلال بیله کردون‌دوند سمندلاریکا رکوب قیلیب شهر جانبی‌غه تورلوک اشتیاق و آمال و تومان مینک فرحت و بهجت مالامال بیله اول نیکوخصال حرکت قیلیب سپاه نصرت‌همراه‌لاری بیله بیراز راه قطعین تقدیمغه |121b| بیتکوروب کته باغ آتلیغ مرحله‌دین عبور ایتیب میدانیغه‌کیم مرحله مذکوره بیله صیاد اورتاسیدا واقع‌دور بیتوشکان چاغدا شهردا حضرت پادشاه دولت‌پناه کیوان‌بارکاه قبله‌کاه‌لاری خوارزمشاه وسع الله ملکه و دولته‌نینک سراسرخاصیت خدمت‌لاریدا قالغان سلطنت ارکانی‌نینک جزو اعظمی و خلافت اعیانی‌نینک رکن اهمی عظمت‌دثار

شوکت‌آثار[1] رحمانبردی بی باشلیق تمامی علما و امرا غایت‌سیز خوشحاللیق‌لار بیله استقبال قیلیب ایردیلار نمایان بولدیلار چون قریب‌راق یتی‌لار بارچه‌لاری آت‌دین نزول قیلیب دست‌بوسلیق شرفی‌نینک ادراکی اوچون سلطان کشورستان عظم الله شأنه طرفیکا یوکوردیلار سلطان صاحبقران داغی آت‌دین توشوب آلارغه التفات‌لاری |122a| کمالیدین بیر بیر قوچوشوب کوروشوب مرحمت و عاطفت سلطانیه بیله هر بیرلاریکا سرافرازلیق بیتکوروب مفارقت‌لاری اوتی‌غه مواصلت‌لاری آب صافی بیله انطفا بیتکوردیلار و چون سلطان صاحبقران اعلی الله مرتبته علما و امرای مذکوره‌نی دیدار دولت‌مدار فرحت‌آثارلاری بیله بهره‌مند و بو نوع التفات‌لاری بیله ارجمند قیلدی‌لار اوزلاری آتلانیب بارچه‌لارین اجازت ذی‌سعادت‌لاری بیله آتلانتوروب مقصد ساری توجه کورکوزدی‌لار و اول اثنادا مزبور بهادرلار بورونغی دستوردا اویون‌لار آشکار ایتی‌لارکیم عقل کل بیانیدین عاجز و قاصر و چرخ منشی‌سی آنینک تحریری بابیدا قلمی کُند و فاتِردور نظم

آتیب هر لحظه شمخالُ جزایر
کورونمای دودیدین |122b| بو چرخ دایر

جهاننی قوزغابان کرنای اداسی
فلک‌نی تیبراتیب توب‌نینک صداسی

سنان‌لار نجم ثاقب‌دیک درخشان
ایرور هر بیریسی چون برق لمعان

قیلیچ‌لار هر بیری تابان هلالی
مسرت باعثی بیرام مثالی

لوالار مهجه‌سی تابنده اختر
بولوب پرچم‌لاری هم عطرپرور

بهادرلار ایتیب کوب لعب اظهار
فلک‌نی حیرت ایتی مضطرب‌وار

---

[1] شوکت‌اثار.

توشوب عالم ارا انداق علالا — که کویا بولدی پیدا حشر کبری
بو نوع شوکت بیله سلطان مذکور — روانه بولدی یولغه شادُ مسرور
قدومی بیرله اول فرخنده‌طلعت — بیتوردی ایلکا فرحت اوزره فرحت
بو اثنادا چیقیب سرباز جانباز — اویون‌لار ایلادیلار طرفه آغاز
که تیل قاصر آنینک تقریریدین هم — قلم عاجز آنینک تحریریدین هم
بیتوشمای آنکا عقل و فهمُ ادراک — |123a| تحیربارماغین‌هم‌تیشلاب‌افلاک

بو نوع شکوه و کیرودار بیله کیلیب خیوق صانها الله عن الحرق و الغرق دار السلطنه‌سیغه سعادت‌وصول دخول‌لاری بیله آبادلیق و دیدار مسرت‌آثارلاری بیله سُکّانی دیده‌لاریغه انوار و خواطرلاریغه اسرو شادلیق بیتکوروب حضرت پادشاه والاجاه کردون‌بارکاه جناب مستطاب قبله‌کاه‌لاری خوارزمشاه دام فرحته‌نینک دست‌بوسلیق‌لاری شرفیغه مُشرَّف بولوب غایت‌سیز مرحمت و نهایت‌سیز التفات‌لاریدین سربلندلیق و ارجمندلیق تاپتی‌لار نظم

اوشبو کون خوارزم ارا ایلاب دخول — پادشه درباریغه تاپتی وصول
خاکپایین اولدم ایلاب توتیا — بیردی سلطان کوزیکا آندین ضیا
|123b| قرة العیبی‌نی شاه بختیار — کوردیُ قیلدی آنی بوس و کنار
بیر بیری دیداریدین تاپیب نشاط — ایتی‌لار غایت‌دین افزون انبساط
ایل داغی تاپیب فرح حددین فزون — قیلدیلار عشرت اویی ایچرا سکون
حق آلار اقبالین ایلاب بردوام — هر بیری‌نینک عمرین ایتکای مستدام
هر قایان بارسه اول ایکی کامکار — بو صفت بولغای ظفر هر بیرکا یار

چون خوارزمشاه بیله سلطان گردون‌دستگاه ادام الله تعالی مسرتهما بیر بیرلاری‌نینک دیدار فرحت‌آثارلاریدین بهره‌ور بولدی‌لار ایرتاسی شنبه کونی حضرت پادشاه انجم‌سپاه جناب مستطاب خوارزمشاه مدّ ظله العالی سلطان سپهرمکان دام نصرته خدمت‌لاریدا بارغان سپهبدلار باشلیق سپاه اهلیغه |124a| زرین لباس‌لار بیریب التفات‌لاری بیله بارچه‌سین سربلند و ارجمند قیلدی‌لار عرض بطریقهٔ دعا نظم

عرض احوالیم ایشـیتکیل بیر زمان　　لطف ایتیب ای داور کشورسـتان
حق سنینک اقبالینک ایتکای بردوام　　دولتُ بختینک اساسـین مستدام
یتـی اقلیـم اوزره چالغای نوبتینک　　یتی گردون اوزره چیقغای رفعتینک
مهر یانکلیغ پنجهٔ جودینک آچیب　　عالم اهلی باشی اوزره زر ساچیب
ایلاسانک اول ایلنی اوزدین شادمان　　قویما بو محزوننـی محروم اولزمان
داورا لطفونک‌غـه توتمیش‌من اُمید　　اوزکالاردیـن ایلاب اوزنـی نااُمید
لطفُ احسـان وقتی ای عِزّت‌پناه　　ایلامـا محـروم بـو حالـی تبـاه
چون جنابینک تکیه‌کاهیم‌دور منینک　　|124b| تورلوک آفتدین پناهیم‌دور منینک
اوزکا یان یانماق‌لیغیم کیلدی محال　　بولـدی بو درکه‌غه باشـیم پایمال

فهرستلار

شخص اسملاری فهرستی

اتا مراد قوشبیکی (قوشبیکی بیک؛ وزیر) 4b، 9a، 10a، 11a، 13b-12b، 14b، 15a، 16b، 17a، 19b، 20b، 21a، 106b، 107a، 111b، 112a، 114a، 116b-115a، 118a

احمد زمچی ← پهلوان احمد زمچی

احمد سلطان – جمشیدی 56b

آدینه بای اتالیق 106b

آدینه محمد بیک 40a

اسکندر (سکندر) 2a

اسلام شیخ 62b، 63a

اسماعیل بای 99a

آصف الدوله [الله یار خان] 43b، 104b، 105a

اکرم 76a، 77a، 95b

اکرم خان ابن عبد الجبار خان – جمشیدی 56b

الله داد ایشیک اقاسی 49a

الله قلی ایشان 118b

الله قلی بیک – جمشیدی 69a

الله قلی خان (خوارزمشاه) 2a، 12a، 14a، 15a، 15b، 18b-17b، 19b، 36b، 37a، 39a، 41a، 42a، 46b، 47a، 49b، 53b، 58b، 61a، 61b، 76a، 81a، 83b، 84a، 88a، 89a، 95b، 103a، 103b، 106b-105a، 107b، 108a، 109a، 113a، 115a، 121b، 123a، 123b

[الله یار خان] ← آصف الدوله

الیاس 7b، 119a

امام بکتاش 51a

امام جعفر صادق 32b، 33a

امیر دوست محمد خان 72a

امیر نصر الله 15b

انه نیاز ایناق 40a

اوراض خان – تکه 99a

ایشان اوراغ 65a، 69b، 109a

ایشان قاضی اسماعیل – جمشیدی 56b

[ایش مراد ابن آدینه محمد العلوی] (مرادی؛ فقیر) 4a، 42a، 79b، 80b

بابا بیک سردار – یموت 71a، 71b ← بابا سردار

بابا بیک محرم 91b، 92a ← بابا بیک سردار

بابا جان توره [محمد امین توره ابن الله قلی خان] 116b

بابا خان فرمانه‌جی 40a

بابا سردار – یموت 46a، 46b، 69b، 109a ← بابا بیک سردار

بکنیاز دیوان بیکی 113a

بهبود بهادر 90a، 92b، 98a

بیرام علی خان 108b

بیرام یاغلی 76a، 77a، 95b، 103b، 115a
بیردی بیک – یموت 38b، 71a، 71b، 89b، 91b-92b، 93b، 94a، 97b
بیردی خان – یموت 55a-56a ← بیردی محمد خان
بیردی محمد خان – یوموت 38b ← بیردی خان
بیک نیاز دیوان بیکی ← بکنیاز دیوان بیکی
بیکیش خلیفه ← خلیفه بیکیش

پهلوان احمد زمچی (احمد زمچی) 31b، 32a
پهلوان نیاز کاکل‌لی (پهلوان کاکل‌لی) 61a، 89b

توردی قیلیچ سردار – یموت 38b

جعفر صادق ← امام جعفر صادق
جمشید 3b

حضرت قلی بیک 67b، 68b، 73b-74b، 100a
حضرت قلی یوزباشی 41b
حیدر قلی بیک 90a، 93b، 97b

خانگ سردار 53b، 54b
خان نایب [محمد ولی خان] 105a
خدای بیرکان بای ابن نیاز محمد بای 107a
خدای بیرکان یوزباشی 52a
خدای یار بی 4b، 52a
خضر 7b، 119a

خلیفه اسحاق – جمشیدی 56b
خلیفه بیکیش 58b، 106b
خلیفه محمد نیاز 101a ← محمد نیاز خلیفه
خواجم شکر آقسقال – تکه 99a
خواجه محمد صالح – جمشیدی 56b
خواجه یوسف همدانی 30b

دارا 14b، 110b
درویش 74b، 90a ← درویش بیک
درویش بیک 93b، 94a ← درویش
دوست محمد بهادر 65a، 67a
دوست محمد خان ← امیر دوست محمد خان
دولت نظر بی ← ملا دولت نظر بی

رحمان بردی بی 121b
رحمت الله یساولباشی 4b، 58b
رحیم قلی بهادر سلطان (ایناق) 1b، 4a، 42b، 49b، 59a، 104a ← رحیم قلی توره
رحیم قلی توره (توره خان) 54a، 96b ← رحیم قلی بهادر سلطان
رستم 11a
رستم خان 38b

سردار محمد اکبر خان غازی ابن امیر دوست محمد خان 72a
سلطان passim ← رحیم قلی بهادر سلطان
سلطان سنجر ماضی 31a، 85b
سلیمان خان 106a
سید احمد خواجه ← قاضی سید احمد

خواجه
سید نظر بی 4b

شاه پسند یوزباشی 49a
شاه کامران 37b، 38a، 43b-42b، 60b، 62b، 63b، 101a
شاه مراد ایناق 106b
شاه ولی خان 38b، 41b، 46b، 65a، 90a، 93a، 97b، 109a
شجاع الدین خان 38b، 65a، 109a

صدر العلما 49b
صوفی دادخواه 69b، 90a

طالقان بابا 45a، 45b، 87a

عابدین محرم 105b
عبد الجبار بیک – جمشیدی 60b ← عبد الجبار خان
عبد الجبار خان – جمشیدی 56b، 58a ← عبد الجبار بیک
عبد العزیز خان – هزاره 55a، 56a، 82b، 83a، 97a
عبد الله بیک (عبد الله بیکلاربیکی) – جمشیدی 62b، 69a
عبد الله خان [ابن اسکندر] 20b، 21b
عبد الله یساولباشی 4b، 55a، 107a
عزیز قلی دیوان بیکی 89a
علی مردان یوزباشی 40a، 41b، 46a
عنایت الله بیک – جمشیدی 56b
عوض خواجه شیخ الاسلام 4a، 55a

عیسی (مسیح؛ مسیحا) 33a، 39b، 44b

فرج الله 25b
فردوسی 53a

قاچار 43a، 43b
قارلی محرم 79b، 82b
قاضی سید احمد خواجه 77a، 78a، 78b
قاضی محمد صادق خواجه ایشان 118b
قاضی محمد نیاز 40a
قاضی نور محمد 40a
قلندر محرم 74b
قوتلوق مراد 47b
قوتوش محرم (محرم‌باشی) 38b، 67b، 82b، 83a، 96a، 96b، 97a

کریمداد خان – هزاره 38b، 55a، 77a، 78b، 82b، 83a، 96a

لاله خان – سمندوک 73a

محمد (پیغمبر؛ سید المرسلین؛ سید المختار) 32b، 65b، 91a، 102a
محمد اکبر خان غازی ابن امیر دوست محمد خان ← سردار محمد اکبر خان غازی
محمد امین بیک 26b، 52a، 60b، 89a
[محمد امین توره ابن الله قلی خان] ← بابا جان توره
محمد امین مینکباشی 4b
محمد بیردی سردار 65a
محمد بیردی یوزباشی 41b

محمد حسن بیک تبریزی 104b
محمد حکیم خان 104b
محمد رحیم بیک 72a
محمد شاه قاچار 43b، 105a
محمد صادق خواجه ایشان ← قاضی محمد صادق خواجه ایشان
محمد علی خان 24b، 27a، 89b، 94b، 98b، 99a
محمد قربان بهادر 65a
محمد قلی بیک 24b، 25b، 27a
محمد مراد بای محرم 4b
محمد نظر بیک 92a
محمد نیاز خلیفه 73b، 74b، 99b، 106a ← خلیفه محمد نیاز
محمد والی آقسقال 69b
[محمد ولی خان] ← خان نایب
محمود [غزنوی] 5a
محمود خان 38b، 65a، 109a
مضراب خان 38b، 67b، 73b، 99b
ملا دولت نظر بی 63a، 64a، 64b، 102a-101a
ملک امان بیک 69b
منکلی بای بهادر 69b، 72b، 92a
میر احمد خان – جمشیدی 38b
میرداد سردار 73a
میرزا ابو القاسم ابن اسلام شیخ 60b، 63a، 64b، 102a
میرزا خان خلیفه 37b، 38a، 60b، 61a، 89a

نظر بای – یوموت 36b، 37b، 103a، 106a ← نظر سردار
نظر سردار 54b ← نظر بای
نیاز محمد بای (بای) 24b، 34a، 35b، 36a، 52a، 107a، 108a
نیاز محمد یوزباشی 52a

والی بیک 38b، 39a، 40a، 41b، 46a، 65a، 69b، 90a، 97b، 98a، 109a
وزیر یار محمد خان ← یار محمد خان
ویس محرم 81a، 88a، 103b، 107b

یار محمد خان (یار محمد وزیر؛ وزیر) 43b-42b، 49a، 50b، 60b، 64b-63a، 101a، 101b
یخشی مراد یوزباشی 4b

جای ناملاری فهرستی

آتخور 17a، 115a، 115b
احمد زمچی ← پهلوان احمد زمچی
اخال 69a
آص ← عاص
آقچه قایه 58b، 62a، 73a، 76b
آق رباط 16b
البرز 57a
امام بکتاش (مزار) 51a
امام جعفر صادق (قدمجا ؟) 32b، 33a
آمو (آمویه، دریا) 113b-115b، 117a، 118a ← جیحون
انتخوی (آنتخوی) 38b، 41b، 65a، 69b، 74b، 89b، 90a، 97b، 109a
[اندخوی] ← انتخوی
اوجارلی 111b
اوچ تیفه 10a
اوروش توشکان 52a، 80b
ایران 2a، 4a

بادغیس 43a
بت خاک 72b
بخارا 15b، 102b
بلخ 65a، 69b، 74b، 89b، 109a
بند نادر 75b، 76b
بوز بورون 55a
بیرام علی خان قلعه‌سی 108b

بیش یاغاچ 11b

پنجده 40a، 47b، 73a-74a، 76b، 79b، 82b
پهلوان احمد زمچی (مزار) 31b، 32a

تاش قورغان 38b، 39a، 40a، 69b، 74b، 89b، 90a، 109a
تبریز 105a
تجن ← طژن
تخت 22a، 112b
ترخان قودوقی 26a، 26b، 110b
توران ← طوران
تیوه بویون 10a، 118a

جلال آباد 72b
جیحون 114a ← آمو
جیکیرداکلی ساومه 85a

چار دره 59b، 60b
چاپیق خواجه کاوی 48a
چانکلی کذر 84b، 85a
چیشلی قرا آیغیر 16b ← قرا آیغیر
چوبلی تیفه 48b، 49a
چهارشنبه 98a
چهار ولایت 41a، 66b

چین 20a، 23b

حصار 69b، 74b، 90a
حوض خان 21b، 22a، 113a ← عبد الله خان سردابه‌سی

خراسان 2a، 4a، 102b
خواجه قلندر 76b
خواجه کاوی 48b
خواجه یوسف همدانی (مزار) 30b
خوارزم 29b، 89a، 99b، 105a، 108b، 123a
خیوق 5a، 85b، 120b، 123a

دایه خاتون 20a، 20b، 114b
دریای آمویه ← آمو
دری‌جز (دریجز) 106a
دهن شیر 15a، 15b

زره 5b
زیره آباد 43b

ساری حاجی 9a
سرپل (سر پل) 38b، 65a، 69b، 71b، 74b، 89b، 92a، 109a
سر چشمه 59b، 60b، 76b
سرطلانلی 22b، 23a، 111a ← سرطلانلی قودوقی
سرطلانلی قودوقی 111a ← سرطلانلی
سلطان اویوقی 112a
سلطان سنجر ماضی (مزار) 31a
سلطان سنجر ماضی بندی 85b
سلطان قلعه‌سی 108b، 109b
سودوک 14b، 15a، 116b

شاه مردان 38b، 65a، 69b، 74b، 89b، 109a
شهر خلیل 59b، 60b، 76b
شیبرغان 38b
شیخ آریقی 9b

صدبر 14a
صفالی 16a
صندوق قاچغان 83b، 84a
صیاد 5b، 85b، 121b

طالقان بابا (مزار) 45a، 45b، 87a
طژن 25b
طوران 101b

عاص 6b
عبد الله خان [کاروان] سرایی 20b
عبد الله خان سردابه‌سی 21b ← حوض خان
عراق 2a

فتناک 9a، 118b

قاباقلی 21a، 113a، 113b
قازوقلی بندی 85a
قاقچی 76b
قرا آیغیر 115b ← چیشلی قرا آیغیر

قرا تیفه 57a، 58a، 59b، 60b، 76b
قراول‌خانه 98a
قلعهٔ نو 38b، 77a، 96a
قوش آسیا 59b، 60b، 76b
قوشلی قایه 51b
قوی قلعه‌سی 108b
قیزیل مست 48a

کابل 72a، 72b
کاریز 76b
کاوبر 29b، 30a
کته‌باغ 121b
کشمان 27b، 110a
کلات 24b، 89b
کل پر 33b
کندمکان 5b
کوشک 38b، 62b، 68b، 76b
کوکارجینلی 20a
کوه قاف 57b

مارچاق 102b، 103a ← مرچاق
مازندران 28b
مجاور کولی 109b
مرچاق 47b، 73a، 74a، 75a، 76b، 77b، 78b ← مارچاق
مرو 24b-25b، 29b، 30b، 36b، 37b، 39a، 47b، 49b، 54b، 61a، 62a، 66b، 73b، 75a، 76b، 84b، 87b-88b
مرو دریاسی 33b، 85b
مشرق 2a
مشهد 43a، 43b، 104b، 105a
مغرب 2a
موری دریاسی 73a، 73b، 79b، 80a
موری کوپروکی 55a، 79b
میمنه 38b، 66b، 67b، 73b، 99b

نیاز محمد بای قلعه‌سی (حصاری) 36a، 36b، 108a

هرات 37b، 43a، 49b، 60b، 63a، 101a
هزاراسب 6b، 7a، 8b، 117b، 118b، 120a
هفت ریك خوارزم 21b، 29b، 113b
هندستان 2a

یانتاقلی 23a، 23b، 110b، 111a
یانکی آریق 6a، 120b
یثرب 2a
یکه چیقیر 8b
یول اوتان 86a، 86b
ییلغینلی 55a

قبیله‌لار فهرستی

اوتامیش – تکه 52a، 69a، 83a، 99a
ایرساری 40a، 79b
آیماقیه 29b

ترکمان ← تورکمان
تکه 52a، 83a، 96b، 98b، 99a
توختامیش – تکه 52a، 69a، 83a، 99a
تورکمان (تورکمانیه) 29b، 94b، 96b

جمشیدی 1b، 38b، 43a، 52a، 56a، 60b، 62a، 62b، 76b، 84b، 88b، 99a، 106b، 113a

چادور [چاودر] 94a
چارشنکی 40a، 79b، 83a ← چهارشنکغی
چهارشنکغی 96b ← چارشنکی

ساریق 24b، 52a، 83a، 94a، 96b، 107b
سالور 26b، 52a، 60b، 83a، 89a، 94a، 96b، 105a، 107b
سمندوک – جمشیدی 73a

فرنکی 72a، 72b

قیزیلباش 43a

کوکلان 52a

منقیتیه 67a

هزاره 38b، 55a، 77a، 78a

یموت (یوموت) 36b، 38b، 46a، 55a، 58b، 69b، 89b، 94a، 106a، 109a

اصطلاحلار، منصب‌لار و لقب‌لار فهرستی

اتالیق 106b
احسان 2a، 3a، 8a، 24a، 69b، [82b، 94b]، 124a
اسلام 6a، 44a، 60a، 72a، 72b
آق اویلی 84b، 88b، 89a
آقسقال 69b، 99a
امام 16a، 32b، 33a، 51a
امر 2b، 5b، 7b، 43a، 53a، 56a، 71b، 72a، 78a، 83a، 84b، 89a، 97a، 109b، 119a
امرا 4b، 5b، 6a، 7a، 7b، 18a، 18b، 24a، 81b، 94a، 99b، 107b، 117b، 120b، 121b، 122a
امیر 15b، 72a
امیر الامرا 9a، 11a، 106b
انبیا 7b، 43b
انعام 8a، 24a، 50b، 57a، 62b، 74b، 78a، 80b، 81b، 82b، [94b]، 97b، 117b، [124a]
آو 9b، 11b، 12b، 14a-15a، 16a، 17a، 21a
اولاغ 99a
اولوس 3b، 8b، 45a، 57a، 94b، 95a
اولیا 31a، 31b، 45a، 87a
ایشان 56b، 118b
ایشیک اقاسی 49a
ایل 2b، 3b، 7a، 9a، 69a، 73b، 87a، 87b، 95a، 97a، 120a، 122b، 123b، 124a
ایلچی 15b، 37b، 45b، 55a، 94a، 104b، 105b-106b
ایناق 40a، 49b، 106b

بابا 45a، 45b، 87a
بای 4b، 24b، 34a، 35b-36b، 37b، 52a، 69b، 72b، 92a، 99a، 103a، 106a-107a، 108a
بایراق 18b، 95b
بویروغ 26a، 41b، 74a، 80a، 99a
بهادر 1b، 4a، 28a، 28b، 65a، 67a، 69b، 72b، 90a، 92a، 92b، 98a، 118b-119b، 120b، 122a، 122b
بی 4b، 52a، 63a، 64a، 64b، 101a-102a، 121b
بیک 10a، 11a، 15a، 21a، 24b، 25b، 26b، 27a، 38b، 39a، 40a، 41b، 46a، 52a، 53b، 56b، 60b، 62b، 65a، 67b، 68b-69b، 71a-72a، 73b-74b، 85b-86b، 89a-90a، 91b-92b، 93b، 94a، 95b، 97b، 98a، 100a، 104b، 107b، 109a، 117a
بیکزاده 5b

بیکلاربیکی 62b

پادشاه (پادشه) 1b، 11b، 13a، 13b، 16a، 37a، 41a، 43b، 47a، 58b، 61a، 76a، 81a، 84a، 95b، 99b، 100b، 103a، 103b، 105b، 106a، 107b، 109a، 113a، 115a، 121b، 123a، 123b
پادشاهزاده 67b
پهلوان 11a، 18b، 28b، 31b، 82a، 95a، 117b
پیشکش 15b، 24b، 25b، 36b، 40a، 56a، 89b

تاریخ 42a، 42b
تحفه (تحایف) 15b، 24b، 26b، 36b، 40a، 55b، 86a، 86b، 89b
تقسیم 86a
توب 5b، 7b، 8a، 9a، 9b، 16b، 30b، 33b، 34b، 44b، 87a، 107b، 108a، 119b، 122b
توبخانه 72b، 102b
توره 54a، 96b، 116b
توره خان 96b

ثنا (اثنیه) 37a، 47a، 61b، 77b، 84a، 88b
ثواب 44a

جار 34a
جارچی 34a، 34b
جریب 22a
جلوس 2b
جماعه 24b، 40a، 44a، 52a، 58a، 60a، 61a، 67a، 72b، 83a
جهاد 42b، 44a

چاکر 2a، 21a، 43b، 49a، 50a، 62b، 96b، 97a، 114b
چاووش 21a، 49a، 62b
چاونی 72a، 72b

حاکم (حکام) 24b، 26b، 38b، 39a، 40a، 41a، 41b، 43b، 52a، 62b، 65a، 66b، 69b، 77a، 82b، 90a، 97b، 104b، 105a، 106a، 107b، 109a
حدیث 79b
حصار 44b، 57b، 58a، 87b، 108a، 108a، 120b
حکم (احکام) 61a، 62a، 87a، 96b
حکومت 47a، 54a، 55b، 70b، 91b، 101b، 104a، 116a، 116b
حولی 6a، 6b، 120b، 121a

خاقان (خواقین) 1b، 2a، 19b، 42a، 76a، 85b، 88a، 95b
خان (خوانین) 2a، 15b، 20b، 21b، 22a، 24b، 27a، 37b، 38b، 40a، 41b، 42b، 45b، 46b، 50b، 55a-56b، 58a، 61a، 63a، 63b، 64b، 65a، 66a، 67b، 72a، 73a، 73b، 77a، 78b، 82b، 83a، 89b، 90a، 91a، 93a، 94a، 94b،

97b-96a، 99b-98b، 104b، 106a،
108b، 109a، 113a
خانزاده 40b، 65b
خان‌نایب 105a
خذمت 2b، 4a، 13a، 25b، 27b، 37b،
39b، 41b، 46a، 46b، 50a، 51a،
53b، 56a، 60a، 62b، 67b-66b، 72a،
76a-74a، 77a، 81a، 82b، 83b، 84b،
85b، 86b، 88b، 92a، 93b، 95b،
98b-97b، 100b، 102b، 103a، 105b،
106b، 107b، 108a، 109b، 115a،
121b، 123b
خذمتکار (خذمتکارلیق) 4b، 10a، 34a،
36b، 38a، 40a، 41b، 50a، 53b، 55a،
61a، 64a، 65a، 71b، 86a، 88a، 90a،
92b، 93b، 97a، 98b، 99a، 100a،
100b، 113a
خلعت (خلاع) 24a، 50b، 63b، 69b
خلق 3b، 26b، 60b، 69a، 79b، 89a،
99a، 105a
خلیفه 37b، 38a، 56b، 58b، 60b،
61a، 73b، 74b، 89a، 99b، 101a،
106a، 106b
خواجه 4a، 30b، 55a، 56b، 77a، 78a،
78b، 118b
خوارزمشاه 2b، 12a، 15b-14a،
18b-17b، 19b، 36b، 37a، 39a، 41a،
42a، 46b، 47a، 49b، 53b، 58b،
61a، 61b، 76a، 81a، 83b، 84a، 88a،
89a، 95b، 103a، 103b، 106b-105a،
107b، 108a، 109a، 113a، 115a،
121b، 123a، 123b

دادخواه 69b، 90a
دار السلطنه 43a، 63a، 72a، 85b، 105a،
120b، 123a
دعا (ادعیه) 3b، 5b، 8b-7a، 18b،
41a-40a، 47b، 54a، 59a، 61b، 67a،
77b، 78a، 82a، 84a، 85b، 87a، 88b،
90a، 104b، 117b، 119a، 120b، 124a
دین 3a، 43a، 102a
دیوان بیکی 89a، 113a

رایت (رأیت) 9a، 13b، 15a، 17a، 33b،
39a، 98b، 109b، 115b، 119a
رعایا 39a، 41a، 104a

زایر 30b
زکوت 79b
زندان 105a
زیارت 13b، 32a-30b، 33a، 87a، 104b

سایس 19a
سپاه (سپه) 5a، 6b، 14a، 16b، 17b،
18a، 23b، 26a، 35a، 35b، 44a، 45a،
48b، 52b، 53a، 56b، 58a، 80b، 86a،
87a، 102b، 110b، 111a، 121a، 123b
سپهبد 4a، 4b، 11b، 14b، 60a، 106b،
112a، 116a، 118a، 123b
سرادق 8b، 50b، 110a
سرباز 122b
سردابه 21b

سردار 38b، 46a، 46b، 53b، 54b، 65a، 69b، 73a-71a، 81b، 109a

سرکرده 5a-4a، 6b، 9a، 10a، 13b-12b، 16b، 17a، 19b، 52b، 55a، 56b، 57a، 58b، 60a، 68b، 81b، 86a، 106b، 114a، 115a، 116b

سروپای 46a، 57a، 60a، 62b، 74b، 78a، 82b، 97b، 98b، 107b

سرهنک 52a

سفارت 60b، 63a، 67b، 69b، 89b

سفیر 99b

سلطان (سلاطین) 1b، 4a، 5b، 6a، 7a-8b، 10b-9b، 12a، 13a، 14a، 15a، 17b، 18b، 20b-19b، 21b، 23b-22b، 24b، 26a، 26b، 31a-29a، 32a، 33a، 33b، 34b، 35b، 36a، 42a، 42b، 45b-43b، 51a، 54b، 56b، 57a، 60a-59a، 73a، 76a، 78a، 80b، 82a، 83b، 85b، 86b، 87b، 88a، 95a، 96a، 99b، 101b، 104a، 106b-105b، 108b، 110b-109b، 111b، 114b-112b، 116b-115b، 118a، 119a، 120a، 123b-121a

سید (سیادت) 4a، 32b، 55a، 65b، 77a، 78a، 78b، 91a

شاه (شه) 2a، 2b، 3b، 12a، 13a، 14a، 14b، 15b، 37b، 38a، 43b-42b، 60b، 63b-62b، 101a، 105a، 123b

شاهزاده (شهزاده) 1b، 4a، 5a، 5b، 12b، 13a، 14b، 42b، 53b، 55b، 59a، 65b، 66b، 68b، 70b، 77b، 85b، 86a، 90b، 95b، 103b، 104a، 116b، 117a

شکار 9b، 10a، 11b، 13b، 17a، 21a، 85b

شهزاده ← شاهزاده

شهنشاه (شهنشه) 2a، 3a، 11b، 37a، 47a، 76a، 103a، 115a

شیخ 60b، 62b، 63a، 64b، 102a

شیخ الاسلام 4a، 55a

شیعه 105a

صاحبقران 5b، 6a، 7a، 8a، 8b، 9b، 10b، 15a، 16a، 17b، 18b، 20b-19b، 22b، 24a، 24b، 26a، 26b، 29a، 29b، 30b، 33a، 33b، 36a، 45b-43b، 51a، 54b، 57a، 59b، 60a، 73a، 78a، 80b، 82a، 83b، 88a، 95a، 96a، 105b، 106b، 108b، 109b، 110b، 111b، 114a، 115b، 117a، 118a، 119a، 120a، 122a-121a

صدقه (صدقات) 18a، 33a، 87a

صلح 44a، 65a، 72a، 101a

صلوة (صلوات) 104b، 113b

صوفی 62b

صید 9b، 14a، 15a، 21a

ضیافت 7b-6b، 36a، 69a، 94b، 107b، 117b، 120b

طایفه (طوایف) 1b، 6a، 17b، 18a، 38b،

43a، 52a، 52b، 53b، 56a-57a، 60a، 60b، 62a، 62b، 68b، 73a، 76b، 84b، 88b، 89a، 97a، 98b، 99a، 100b، 106b، 107a
طواف 33a
طوغ 10a، 14b، 16b، 21a، 34b، 114a، 115a

عرضه‌داشت 24b، 25b، 26a، 27a، 36b-37b، 39a، 40a، 40b، 41b، 46a-47b، 49a، 50b، 55b، 59b، 61a-62a، 63a، 64b، 65a، 67a-68a، 69b، 72a، 73a، 74a، 75a، 76a، 77a، 78a، 78b، 83b-84b، 88a-89a، 90a، 93a، 94a، 96a، 97a-98a، 99b، 101b، 103a، 103b، 104b، 106a، 107b، 115a
عسکر (عساکر) 9a، 23a، 23b، 33a، 57a، 72a، 73b، 84b، 92a، 116a
عَلَم 20a
علما 5b، 6a، 7a، 7b، 8b، 18a، 18b، 56b، 81b، 94a، 107b، 117b، 120b، 121b، 122a
عنایت‌نامه 27a، 27b، 38b-39b، 46a، 50b، 51a، 54b، 55b، 59b، 63b، 64b، 65a، 68a، 73b، 74b-75b، 79a، 82b، 83a، 97b-98b، 104b، 106a، 109a، 109b

غازی 72a، 72b، 105a
غزا (غزات) 44a، 72a
غلام 24b، 36b

فاتحه 19b، 53b، 57a، 85b
فرسخ 28a، 34a، 109b
فرمان 5a، 42b، 52a، 56a، 60a، 71b، 72a، 83a، 89a، 107a، 111b
فرمانه‌جی 40a
فرمایش (فرمایشات) 25b، 37b، 50a، 96b، 103a
فرنکی 18a، 81b
فقرا 41a، 77b-79a، 104a

قاضی 40a، 56b، 77a، 78a، 78b، 118b
قران 12b، 13a، 117a
قلعه (قلعجات) 7a-8a، 9a، 20a، 20b، 30b، 36a، 36b، 43b-44b، 58a، 59b، 62b، 68b، 73a، 76b، 79b، 82b، 85b، 88a، 95b، 108b، 109b، 118b، 120a، 120b
قودوق 26a، 26b، 110b، 111a
قورخانه 102b
قورغان 36a
قوش 9b، 10a، 12b، 13a، 15b، 18b، 82a
قوشبیکی 4b، 9a، 106b، 111b، 114a
قوشبیکی بیک 10a، 11a، 15a، 21a
قوشون 41a، 66b

کاروان‌سرای 20b
کافر ← کفار

کدخدا 24b، 69a، 73a، 79b، 82b، 107b
کرنای 5b، 7b، 9a، 9b، 30b، 33b، 34b، 44b، 87a، 107b، 108a، 119b، 122b
کفار 72a، 72b، 100b
کفر 6b، 44a
کوچ 52b، 60b، 62a، 69a، 73b، 76a، 107a، 113a
کوراش 18b، 19a، 82a، 95b، 117b
کولوک 99a

لشکر 4a، 6a، 8b، 10a، 11b، 13b، 15b، 16b، 21b، 23b، 28a، 29b، 30b، 35a-34a، 43b، 44a، 47b، 48b، 55a، 56b، 57a، 58a، 61a، 68b، 69a، 73b، 74a، 79b، 80a، 83b، 102b، 105a، 110a، 112b، 114a، 119a
لوا (الویه) 11b، 34b، 116a، 122b

مجاور 32a، 33a، 87a
محبت‌نامه 15b، 38a، 38b، 62b، 63b، 64a
محرم 4b، 11b، 38b، 67b، 68a، 74b، 79b، 81a، 82b، 83a، 88a، 91b، 92a، 97a-96a، 103b، 105b، 107b، 114b، 115a
محرم‌باشی 97a
مرید 62b
مزار 31a، 31b، 45a، 45b، 51b، 87a
مسلمان 100b
مصری 18a، 81b
مفتی 42a
مقرب 24b
مکتوب 54b
ملا 63a، 64a، 64b، 101a، 101b
ملازم 2b، 4b، 15b، 18a، 24b، 25a، 27a، 27b، 36b، 40a، 46a، 55a، 58b، 59b، 63a، 65a، 72a، 74a، 75a، 77a، 90a، 91b، 93a، 98a، 101b، 104b
منشور 62b
موروثی 6a، 120b
میسره 10b، 34a، 107a
میمنه 10b، 34a، 107a
مینک‌باشی 4b

نامه 101b
نایب 105a ← خان‌نایب
نذورات 33a، 87a
نماز 5a، 11b، 23a-22a، 24a، 27b، 28a، 52a، 55a، 56a، 58b، 69a، 81a، 107a، 110b، 111a، 112b، 113a، 114b
نوکر (نواکر) 29b، 55a، 61a، 89a

والی 52a، 69b
وزیر (وزرا) 4b، 9a، 10a، 11a، 13b-12b، 14b، 15a، 16b، 17a، 19b، 20b، 43b-42b، 49a، 50b، 60b، 64b-63a، 101a، 101b، 106b، 107a، 112a، 116b-115a، 118a
ولایت (ولایات) 25a، 25b، 29b، 36b،

37b، 39a، 41a، 44a، 47b، 49b،
60a، 62a، 66b، 67b، 69b، 71b،
75a، 76b، 84b، 88b-87b، 92a، 98b

هدیه (هدایا) 55b، 86a، 86b

یارلیغ 27a، 39a، 39b، 46a، 46b، 49b،
50b، 53b، 54a، 58b، 59a، 62b،
64b، 73b، 75a، 78a، 78b، 81a،
83a، 89b، 96a، 96b، 97b، 98a،
99a، 104a-103a، 106a، 109a
یالاو 34a، 35a
یر 43a، 43b
یسار 61a
یساولباشی 4b، 55a، 58b، 107a
یمین 61a
یورت 43a
یوزباشی 4b، 40a، 41b، 46a، 49a،
52a، 111b، 112a
یوللوق 53b
ییغین 92a، 102b